Preaching
as Worship

Preaching
as Worship

An **Integrative Approach**
to Formation in Your Church

Michael J. Quicke

BakerBooks
a division of Baker Publishing Group
Grand Rapids, Michigan

Published by Baker Books
a division of Baker Publishing Group
P.O. Box 6287, Grand Rapids, MI 49516-6287
www.bakerbooks.com

Printed in the United States of America

Library of Congress Cataloging-in-Publication Data
Quicke, Michael J., 1945–
     Preaching as worship : an integrative approach to formation in your church / Michael J. Quicke.
        p.   cm.
     Includes bibliographical references (p.   ) and index.
     ISBN 978-0-8010-9226-8 (pbk.)
     1. Public worship—Protestant churches. 2. Protestant churches—Clergy—Office. 3. Evangelicalism. I. Title.
BV15.Q53 2011
264—dc22   2011012338

11   12   13   14   15   16   17   7   6   5   4   3   2   1

To
the latest generation of Quickes,
Luca, Anton, Elliot, and Sophie,
praying that they may grow up into
big-picture worship of God.

Contents

Figures

Acknowledgments

If someone had told me eight years ago that I would write a book on worship, I would have laughed at the idea. My reply would have been that my focus as a teacher and author is on preaching, and I have had my work cut out for me just to write a couple of worthwhile books on that topic. But in recent years, I have been propelled into a fresh understanding of how worship includes *everything*. Whenever definitions of worship limit and shrink it down to small-scale stuff, great damage is done to God's cosmic purposes. We need to see not only how preaching belongs within worship but also how the whole of church life and mission is part of worship too. My convictions about worship have grown in dimension so much that they have radically deepened my life and ministry and reordered its goal. That's why I hope you will take the time to read this book.

Many people have helped me on my worship journey, some of whom have played a large role. In the first chapter, I describe Bob Webber's impact on me as well as my work with Karen Roberts. Early on, Dr. Jim Stamoolis read some of my writing, and later six readers formed a formidable team who read my final drafts and privileged me with insights. I offer profound thanks to these six friends: Stu Heiss, skilled musician and former student; Dr. Barry Morrison, pastor and former professor; Dr. Karen Roberts, my colleague at Northern Seminary; Dr. David Schlafer, gifted author and homiletician; Dawneen and Bill Suriano, both remarkably thoughtful worshipers in the pew. Worshipers all, these six brought eagle eyes, lively minds, and warm hearts to the task. Together they greatly improved this book, even rewriting some sections. I remain responsible for its many imperfections, but there would have been even more without their intervention.

I owe a great debt to Northern Seminary for granting time and opportunity to study and write over the last three years, which included freedom to lead several workshops and conferences that opened my eyes to so many worship issues. In particular, the 2009 Ockenga Lectureship Series at Gordon-Conwell Theological Seminary enabled me to focus on closing the gap between preaching and worship. Friends in different churches, especially Calvary Memorial Church in Oak Park, Illinois (a Chicago suburb), have also interacted with me, often through postings on my blog. Some elements were developed in other publications, especially *Preaching* magazine, which published a three-part series on "Preaching and Trinitarian Theology" (January–June 2008) and an interview with me that sparked considerable debate (July–August 2009).

I will always be thankful for the many conversations and insights that have contributed to my learning. On the publication trail, I am immensely grateful for the professional skills and patience shown by Robert Hosack and Kristin Kornoelje, as well as other people at Baker Books. Talking of patience, I especially thank my wife, Carol, who has tolerated the shut study door for almost more hours than she could bear. Most importantly, because I believe that worship participates in fellowship with Father, Son, and Holy Spirit, I am profoundly humbled by God's help in writing this book. Like my six readers, he is not to be blamed for its faults. But if there's something here that lights us up about worship, it is because he put it there.

1

An Ocean and a Bucket

Give me new Christians before they have heard too many sermons
and been to too many worship services.

I spent several summers at the International Baptist Seminary when it was
based at Ruschlikon, Switzerland. The seminary overlooked Lake Zurich,
which stretched into the distance and was surrounded by low mountains on
both sides. To my surprise, a postcard on sale in the seminary office showed
the same lake view but with a vast, snow-covered mountain range in the distance. This seemed rather fanciful. On earlier visits I had never glimpsed these
mountains, and no one had even mentioned them. I know postcards are sometimes doctored for effect, and without much further thought, I concluded this
represented an imaginary scenario. So I put the mountains out of my mind.

On one unforgettable early morning, however, I glanced across the lake and
there to my utter astonishment, snow-covered and dazzling in sunshine, was
an alpine range filling the horizon. Soon the sight was lost as clouds moved
in, but not before I had excitedly called my wife and all the friends I could
find. With me, they gasped at the sight. I breathlessly checked with those who
lived at the seminary. "Oh yes," they told me, "sometimes you see that view
for a few hours. It's awesome, isn't it?"

Parallels with writing this book about worship may become obvious. All
my life, from my earliest worship experiences in church, I have been aware
that there might be more. Beyond uncomfortable pews and often stark chapel
walls bearing fading painted texts, I imagined more dazzling encounters with

11

God than the pedestrian, predictable services offered—more mystery, wonder, and danger. At best these worship services hinted at more profound realities of experiencing God's sheer *godness* and of loving, joyous, and peaceful relationships in a community shining with holy-nation, royal-priesthood possibilities. First Peter 2:9–10 excited me not just about gathering with brothers and sisters in bricks and mortar but about God's much bigger mandate. I imagined progressing on a journey together, once not a people but now God's people, destined to impact those around us as a community united in living for God's greatest purpose as a holy nation and a royal priesthood (1 Pet. 2:11–12), being a church that overflowed walls and Sundays.

Dan Kimball claims that church success is measured by "looking at what our practices *produce* in the called people of God as they are sent out on a mission to live as light and salt in their communities (Matt. 5:13–16)."[1] And a powerful New Testament example of such a church is found in the emerging Thessalonian church of the first century: "You became an example to all believers in Macedonia and in Achaia. For the word of the Lord has sounded forth from you . . . in every place your faith in God has become known . . . and how you turned to God from idols, to serve a living and true God" (1 Thess. 1:7–9). These believers are urged to continue pleasing God "so that you may behave properly toward outsiders" (1 Thess. 4:12).

During my years as a pastor serving two churches for a total of twenty-one years, I helped plan weekly services of worship, ever yearning for fresh experiences of God's awesomeness, intrusiveness, inclusiveness, and community formation. My vision of worship occasionally opened up to high mountain possibilities "so that through the church the wisdom of God in its rich variety might now be made known to the rulers and authorities in the heavenly places. This was in accordance with the eternal purpose that he has carried out in Christ Jesus our Lord" (Eph. 3:10–11). Sometimes I sensed that what was happening within inauspicious four walls was cosmically connected with humankind's ultimate destiny.

Yet over time, in spite of yearning for bigger experiences in worship, I found myself settling for less. What else could I do? My church held worship services every week; I felt trapped by repetitive practicalities and routines. After living with a small picture of worship for a time, you eventually settle for its familiar scale and stop yearning for something more. Someone wryly commented, "Give me new Christians before they have heard too many sermons and been to too many worship services." For, unhappily, routines set in, expectations are lowered, self-interest grows, and worship can become trifling and banal.

The result is tragic. We actually downsize worship, dooming it to live in small boxes. With shortsightedness, we look through the wrong end of the binoculars. Worship has high claims about believers joining in the worship of heaven (Rev. 7:11–12), sharing in a new creation being formed (2 Cor. 5:17), and living praiseworthy lives before a watching world (1 Pet. 2:11–12). But instead, the term *worship* becomes locked down into planning Sunday services, especially the music. Those who plan Sunday services, especially the music, are called *worship leaders*. In spite of huge biblical promises about worship's all-inclusive nature, we trap ourselves in little boxes of worship services crammed full of concerns about power and control, preferences, and even selfishness.

So we settle for lowlands that treat higher ranges as fantasy, unlikely ever to be seen. Over time it appears increasingly unlikely that worship can be different. How could worship be more real, astonishing, closer, and higher for us than we could possibly imagine? Being "lost in wonder, love, and praise" remains only a line in an old hymn rather than an authentic possibility.

Seeing the Bigger Picture

This book tells of my journey from small-picture to big-picture worship and of some surprising people and events that challenged me to pick up binoculars and look through them the right way. In contrast with that brief glimpse in the Swiss lowlands that took my breath away, this journey has been lengthy and disturbing, tearing apart many of my assumptions, breaking open old habits, and forcing me to face uncomfortable questions. Gaining a bigger picture has forced me out of my comfort zone. As someone who thought he had preaching and worship safely buttoned down and sorted, I feel wildly alive as worship sorts out me!

Lytton Strachey's description of the historian's task aptly pictures my journey: "He will row out over the great ocean of material, and lower down into it, here and there, a little bucket, which will bring up to the light of day some characteristic specimen, from those far depths to be examined with a careful curiosity."[2] An ocean and a bucket sum up both the scale of this project and my inadequacies. Actually, one friend suggested it would be more accurate to say little buckets and several oceans, for worship comprises oceans of material with the widest of perspectives, complex theological depths, and a thousand different practical expressions. Worship can seemingly embrace everything and anything, stretching toward the widest of horizons and overwhelming by its scope that encompasses all of life.

For example, Susan White's survey of the foundations of Christian worship offers six basic theological models that Christians have used over two thousand years to understand worship:

1. *Service to God*: worship offers what we have and are ("offer your bodies as living sacrifices" [Rom. 12:1 NIV]).
2. *Mirror of heaven* (Rev. 4–5): worship enters ceaseless praises of heaven, associated with Orthodox and Eastern rites.
3. *Affirmation*: worship reinforces the Christian ethic for vocation (Ps. 56).

4. *Communion*: worship forms and sustains essential relationships (Acts 2:42).
5. *Proclamation*: worship is the principal place where Christians gather together to make public affirmation and witness (1 Pet. 2:9).
6. *Arena of transcendence*: worship enters the presence of the living God, overwhelmed by awesome holiness, majesty, and power (Exod. 3:5).

While analyzing the strengths and weaknesses of each model embedded in Scripture and church history, White recognizes that they must all live together in tension. "Worship is at the same time service and affirmation and proclamation; it is a place to encounter transcendence and it is a place to renew and celebrate our communion with God."[3] I echo her desire for a wide, comprehensive overview, but I confess intimidation by its dazzling reach of theology, spirituality, and history—especially when I consider the size of my bucket.

A little bucket speaks of inevitable limitations. Much of my ministry has been in Baptist churches in the United Kingdom and the United States, which means a largely nonliturgical background—by which I mean one lacking a historical (denominational) pattern of liturgy. Of course, as we will see, all worship patterns, no matter how informal, actually create liturgical forms. While I hope that my own leadership as a local church pastor showed some sensitive awareness of worship issues while I heeded the Christian year pattern, I needed to listen to those from strongly ordered liturgical backgrounds as well as to those who are so-called *worship specialists*. At any one of a hundred different points, worship demands specialist attention, such as in areas about liturgy, the Lord's Supper, baptism, music, the arts, and the role of culture.

Frustration levels have inevitably been high as more and more implications of worship have demanded attention. My wife recently burst out in exasperation, "If you go on reading book after book and keep telling me there's more and more you want to cover, you'll never reach the end. And you won't get *your* book written. Quit reading and work with what you have." Several times I have sensed that I have dipped my bucket enough, only to be faced with more critical omissions that demanded attention. One such concern hit me after I had completed the first draft. I had completely omitted mention of what I now call the "architecture of community formation"—how worship helps build God's new community not only through church services but also through service, witness, and ethics in the world every day of every week. So often attention focuses on patterning worship for one to two hours a week in church, but I have increasingly recognized that this should be only a shop window onto the total daily living of a people who offer the whole of their lives and relationships in true worship. So dipping a bucket into a great ocean remains an appropriately humbling analogy.

Encounters

Along the way, I made several serendipitous encounters through my bucket-dipping. Apparently the word *serendipity* ("the faculty of making fortunate discoveries by accident") originates from a Persian fairy tale. But I dare to believe that my discoveries—and some of them have been genuine surprises—have been by God's grace.

The most obvious encounters were with Robert Webber (1934–2007). Those who knew Bob will readily understand his impact on me during his last seven memorable years working at Northern Seminary. His larger-than-life persona contagiously caught the whole seminary community up into his life's passion for worship. With intellectual and spiritual zest, his writings and irrepressible fervor left few of us unaffected.

Reading his *Worship Is a Verb* set me alight in several ways. His diagnosis that much worship is in trouble today struck home. "Traditional worship seems over intellectualized, dry and something apart from where we live. And contemporary worship is too focused on 'my' experience."[4] His own experiences of shallow evangelical worship resonated with me as he identified four disturbing issues: (1) too much of our worship is dominated by the pastor; (2) the congregation is little more than an audience; (3) "free worship" is not necessarily free; and (4) the mystery is gone.[5]

I heard his plea to see worship as the primary work of the church. I was exhilarated to read his principles of worship that emphasize how worship celebrates Christ with wonder and festivity because God has spoken and acted. God's mighty deeds of salvation are the cause of worship that tells out and acts out the Christ event. Worship is meeting with God on his terms and for his purposes, and it sounds out the triumphant claim: "Christ has overcome the powers of evil. Be at peace."

Yet tragically, this message of God's mighty deeds goes missing.

> Often the service tells me what *I* have to do rather than celebrates what *Christ* has done. I'm told to live right, to witness, to get myself together, to forgive my enemies, and to give more money. But that's only part of the story. I also need to hear and experience the triumphant note that God has put away evil through his work in Christ.[6]

Webber startled me about preaching. While he made few direct references to preaching (and not always complimentary ones either), I kept seeing how much his critique and proposals involved the preacher. I was challenged not only about what positive differences these worship principles might make to preachers if they took them seriously, but also about how much damage preachers cause when they disregard them. The more urgently Webber presented this God-centered perspective on worship, the more he pushed me as a preacher to reexamine my own principles and practice.

His passion for God-focused worship led to his fathering the Ancient-Evangelical Future Call to the contemporary evangelical church, which includes these words:

> We call for public worship that sings, preaches and enacts God's story. . . . Thus, we call Evangelicals to turn away from forms of worship that focus on God as a mere object of the intellect, or that asserts the self as the source of worship. Such worship has resulted in lecture-oriented, music-driven, performance-centered and program-controlled models that do not adequately proclaim God's cosmic redemption. Therefore, we call Evangelicals to recover the historic substance of worship of Word and Table, and to attend to the Christian year, which marks time according to God's saving acts.[7]

I shivered when I first read that. Have I contributed to "lecture-oriented, music-driven, performance-centered and program-controlled models" of worship? Do I need to think harder about historic patterns of worship and the Christian year? Oh yes. Webber opened my eyes to see a bigger picture of worship, far beyond my limited practice.

Further, and even more devastating, he challenged me about how teaching preaching in seminary can become an end in itself. It can reinforce small-picture worship.

> Many seminaries do not even require worship courses or training. The training that pastors do get is in the art of preaching. . . . Unfortunately, because of this training and perhaps even because of their gifts, most pastors feel that preaching is the essence of worship. A few outstanding and gifted preachers build the church around their preaching and feel they are quite successful at it, but this is neither biblical nor is it, in the end, a means to good worship.[8]

This hit me between the eyes. Could my teaching develop in preachers a mind-set that "preaching is the essence of worship"? Could students emerge with an A in preaching without any wider understanding of worship? Since preachers are de facto leaders in most local churches, might seminary training continue to elevate preaching to the detriment of practicing worship? Webber profoundly distrusted any who acted as though God uses only preaching as *the* vital, solitary engine of church life and mission.

Along the way, many other authors have contributed to my journey. I was rocked by Harold Best's *Unceasing Worship: Biblical Perspectives on Worship and the Arts* and Mark Labberton's *The Dangerous Act of Worship*. Russell Mitman's *Worship in the Shape of Scripture* alerted me to a liturgical preacher's vision for Scripture's dominant role. James B. Torrance provided a powerful trinitarian theology for worship, and Marva Dawn and Dan Kimball offered insightful challenges from changing culture. Other striking themes included worship and spirituality (Don Saliers), community formation (Tod Bolsinger), and understanding worship as narrative (Cornelius Plantinga and Sue Roze-boom). And *Worship by the Book* and *Designing Worship Together* provided rich details about worship planning.[9] My quotations and reference notes will reveal some of the debt I owe to the thinking of others.

In addition to reading about worship, I encountered an unusual worship experience due to my seminary's desire for a new online course called "Preaching and Worshiping through the Christian Year." Co-writing and team teaching this course was a yearlong project during 2007 that involved collaboration with a worship specialist, Karen Roberts, who at that time taught worship at the seminary. I learned so much from our intensive teamwork.

Karen has preached only occasionally. She would say she is a novice at preparing sermons. While I have led worship services, I possess none of her rich knowledge of worship resources and liturgical flair developed over years of experience (to say nothing of her singing and keyboard skills). Her bookshelves are full of worship resources—many volumes of prayers, hymns, and visuals. Indeed, her seminary room delights eyes and ears with aesthetically placed pictures, icons, and inspiring music. Her work space beautifully expresses worship. In contrast, my shelves are stacked higgledy-piggledy with books—homiletics, theology, and commentaries. Scarcely anything is beautiful. Occasionally, CDs and DVDs of sermons can be heard, but frankly, little inspires.

We both agree that our collaboration on this course stretched us in unimaginable ways. Gleefully, Karen opened up literature on preaching and talked excitedly about how preachers prepare sermons and what this means for worship. Yes, really, she was truly excited to learn about preaching. Several times she lamented that many of her fellow worship specialists never have an opportunity to talk with their senior pastor about anything, let alone about their preaching preparation. And from the other side, working closely with a worship leader made me look at my preaching task in entirely fresh ways. I owe much to this period of collaboration, as will be evident in the last part of the book.

All the time as I was on my bucket-dipping journey, innumerable conversations with pastors and worship leaders, sometimes in the context of conferences and workshops but more often informally, further challenged my growing perceptions. Fortunately, continuing practical experience of preaching and leading worship in local churches also kept my feet on the ground and even enabled me to test some of my insights. Later I will mention my experience with blogging.

Urgency

The metaphor of rowing across an ocean with a bucket should not be pictured as a serene journey borne along by fair winds in pleasant sunshine. Rather, turbulent currents rage beneath and storms roar overhead. Worship is in trouble in many places for many reasons.

1. Most seriously, some worship palpably lacks a sense of encounter with God. Many echo Webber's criticisms—especially that the mystery has gone. William Hendricks interviewed people who had left the church and found two common themes. First, although they left the church, they claimed not to have left God. Second, they expressed disappointment because "people in church weren't religious enough and they couldn't find a sense of true communion."[10] Worship was found to be all too human in content and direction. As Marva Dawn comments, "Not one of them left because worship was too deep."[11] She is particularly associated with the critique that much current worship has been so dumbed down that it lacks spiritual reality. A Barna poll asked regular churchgoers how often church worship services brought them into God's presence. The results were as follows: 27 percent "always," 12 percent "usually," 27 percent "rarely," and 34 percent "never."[12] Mark Labberton lambasts much contemporary worship, saying that it settles for personal comfort instead of facing the dangerous reality of encountering the real God.

2. Culture has insidiously impacted worship. Understanding the relationship between gospel and culture is complex, and it opens up areas beyond this book's scope. David Fitch tellingly summarizes how evangelical worship has tended to develop into two dominant models. On one hand, "Lecture Hall worship" elevates the sermon and, encouraged by modernity, stresses individual appropriation of truth in terms of words, proposition, and reason. Such confidence in autonomous thinking worked effectively in modern culture, but postmodernity has undercut such confidence in individual human reason. Even more powerfully, culture has become the primary shaper of experience. "Souls, character, and imaginations are being formed by the culture technologies of the Cineplex, the television, the university, or the local Starbucks." So hearers may agree intellectually with sermons, but "their so-called autonomous minds are being compromised before they even come to church."[13]

On the other hand, however, he argues that "Rock Concert and the Feel-Good Pep Rally worship" centers on praise and musical self-expression. Again, influenced by modernity, it assumes that "personal self-expression, freedom in the Spirit and personal experience are the basis for authentic engagement with God."[14] Dangerously, it may put self at the center of worship, bringing in cultural assumptions, but in pursuing the arousal of emotions, the worship experience becomes an end in itself. Fitch points out historical and biblical reasons why evangelicals have espoused these models, but he warns that *both* models give away the formation of minds and imaginations to cultures that are foreign to the gospel. Worshiping God in his glory should be the primary influence on the thinking and behavior of individuals within the Christian community, not the influence of the surrounding culture.

To underline how complex this subject is, it is worth noting that worship as *spectacle* may not necessarily lead to self-indulgence. Indeed, in the Old Testament worship was a carefully planned spectacle to confront the nation with God's transcendence. While well aware of dangers of performance, Tex Sample argues that today "spectacle and performance are basic indigenous practices in an electronic culture" and that "the use of image, beat and visualization has encoded younger generations in new ways and that music traditions reflect and enact soul."[15] His challenge that the church join the practices of an electronic culture while keeping faith with God's story and appropriate liturgy requires a careful response.

3. *Aided and abetted by cultural preferences, worship dominated by debate over musical styles has ironically caused congregational conflict in too many places.* Marva Dawn begins her book *Reaching Out without Dumbing Down* by saying, "I am worried about the Church. The 'worship wars' that rage in so many congregations are preventing us from truly being the Church."[16] Warren Wiersbe's book *Real Worship* is subtitled *Playground, Battleground, or Holy Ground?*[17] Sadly, for many churches the prime cause of tension is music—though other worship issues can also stir dissension. For example, a Presbyterian pastor informed me that the bitter divide in his church is about whether the offering should come before or after the sermon.

4. *There are certain specific, identifiable, current weaknesses in acts of worship.* For example, William Willimon notes common failings in much Protestant worship:

1. lack of focus and coherence in the acts of worship
2. inadequate treatment of Scripture
3. inadequate opportunities for congregational participation
4. insufficient attention to the acts of gathering for worship
5. architectural setting not always conducive to the type of worship climate we wish to create
6. exclusion of children
7. poor formation and leadership of public prayer
8. woeful neglect of baptism and the Lord's Supper[18]

While some bright exceptions exist, much worship sadly lacks holy encounter with God, fails to build communities that make a difference, is riven by music discord, and practices sloppy, lazy patterns. But when worship fails, the church completely misses its reason for existing.

What This Book Is Not

While noting some of these urgent problems, I must emphasize what this book is *not* about. First, it does not browbeat by a loaded *agenda*. I recognize that earlier references to Robert Webber might suggest that I will be promoting an *ancient-future evangelical* emphasis, particular orders of worship, the Christian year, or a strong link between the Word and the Lord's Table. It is true that each of these emphases (and many others) will emerge, but it will be within the much wider framework of big-picture worship that forms community.

Equally, this is not a personal *fad*, as though a worship bug has bitten me that now displaces other enthusiasms. Previously I have written ardently about preaching, but this is not a lessening of earlier convictions. Rather, as you will see, this new vision of worship has enriched both my understanding and my practice of preaching and has actually increased my enthusiasm as a preacher.

Obviously, given the bucket-ocean metaphor, this is not an *encyclopedic* approach that attempts to sum up all important aspects of worship and thread them into a TOE—a Theory of Everything. Experts in worship will note many gaps and lament my partial reading and oversimplifications. Inevitably, much is omitted, and my work-in-progress needs abler minds and experienced practitioners to join in. The ocean remains too wide and deep for one small book.

Neither is this *lightweight* in content. Theological and missiological dimensions of worship will be introduced to stretch readers. The journey to big-picture worship demands thoughtful responses. Someone commented, "It doesn't take a great brain to be a Christian, but it takes all the brain you have." I believe that claim applies particularly to understanding worship. Rather than introduce preachers to a new idea here or there, this book seeks to revolutionize preachers' perspectives of everything, because worship involves everything, including preaching.

Finally, this book spends little time on *styles* of worship. Commonly, individual churches now offer different styles in separate worship services, generally based on music, such as traditional, contemporary, classic, and blended. Music inevitably requires consideration, and tensions about style will certainly emerge in discussion about community formation. But there is no style blueprint that subtly, or otherwise, advocates a preferred format.

What This Book Is

While admitting to the limits of bucket-dipping, I nevertheless have a bold goal: to open preachers' eyes afresh to glorious big-picture worship. I urge them help to restore worship as an encounter with God. He calls us to worship in spirit and truth, with depths of spirituality and unity that help form us as his people. This book proffers a heavyweight call for preachers to retake their worship responsibilities for God's sake.

The following pages tell how my journey shredded some of my assumptions, upended some preaching principles, and complicated my practice. But I consider these *glorious* shreddings, upendings, and complications. They have given me an enthusiasm for preaching that now belongs within an awareness of how much bigger worship is—growing a people beyond worship services into worshipful living. With wonder and excitement, I now believe in big-picture worship that makes for larger preaching and deeper living. This book has high ambitions to turn preachers around, challenging them *to become worshipers first and to commit to sharing God's biggest purpose, which is called* worship.

Glimpsing worship's big vista as God intends places sermon-making within its scope, and as a result, many preachers will face a revolutionary concept that worship proclaims and preaching worships as God's new creation is formed in Christ. They will be challenged to relocate preaching within worship, with theological, spiritual, and practical integrity. In short, this book calls for preaching as worship.

Moving preachers from small-picture to big-picture worship means a major change from seeing worship as an activity alongside preaching and pastoring to viewing it as *the* integrative activity that holds everything else together. For those of us who once viewed preaching as all-important, I plead for a shift of worldview. Instead of claiming the supremacy of preaching, I dare to claim the supremacy of worship, which includes preaching and much else.

The Preacher's Role

As you can tell from the book's title and this introduction, I especially focus this book on preachers. Why? Because preachers have the major responsibility. Their highly visible public leadership role inevitably influences local churches' understanding and practice of worship. By attention or inattention, by domination and manipulation, or by avoidance of responsibility, preachers impact worship for better or worse. They reveal (wittingly or unwittingly) their own convictions about church priorities by allocations of time and commitment. When a senior pastor thinks little about worship (we will see some symptoms and causes in the next two chapters), it is unlikely that many in the congregation will think much of it either. Low expectations of worship from the pulpit reinforce low expectations everywhere else.

In my reading and discussion with others about worship, I discovered immense creativity and commitment. But unless preachers connect with this creativity and commitment, they are unlikely to flourish. Perhaps it is a blinding grasp of the obvious, but if preachers do not see the big picture of worship, others won't either. By their action or inaction, preachers bear great responsibility for community formation and how communities worship. Preachers are *critical* to how communities worship.

What Lies Ahead?

This book is divided into three parts: Part 1 begins the journey "From a Small Picture of Worship." Chapter 2 highlights an incident that seems symptomatic of the often-troubling relationship between preachers and worship that leads to some sober reflections on why preachers usually are not interested in worship. Chapter 3 follows with a critical assessment of any preaching that is disinterested in worship. Ten characteristics spell out such *myopic preaching* and underline the disaster facing preachers who blithely ignore the implications of big-picture worship. Addressing each of these characteristics requires the rest of the book.

Part 2, "Toward a Bigger Picture of Worship," offers a new framework for understanding preaching as worship. Chapter 4 tackles the first two characteristics of myopic preaching, advocating a fuller definition and a more adequate theology of worship, exploring the dynamics of trinitarian worship, and applying the first of six principles to preaching itself. Chapter 5 describes the revolutionary outcome this brings to preaching and offers a fresh model that integrates various insights. Chapter 6 pursues how Scripture can direct both general worship structures as well as specific patterns for acts of gathered worship. Chapter 7 examines the relationship between Scripture and liturgy focusing on the Christian year, the lectionary, and other worship resources. Chapter 8 opens up the large subject of community formation, describing its missional theology and various interacting dynamics involved. Chapter 9 attempts to integrate the many elements involved in community formation by delineating four progressive stages. Throughout part 2, six questions emerge that form a *question toolbox* that needs to be applied when planning gathered worship.

Part 3 introduces a fresh process of planning for big-picture worship. Principles emerging from parts 1 and 2 are practically grounded, though practices will inevitably vary greatly as preachers collaborating work through implications of big-picture worship in many different contexts. Chapter 10 provides an overview of the new pattern that involves preachers with other worship planners through six stages of the *worship swim*. Chapter 11 describes stage 1, "commit to worship," by seeking unity of heart, head, and hand. Chapter 12 continues with stages 2 and 3 by emphasizing the responsibility of letting Scripture shape sermons and gathered worship, while chapter 13 considers stage 4, "help shape gathered worship," which involves rigorous application of the question toolbox. It also deals with outcomes when delivering sermons and leading worship (stage 5). Finally, chapter 14 considers the complex yet vital need for evaluating outcomes of big-picture worship (stage 6).

Hopefully you will share some of the shocks but also the delights of my journey and you will come to understand why I, as a preacher, am so passionate in my beliefs about worship. I recognize that your starting point may be far removed from mine. Perhaps you already have a fully formed appreciation of worship and preaching's role within it. Certainly you are likely to add many significant issues that are not covered here. But in talking with many other pastors, especially those sharing a similar background, I have often found both honest confession that admits to small-picture thinking and genuine desire for fresh thinking.

As a seventeen-year-old, I met sculptor Henry Moore. With youthful naivete, three of us turned up unannounced at his front door and invited ourselves to spend some time with him. The hour he generously gave us, talking about his work, engaging with us, and allowing us to wander around his studio and then roam his grounds, is unforgettable. His creativity was extraordinary to witness firsthand. But something he wrote stuck with me. It expresses both the passion and the tension that I have discovered about worship: "The secret of life is to have a task, something you devote your entire life to, something you bring everything to, every minute of the day for the rest of your life. And the most important thing is, it must be something you cannot possibly do."[19]

Of course, along the way God enables you to worship in spirit and truth. Yet once you have tasted the glories ahead, you know real worship is something you cannot fully experience this side of heaven. But we live this side of heaven and must get down to business.

PART 1

From a Small Picture of Worship

2

Preaching and Worship

Is There a Problem?

Pastors aren't usually interested in worship.
comment at a worship conference

My thinking about worship began with a nagging problem: the widening gap between preaching and worship. Earlier Christian worship assumed that preaching and worship—Word and sacrament—were indissolubly linked. Older books on preaching often emphasized how closely preaching and worship belong together. But this relationship seems to have broken down in many places.

Let me illustrate. In 2006, I attended the Calvin Symposium on Worship in Grand Rapids, Michigan, along with 1,600 others. One of the organizers said to me, "Do you know that we have over 250 pastors here this year?" Unable to detect the speaker's point of view from his tone of voice, I asked whether this was a good or bad thing. "Oh, very good," came the reply. "Pastors aren't usually interested in worship."

That reply shocked me. By *pastors* he meant senior pastors who are generally preachers. Was such a sweeping statement justified? Maybe lack of money or time, rather than a lack of interest, meant some preachers were absent. And anyway, at least 250 *had* turned up. But his assertion got under my skin.

Lack of Interest in Worship

Over the following months I listened closely to fellow preachers' opinions about worship as well as reflected on my own thinking and behavior. With regret and embarrassment, I concluded that his statement is largely correct: many preachers aren't usually interested in worship. This book is dedicated to finding out why this is so and to revealing how preachers have succumbed to the same influences that have impoverished the understanding of worship in general. They are victims of small-picture worship. We will discuss eight symptoms of this lack of interest.

1. Worship Is Considered Less Important

Worship lies lower down the priority list behind preaching, leadership, pastoral care, and administration. Hubris plagues the act of preaching; rightly convinced of preaching's importance, preachers can wrongly become self-important. Investing all their effort in sermon-making, and claiming its importance for proclaiming the gospel (Rom. 10:9), they can sideline worship as a secondary matter. Charles Rice mischievously describes such an attitude as viewing the sermon as "a kind of homiletical ocean liner, preceded by a few liturgical tugboats."[1] Worship is reduced to tugboat scale.

Consider John Killinger's assertion:

> There is no substitute for preaching in worship. It provides the proclamatory thrust without which the church is never formed and worship is never made possible. It complements the creedal, poetic nature of the liturgy and keeps before men the absolute contemporaneity of the Gospel, as of a Word made always present and personal to them under the pressure of their current life-situations. . . . Above all it provides better than anything else the necessary encounter between the lackadaisical worshiper and intensity of Christ's lord-ship. It, of all the elements in the liturgy, is primary, for it and it alone is able to guarantee the success of Christian worship and the Christian sacraments.[2]

I thrill to this high view of preaching's "proclamatory thrust," but though he uses the word *complements*, I am uneasy about the implication that worship is almost useless without a sermon. Is it true that preaching "alone is able to guarantee the success of Christian worship and the Christian sacraments"? Is it not possible that a congregation might encounter God and proclaim the gospel just as powerfully in the bread and cup as in the spoken word (1 Cor. 11:26)? And just how necessary is a liturgy involving everyone in congregational praise, confession, and intercession for worship to be effective?

A Christian leader recently blurted out despairingly, "I find many preachers are so smug. They think everything revolves around them." Hopefully, very few deserve that indictment—but it made me nervous.

2. Worship Is Viewed as Burdensome

Worship planning is an extra hassle added to a conscientious pastor's heavy workload, so many seek to delegate responsibility for it if at all possible. Probably, frowns and yawns are the preacher's most common reaction to worship. Already needing to prepare one weekly sermon (or more), pastors just try to keep afloat among daily pastoral and administrative pressures of church and community. Worship understandably seems a bridge too far. "Why get us more involved in worship?" said one exasperated pastor. "Isn't it enough to produce sermons every week while trying to keep our heads above water among all the pastoral, administrative, and leadership demands? How can you seriously expect us to be involved with worship too?"

Pastoral fatigue is understandable, and no one should deny that responsible worship planning *is* hard work. But properly understood, worship invites preachers to a new way of working with fresh power and perspective, as I will seek to show.

3. Worship Is Seen as a Specialist Subject

This symptom needs lengthier description. Perhaps the main reason why relatively few preachers attended the Calvin Symposium on Worship stems from its title—it sounds like a conference for worship leaders only. Later I will suggest that the term *worship leaders* is unhelpfully limited, but conventionally it describes those who design and lead congregational services. In larger churches, these are paid roles, sometimes with significant budgets dedicated to excellence in Sunday worship, which is sometimes erroneously limited to the music program. Yet even in smaller churches, where the pastor is more likely to be responsible for both preaching and leading of worship, volunteer musicians and others are increasingly developing roles alongside the preacher, often gaining their own spheres of influence.

Understandably, preachers may hesitate about being involved in this special worship world—looking after choirs, singing groups, organs, guitars, and all the rest. Surely this is best left to people who are gifted and trained. Let those responsible for worship services get on with their task.

Our seminary welcome lounge has magazines for browsing. Among them are *Preaching: The Professional Magazine for Preachers* and *Worship Leader Magazine: More of What You Need to Lead*. Most visitors pick up one or the other; there seems to be minimal overlap. Prospective students can opt for the Master of Divinity course of study, which includes preaching, or the Master of Arts in Christian Worship. Those studying worship feel no need to take any preaching courses and vice versa.

Aided and abetted by seminaries, various guilds have developed. Dictionaries of liturgy and worship have no entries for preaching, while encyclopedias of preaching have no entries for worship. The North American Academy of

Liturgy has many study groups, but none are for preaching. Probably they expect the Academy of Homiletics to focus on that.

Some guild literature reinforces a professional divide between worship and preaching with minimal reference to each other. For example, Gregory Dix's classic, *The Shape of the Liturgy*, gives space amounting to 2 out of 764 pages to the role of the sermon.[3] Sometimes preaching may be identified as a key component yet receive only slight attention. In *The Complete Worship Service: Creating a Taste of Heaven on Earth*, Kevin Navarro extols the importance of preaching. "The more I think of my preaching as an act of worship and not merely as an act of exhortation, the more gospel I will have in my message."[4] Yet though he likens preaching to the main course in a well-prepared meal, it receives only limited attention in the penultimate chapter. Others highlight inevitable tensions such as how efforts at liturgical renewal have often minimized the role of preaching. "Mainline congregations, discouraged by legacies of poor preaching, tend to minimize the sermon by over-stating the place of the sacraments."[5]

Some homileticians have tried to reach across the gap. Thomas Troeger's *Preaching and Worship* concerns the interrelationship of culture, preaching, and worship.[6] Deploying a cultural analysis of the five senses, he raises important questions for understanding both preaching and worship, though without integrating them theologically. William Willimon's *Preaching and Leading Worship* provides practical checklists and guidelines but also does not pursue how preaching may belong as worship.[7]

Of course, many preachers are sensitive about worship. In *The Preaching Life*, Barbara Brown Taylor describes preaching in her Book of Common Prayer tradition: "The words of the liturgy are theologically correct words that stay the same from week to week. A sermon, on the other hand, is an act of creation with real risk in it. . . . For the preacher, the discipline of the sermon is to respond to the Word of God as one who represents both God and the people of God."[8]

Michael Knowles emphasizes how preaching relates to pastoral concerns in the context of corporate worship in 2 Corinthians 1:1–6:13.

> As worship is the proper human response to divine self-revelation, so preaching itself is an act of praise. It is doxological in the sense that it arises from and responds to God's saving action. . . . Preaching is a function not primarily of form . . . but of spirituality. . . . In particular, properly "Christian" preaching focuses on the person of Christ as instrumental to the relationship between God's creation, God's creatures, and their Creator.[9]

Yet these and other provocative references to preaching and worship (some of which will appear later) seem all too rare in literature that often separates worship from preaching, seeing them as distinctive disciplines. As a painful footnote, I must also admit that my own past writing on preaching failed to honor worship's role.[10]

So preachers can be trained to preach without receiving any teaching on worship itself, and those who lead worship have their own training. Disturbingly, this glaring deficiency allows each to work within his or her own professional box.

4. Worship Is Deemed Controversial

As noted earlier, worship styles have sadly contributed to friction and sometimes even divided churches, causing some preachers to become understandably wary. Someone commented that worship should be spelled "warship," and tragically, the term *worship wars* describes conflict, sometimes bitterly splitting congregations over worship styles. Fault lines divide traditional from contemporary, liturgical from informal, historical from new, boomers from busters, and busters from millennials. Personal preferences can hijack worship's grander, inclusive vision, with believers settling instead for exclusive pockets of choice. Examples abound, as in the annual assembly of the Convention of Atlantic Baptist Churches in Canada, which gives delegates the choice of contemporary (rock band), contemplative, traditional, or global worship. No inclusive possibility there.

Music plays a powerful part in gathered worship and perhaps inevitably leads to strong expression and sometimes even power struggles. "Worship wars may actually be about worship; people do have legitimate concerns and convictions. . . . Just as often, however, these skirmishes reflect a more generalized struggle for power."[11] Sparring over preferred worship styles sometimes reveals tension over who is in charge rather than a desire to worship God. Whatever its reason, such worship controversy endangers the unity and witness of Christ's church.

Sadly, when it comes to worship conflict, preachers may be even keener to pass by on the other side, leaving worship leaders and others to minister to wounded congregations. But worship calls for the noblest and most mature of responses, and opting out is not an option.

5. Worship Is Reckoned an Enthusiasm

Some preachers treat worship like overseas missions—likely to attract only a small number of committed enthusiasts. Undeniably, people with *affective personalities* are visibly moved by worship: from rapt attention to the high aesthetics of organ and choral singing to holistic participation in informal worship with hands raised and feet dancing. One of my affective friends speaks about *losing herself in worship*, and she appears oblivious to everything else during the singing of worship songs. She belongs to a worship planning group that meets enthusiastically each week. Beginning with extended worship and prayer among themselves, members invest considerable amounts of energy and commitment to service preparation. They willingly give hours each week to follow up phone and email contacts.

Such visible engagement sometimes contrasts sharply with others' seeming lack of involvement. Perhaps because of their very public responsibility for leading, most preachers are reluctant to allow themselves to be *lost in worship*—whatever their personalities. But when faced by others' strong passion, preachers may be tempted to leave worship to the enthusiasts.

Ideally, preachers need to identify with such groups and encourage them to see that their particular gifting belongs within the wider fellowship. After all, enthusiasm literally means "in godness" and should benefit the whole community's worship. Incidentally, preachers should continually self-check how they *appear* as worshipers. I remember being surprised by a church member who commented, "I so appreciate it when you really sing the hymns and songs with us and obviously mean it." I responded, "Do you mean that sometimes I don't seem involved?" "Oh yes!" came the emphatic reply. Preachers who appear disengaged may unwittingly impact others, giving the impression that public worship is really for other people and that they have a more important focus elsewhere. The critic, however, may have been focusing too much on the pastor—sometimes people in the congregation are watching someone else (such as the band or pastor) instead of offering themselves.

6. Worship Causes Personal Pain

Perhaps because of issues already mentioned, some preachers and worship leaders have been mired in bad relationships that leave a bitter taste. You can chart relationships between preachers and worship leaders across a broad spectrum—from warm cooperation to competitiveness and even cold hostility. Sadly, anecdotal evidence shows that negative relationships abound; for every one happy team, there seems to be another dysfunctional one. On one hand, preachers may appear to demote worship leaders to a secondary role as service organizers. When sermons are regarded as primary, worship is reduced to plying musical ability and arranging service elements appropriately. On the other hand, worship leaders know the power of communal worship, and smarting from being underrated, they may even question how effective sermons are for creating and sustaining overall congregational life. They are unlikely to be surprised by a survey that showed that a significant percentage of a worshiping community "perceived that other worship acts were just as helpful as the sermon, sometimes even more so."[12]

Thoughtless behavior sometimes reinforces tension. I visited a well-staffed church where the senior pastor ("100 percent dedicated to preaching," he claimed) viewed the church service on a television monitor in his office. Relaxing comfortably until moments before he had to preach the sermon, he then emerged dramatically at the front of the church for the *main event*. In another church, however, I discovered the worship leader obviously absent when it came time for the sermon. Having completed his tasks of leading the choir and orchestra during the first part of the service, he disappeared, perhaps to enjoy a cup of coffee. I have heard pastors complain that music is rated as too important in their church, and worship leaders resent how little interest preachers take in their work. One worship leader criticized the preacher because, in spite of repeated promises, he never provided Scripture and sermon details until late in the week. Another worship leader with a significant choral ministry said, "When I take a choir on mission, singing in different parts of the world, I always feel that our senior minister thinks it's a waste of time. I don't think he believes we have a valid ministry." Some worship leaders may also resent pastors *overstepping boundaries* by being involved in worship—a risk this book will encourage.

How easily tension can flare up whenever people work together. Look at the disciples (Mark 9:34; Luke 22:24) or Paul and Barnabas (Acts 15:36–40). Friction arises in the best of teams, especially when leaders work in the public eye. Admittedly, some preachers find it difficult to relate to others (Thomas Long once reckoned that most *great* preachers are introverts),[13] and some worship leaders may be difficult too. A worship leader said to me, smiling, "Music produces an above-average number of prima donnas." All kinds of issues may cause friction. I recently heard about a worship leader who chooses songs based entirely on which key they are set in. Apparently, making an agreeable musical transition to the next song is the only criterion that matters. Unhappily, both preachers and worship leaders can be awkward, territorial, and uncooperative. One of my readers commented that this inevitably accompanies current *Christian star culture*, which praises leaders for gifts and feeds their self-importance.

7. Worship Is Dismissed as Boring

Over the last three years, several people have asked me, "Michael, what are you working on at the moment?" But when I answer "worship," their faces immediately register a thumbs-down attitude. Some have called this a MEGO complex—"my eyes glaze over." I sense that if I had answered that I was researching the emergent church, missional leadership, or church planting, there would have been a positive buzz. Bluntly, some people find worship a boring subject, though we will see how it encompasses all these subjects and more.

8. Worship Is Just Not Understood

Underlying many of these symptoms is genuine puzzlement among some preachers about what worship really means. Sadly, because it is possible to graduate from seminary without taking any course in worship, preachers can find themselves woefully lacking a biblical and theological understanding of worship, with almost a total lack of exposure to its history and practice in the great traditions of the church. Without theology and biblical spirituality, worship can easily degrade to matters of style, taste, aesthetics, and experience with no bedrock on which to build. Faced by others' expectations about worship, which are often strongly influenced by culture, preachers can find themselves utterly bewildered.

These eight symptoms, and possibly more, are signs that worship is being pushed aside, squashed into a separate box, or regarded as somebody else's business. Of course, for preachers the act of preaching itself occupies a much bigger box, and worship, of smaller concern, is elbowed off to the sidelines. The word *box* may suggest a small vision, but some have a very large view of preaching, almost a worldview in which preaching is central to everything else in ministry and mission.

In Peter Weir's iconic movie *The Truman Show*, Truman (played by Jim Carrey) is unaware that since birth he has been the star of the ultimate reality show. Living under a dome constructed over several square miles, he has no idea that this "world"—all the scenery surrounding him—is under a producer's command, as is the cast of thousands. For thirty years his town, island, and sea are all that he has ever known. Yet the film reveals his growing suspicion that more lies beyond his world. Eventually he sails out, and in a memorable scene, his boat's prow suddenly hits the outer wall of his domed world. Discovering the horizon is painted scenery and the ocean is only knee-deep, he begins to walk along to some steps leading up to a door marked *exit*. His struggle in front of the exit door marks the movie's climax. Will he dare to step out into the unknown world, far bigger than anything he could imagine, or will he stay safely within his known world?

Preachers who live with a *preaching worldview* or within a *preaching dome* may think they see everything that matters. But I want to sound out the disturbing possibility that all they see actually belongs within something immeasurably larger. They have only a small picture, and beyond, a much larger vista exists. Whenever preachers push worship to one side, they settle for a smaller picture. Unknowingly, they suffer from critical shortsightedness. They become myopic.

Physical eyesight can be checked regularly. My ophthalmologist annually tests my eyes and prescribes appropriate strength contact lenses so that I can see in the distance as well as close-up. But the symptoms and treatment of preaching myopia are much more complex because many preachers have no idea of their condition. I certainly didn't.

A Story

The most dramatic incident of my twenty-one years of pastoral ministry didn't seem so at the time. I have told parts of the story elsewhere, though here I will reflect more fully on what happened. I had been at the downtown Cambridge church only a few months. St. Andrew's Street Baptist Church occupies an impressive building situated on one of the main city streets and has a rich history since 1721 of mighty preachers and influential congregations. But from those heady days it had gradually declined through the twentieth century until 1980, when I was called to be pastor. The small, elderly, but eager congregation numbered around seventy people in a building that could seat a thousand.

Its worship services were fairly formal (unusual for a Baptist church), with sung psalms led by a tiny choir both morning and evening. The robed preacher (complete with academic hood) mounted a high central pulpit. The usual pattern of worship included a call to worship with gathering hymn and prayers of adoration and confession (including the Lord's Prayer). A chanted psalm was then followed by a talk with the children (who could be numbered on one hand). Then an offering was taken, followed by special music from the choir and lengthier prayers for others. Scripture reading(s) preceded the sermon, which was followed by prayer and a final hymn before the benediction. With order and dignity, the congregation sang out of the denominational hymnbook, previously revised in 1963.

If you asked me about worship, I would have described it exactly in these terms, explaining that there were two services on Sundays at 10:45 a.m. and 6:30 p.m. Both followed the same pattern, with the Lord's Supper celebrated on the first Sunday in the morning and the third Sunday in the evening. At that time I probably would have been fairly defensive about the church's small numbers and traditionalism. Given the chance, I would have told you that preaching was my main passion and calling and left you in little doubt that worship structures were inherited patterns that could be improved but were strategically much less important than preaching. By saying this, I am disclosing several symptoms that expose what was my lackluster interest in worship.

In May 1980, I was asked to meet someone on the church's front steps. So that morning I bicycled there, leaned my bike against the steps, and waited. The steps led up to solid oak doors that were shut fast. In those next minutes as I waited, I saw dozens of people, all kinds of people: students weaving on bicycles, tourists in excited knots with cameras poised, shoppers with bags of all kinds, young mothers pushing babies in strollers, businesspeople purposefully striding. And especially, I noticed homeless people leaning against the wall, shaking empty cups, and saying, "I'm hungry." People kept moving relentlessly past, four or five deep. I am not sure how long I stayed—probably about fifteen minutes. The person who requested the meeting never showed up, but I believe in those fifteen minutes God engaged me in a fresh way.

I realized with a jolt that I had never been at the church's front doors when the city was alive. I always came down on Sundays, when it was quiet and easier to park, or sometimes in the evenings I slipped in by the side door for private meetings. While the city was awake, packed with people of every kind and every need, we were closed. We only opened for private moments behind almost closed doors.

Seeing those closed oak doors and the many people passing by troubled me more than I can say. I felt overwhelmed. I wasn't sure what we should do. I wondered whether this experience might be a vision from God. Certainly I had been hit by a new awareness about the ineffectiveness of my ministry. Yes, I was preaching Good News, but only at times that were convenient for us but inconvenient for others. We welcomed people in, but only if they fit in with our agenda.

I wondered how the congregation would respond to a challenge concerning the closed doors when the city was alive and open doors when the city was dead. Would there be any concern or energy to act? When I shared my burden with the wider congregation, I found ready sympathy yet, understandably, also a strong sense of being overwhelmed by the challenge. How could a small group of people be equal to the task of opening doors to the city? We agreed to pray for guidance to know what exactly Jesus Christ was calling us to join him in doing. We organized our prayer corporately, agreeing to particular petitions and intercessions for persistent prayer (Luke 11:5–10). We believed God was already at work on the sidewalk and everyone in those crowds mattered to him.

Gradually we grew to realize that this *open doors* vision was God's future for us. He was calling us to proclaim his Good News, on his own terms, every day of the week. Somehow we needed to fling wide those doors and be present in Jesus's name for every kind of person walking by. Momentum developed through fourteen years of praying and preaching to be a community open seven days a week. Alongside the church, a restaurant was opened offering food to passersby. Counseling was given to people lost and disturbed. Young people had a safe space to be with their friends on the top floor. Two job clubs were established to help the long-term unemployed.

The most complex group of people needing help was the homeless. Dozens of them slept outside every night in the city. After Sunday services they waited on the steps with hands open or holding empty coffee cups. We knew Christ was calling for a deeper response than offering money or inviting them in for food. They required shelter, but only our large upper hall was left to accommodate them. If we said yes, it could render other parts of our work vulnerable and would require many support teams of church people. Those who worked with our children and young people were especially apprehensive. Yet the more we learned about Christ's upside-down kingdom where nobodies count and the unloved are loved, the more we knew we had to act. The night the whole congregation convened to vote whether to open up our main hall in order to provide a place for the homeless to sleep was a long-awaited outcome of my church-steps vision. Unanimously the congregation said yes, and we began forming teams of four to stay overnight in order to care, cook, and counsel through the cruel winter months.

Now the important question is how I best describe this fourteen-year story. Most obviously, I have generally summed it up as *mission*—joining in God's work through collective witness that embraced both evangelism and social action. The story of opening up the church to serve the city throughout the week was clearly mission in action. Sometimes I spoke of the open-doors work as "the laboratory where we put Sunday claims into practice Mondays to Saturdays." So it did have a relationship with what was preached on Sundays, but until I gained a deeper understanding of worship deeply rooted in theology and biblical spirituality, I did not conceive of this as *worship* itself.

I have already told you how I viewed worship in terms of church service patterns offered to God behind those doors on Sundays. But I have now come to see I was living in a *preaching dome*. I had separated preaching and mission from what I regarded as worship—the rest of what happened in Sunday services. Worship was downsized to describe orders, hymns, songs, prayers, and sermon. I had forgotten my New Testament theology.

> In the New Testament there is no problem of the connection of worship and mission, because they are seen as unified aspects of God's relation with man. This totality has been fragmented; the two have been placed in separate compartments so that worship and mission, which should be one, have become isolated facets of the Church's life.[14]

The outcome of my new worldview, described in this book, is that I now want to claim the word *worship* as appropriate to sum up all the best that happened over fourteen years. *Worship* does justice to the whole story. It is utterly comprehensive, involving people praising and serving God with all they have and are—both in gathered services and through open doors into the life of the community around. In him we live and move and have our being. Worship embraces vision, mission, and *everything* else, for nothing is more important than living together for God's glory. Methodist preacher Bill Sangster used to speak of service beyond services, and the two belong together in worship as the whole point of Christian living. Within four walls and beyond four walls, militant and triumphant (Heb. 12:22–24), worship is the greatest unifying desire of a new people living utterly for God. *Worship* is *the* theological word to describe living for God's big picture. Magnificently it brings together all the grandest themes imaginable—of our Triune God, mission, and community.

So much of my earlier thinking presumed that worship was restricted to Sunday services. What happened during organized services seemed to sum up 90 percent of worship. That May morning in 1980, I was living within the preaching dome and was suffering from myopic preaching. Now I have come to realize that worship is so much bigger than any of us can imagine. I have stepped through the exit door of the dome! Before I move on to clarify what defines big-picture worship (part 2), I need to examine the serious condition of myopia in the next chapter. But I also need to pause briefly for a reality check.

A Warning—Don't Give Up

One of my friends, having reached this far in the manuscript, sent me a warning. He told me of a recent conversation with another pastor along these lines about worship's importance. The other pastor's response, however, showed he had great difficulty grasping such a comprehensive view of worship. Clearly caught up with the nuts and bolts of worship practice, he couldn't make much practical sense of a bigger picture. It all seemed too complex to take on board. My friend imagined how poorly this pastor might respond to this chapter, with exasperation at its large but vague vision as he stomped off, full of confusion and muttering, "What exactly is worship?"

May I counsel patience to read on? The worship issues I raise are indeed complex for preachers and all those who lead worship within a culture that has long viewed worship in limited ways. Without even realizing it, many of us are deeply embedded within a large, systemic problem caused by a false or inadequate understanding of what God desires worship to be. It's his plan for worship that really matters, and for too long we have been satisfied with our plans.

I hope that my own journey honestly reveals something of the struggles I faced in wrestling with the question: What exactly is worship? The last thing I want to do is paint myopic preaching insensitively or big-picture worship simplistically, as though the process of moving from a small to a large picture is easy. It is demanding—but infinitely worthwhile! Please stay with me.

3

Beware Myopic Preaching

To worship is to experience reality, to touch Life.
Richard Foster

As a young schoolboy, my squinting at the blackboard alerted teachers to my poor eyesight, and I was sent to the optometrist. I guess my vision had worsened so slowly that I was unaware how limited my eyesight had become. The blur in the distance had become an acceptable everyday experience. But I have never forgotten that first visit to the optometrist when he tried out different lenses and, at a stroke, gave me back the vivid details of life. I had grown used to living in a haze.

In the last chapter, I suggested myopia was an appropriate metaphor for small-picture preaching. Myopia is defined as "a visual defect in which distant objects appear blurred because their images are focused in front of the retina rather than on it; nearsightedness."[1] Often unaware how limited its vision has become, myopic preaching misses out on God's long-range worship perspective, on the details of life.

Myopic preaching is marked by ten characteristics, each a serious indicator that preachers have separated their task from worship. Together these features portray a general profile of preachers who aren't usually interested in worship. Please forgive any caricature in my description. Clearly this list is far from exhaustive, and other issues could likely be added. Indeed, each of these signs of myopic preaching could be a chapter in itself. The priority in ordering I have given shows something of their relative importance. In this chapter, I will briefly describe each, and in later chapters I will begin to redress them all.

1. Faulty Definitions

How people define worship shows its relative value to them. When understood in limited ways, worship is inevitably devalued. Below are some shorthand (though popular) conceptions of worship that do just that.

Music Only

Perhaps the most common devaluation of worship labels it *all* about hymns and songs. For some churches, *praise and worship* sums up not only 99 percent of the worship team's responsibility but also worship itself. Since music is deemed all-important, those with musical ability become *worship leaders*, thereby reinforcing the impression that music comprises worship. What they lead is regarded as genuine worship, and any other activity is marginal. I have heard worship leaders say, "Let's have some more worship before we hear the message." Gary Parrett tells of the church where the worship leaders got up the courage to ask the senior pastor whether he would sometimes omit the sermon in order to make more room for worship.[2] This interchangeability of *music* with *worship* is probably the single most damaging misdefinition of worship. Calling those who lead music *worship leaders* dangerously shrinks worship down to their work as musicians.

Paul Beasley-Murray hints that some preachers, because they see worship as mainly music and a cause of conflict, opt out of responsibility with this result: "Worship for the most part lacks form, and therefore lacks direction. Many pastors have abdicated their traditional role of leading worship and handed it over to the church's musicians without apparently realizing that there is a great difference between leading songs and leading worship."[3] This narrowing down of worship to music has hampered preachers from seeing God's big-picture worship, all too often encouraging others to view worship as largely a matter of musical preferences and individual style choices.

Preaching Only

In contrast with defining worship as music only, some have regarded worship as preaching only, especially a generation ago. As William Willimon comments, "Many of us Protestants have conceived worship as preaching and listening to preaching."[4] Elsewhere he says, "Our problem as free-church Protestants is that we have attempted to make the service of the Word bear the total burden of the congregation's judgment, grace, healing, nourishment, response and edification."[5]

Gary Parrett again offers an illustration, contrasting two experiences in the same New York church he visited. During his first visit in 1985, the service began with an overhead projector, guitars, and a rousing twenty minutes of music followed by the pastor saying, "Now we will begin our worship." Clearly, he saw music as preparation before the real worship event—his sermon. Returning in 1998, however, Parrett saw that the music group had expanded in size and led singing for thirty-five to forty minutes. At its conclusion the worship leader said, "Boy, that was a wonderful time of worship!" as though worship was now concluded as they moved into listening to the sermon. In thirteen years the situation had reversed—from viewing preaching as worship to assuming that music is worship. Of course, neither stance is correct.

Liturgics Only

The word *liturgics* (with similarly rather ugly words like *liturgiology*, the study of liturgy, and *liturgiologists*, those who study liturgy) can also define worship and unfortunately give the impression that worship involves a superior, ecclesiastical art form. So *liturgy* becomes a negative word that implies worship is an arcane art that specializes in printed prayer books, set rituals, smells, and bells.

Of course, ritual has often been in tension with preaching throughout church history. "It is noteworthy that the churches which have exalted preaching have generally been indifferent to ritual; and that where ritual has been elaborate, preaching has declined."[6] Such tension particularly surfaces when preachers fear limitations imposed on their freedom to preach. In a recent preaching class, I mentioned the lectionary as a tool for preaching. One bright student raised his hand. "Excuse me, but what's the lectionary? I've never heard of that before." Explaining that it is a set order of Scriptures that follows themes of the Christian year, I was surprised by how few knew of its existence and by the flickers of doubt that it could ever be of benefit.

We need to see that *liturgy* is a positive biblical word, *leitourgia*, meaning literally "the work of the people." Constructively, it describes the "art of crafting and doing liturgy, . . . the sequence of communal acts, verbal and nonverbal, that together form and shape the worship event."[7]

Pragmatics Only

Some define worship solely as the practicalities of choosing content for church services, with no higher motive than creating a smoothly operating program. Even though, in the light of the previous comments, such service structures should properly be described as *liturgy*, this lowbrow end of worship practice may treat them as mere nuts and bolts—just organizing a sequence of hymns, songs, prayers, offering, and message. This is a corporate view of worship as conducting business.

Nothing downgrades worship more rapidly than seeing it as a dutiful weekly round of making choices and coming up with fresh ideas. Of course, choices and ideas are necessary, but concentrating on practicalities can reduce worship to a pragmatic sorting out of necessary bits and pieces with little awareness of big-picture worship that focuses on the Triune God.

Maintenance Only

Some are suspicious that while worship is all well and good for helping saints celebrate, it rather misses what they see as the whole point of being church, which is mission. Assuming that worship focuses people inwardly on preferences, styles, and churchy activity, they see it reinforcing the status quo. Set against Emil Brunner's famous challenge, "The church exists for mission as fire exists for burning," worship is therefore regarded as something of a luxury for the in crowd at the expense of concern for a lost world. They argue, "Surely the priority is for biblical preaching to tell the Good News so that there is repentance and faith."

Compared to confronting people with the message of salvation, worship seems to them to be a lower-order concern. I remember a preacher critiquing another church for its traditional liturgy, with renowned organist, choir, and highly literate preacher: "They spend all their time on performance, and they are not bringing people to Christ." This implied that beautiful acts of worship are inevitably self-serving. It is true that some worship may be self-serving, but some preachers have suspicions about putting any effort into worship design: "That's not where we should be spending our time and money!"

Sunday Services Only

Almost inevitably, most people associate the word *worship* with what happens in church on Sundays (though I realize some churches also have Saturday and midweek worship services). After all, gathered worship best expresses togetherness that gives praise to God (Acts 2:42–47). All aspects of worship mentioned so far, such as music, preaching, and liturgy, presuppose this togetherness.

But the togetherness that worship builds should not be confined to the hour(s) spent in worship services. Rather, God seeks to build a community of people who respond to him worshipfully throughout every day of the week. Such worshipful living challenges that we don't just *go* together to be church but we *are* the church all the time. Whenever worship focuses on churchly activity, restricted to specific times and places, we are in danger of missing the responsibilities of offering our "bodies as a living sacrifice"—a spiritual act of worship that does not conform to the pattern of this world (Rom. 12:1–2).

Regretfully, little help is given to average worshipers about conceiving daily life as worship. Connections between what happens on Sunday in corporate worship and what occurs on working Mondays are often left unclear. Yet *Sunday-only worship* not only shrinks worship down in specific events but also damages the vision of worship that forms a community of people who live in a different way for God (1 Pet. 2:9–12). Several have suggested that worship services should be renamed. For example, R. Kent Hughes comments, "To call our public meetings 'worship' can unwittingly install a resacralization of time and space. It is better to employ terms like 'corporate worship,' . . . or 'gathered worship' works best for me."[8] This contrast between a people gathered together in one place (*going to* church) and then scattered as God's community (*being* church) will receive more attention when we consider community formation.

Each of these six definitions contains some truth, yet by their limited focuses, they confine worship to a small picture and help explain why preachers are not usually interested in worship. Such faulty definitions impoverish worship and need forthright countering (see chap. 4).

2. Thin Theology of Worship

Defective theological thinking underlies many of the faulty definitions above. Instead of giving serious thought to God's relationship with us and his purpose for worship, we trap worship within a lesser vision by focusing on matters such as music and the practicalities of organizing Sunday services. Particularly important is the lamentable absence of trinitarian theology in much current preaching and worship practice. Given the significant role of preachers in framing congregational understanding and practice of worship, weakness in trinitarian theology explains much of worship's current troubles.

Within that large part of the evangelical church that is nonliturgical and noncreedal, mention of the Trinity is increasingly rare. Spared even having to mark Trinity Sunday, much worship seldom makes reference to the Father and the Holy Spirit as part of the Triune Godhead. Jesus is not identified and depended on as the Mediator and Intercessor with the Father by the Spirit, and the Holy Spirit has all too often become the *missing person*. We are witnesses to the incredible shrinking God.

Recent trends in music illustrate this. Robin Parry claims that collections of hymns and songs put together for contemporary singing tend to have fewer trinitarian references. For example, in his survey of twenty-eight worship albums produced by Vineyard Music (1999–2004), he places songs in various categories: "three person songs" (1.4 percent); "two person songs" (8.8 percent); "one person songs" (38.7 percent, of which over four-fifths are to Jesus); and "you Lord songs" (51 percent). He challenges Christian groups to find balance in their singing: "Whatever God-given emphases they have, they must go hand in hand with an emphasis on the *Christian God*—the Trinity."[9]

Strikingly, Michael Pasquarello III claims, "For most of Christian history the practice of preaching was believed to have taken place in, with, and through the initiative and presence of the Triune God."[10] But he finds such trinitarian preaching conspicuously absent today. Arguing convincingly for a trinitarian theology of preaching, he criticizes much current preaching as pursuing entirely pragmatic ends as it concentrates on teaching individuals and increasing congregational numbers rather than on building up Christ's community. Focusing on communication techniques at the expense of helping people encounter God's holy glory and mystery, such preaching justifies itself by securing bottom-line results for successful church business. As long as numbers and finances stay healthy, it is deemed effective. He sums up:

> There is a widespread view that preaching is no longer intrinsic to the worship of God since, for many, worship has been reduced to the matter of individual "religious" preference or taste—a marketed "style" that functions instrumentally to promote the growth of the church or individuals rather than to create and transform a people for the praise and glory of God.[11]

Pasquarello is not alone in this assessment. In his farewell address after forty-two years at Concord Baptist Church of Christ in Brooklyn, Gardner Taylor criticized the contemporary church for its "binitarianism."[12] When Bishop Lesslie Newbigin returned from missionary service in India, he observed that when the average Christian in Britain hears the name of God, he or she does not think of the Trinity, and in consequence, much worship in the West is in practice, if not in theory, unitarian.[13] Others have commented that Christian worship is "mere monotheism" or is marked by the "forgotten Father."[14]

In a provocative analysis, James B. Torrance sharply contrasts what he calls *unitarian* and *trinitarian practices of worship*. Of course, orthodox preachers resent any labeling associated with the formal unitarian doctrine that God is one person only, denying the divinity of Christ and of the Holy Spirit. Torrance demonstrates, however, that ironically, such preachers may actually *practice* forms of worship that *are* unitarian because they are closed to Christ's continuing work and the Holy Spirit. In reality, too much worship is made by human hands for all-too-human purposes.

Admittedly, his broad brushstrokes overstate what many evangelicals believe and practice about salvation and fellowship with God, for in fairness to the evangelical world that I know, many preachers and worship leaders, if not expressly trinitarian in their thought patterns and language, are at the very least binitarian, emphasizing the relationship between Father and Son. While the Holy Spirit may be emphasized less, the person of Jesus is often given a much larger role than Torrance suggests. For example, the common way of offering evangelical prayers is "through our Lord Jesus Christ" or "in the name of Jesus."

But bearing in mind such dangers of oversimplification, note what Torrance describes as the "Existential Experience Model" (adapted and simplified below).

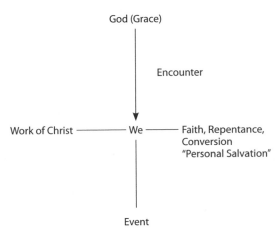

Figure 1. The Existential Experience Model (Evangelical Experience). Adapted from James B. Torrance, *Worship, Community, and the Triune God of Grace* (Downers Grove, IL: InterVarsity, 1996), 27.

Here God's grace is understood primarily as a transaction between *God and me*. God is encountered in a personal crisis of decision because of Jesus Christ's work on the cross. Torrance says, "According to this model, we are accepted by God as forgiven, as his children today, because of the death of Jesus on the cross. . . . The event of the cross, through the event of preaching (the *kerygma*), gives rise to the event of faith."[15] Yet by stressing what Jesus did on the cross, preachers can so emphasize his *work* that they minimize his *person*, making us more interested in our experience of blessing than in Jesus Christ himself. Human response can therefore be reduced to, "Thank you, Lord, for saving me." Even worse, Jesus may be regarded as the *way in* to a relationship with God rather than the person through whom we *continually* draw near to God our Father in the communion of the Spirit. In this model, the interacting persons of the Trinity all recede in importance because Jesus's role as Mediator (Heb. 8:1–2) is diminished.

Notice how this model operates by a single movement as God reaches down in Christ. A descending arrow describes the God-humanward movement in Christ focused on his work on the cross, but the human-Godward movement is all ours. "It emphasizes *our* faith, *our* decision, and *our* response in an event theology that short-circuits the vicarious humanity of Christ and belittles union with Christ."[16]

Not only is such a model highly individualistic, but it flirts dangerously with the notion that faith is a *contract* with God. It suggests that once a person has responded to Christ's work on the cross, the subsequent demands of Christian living are seen as requirements to be met solely by human discipline and energy. "Practical unitarianism" that "has no doctrine of the mediator or sole priesthood of Christ, is human-centered, has no proper doctrine of the Holy Spirit. . . . We sit in the pew watching the minister 'doing his thing' exhorting us 'to do our thing' until we go home thinking we have done our duty for another week."[17] The implication of God's one-way movement is that it is now up to us to make worship work. God's involvement is relegated to the past tense.

Doing our thing aptly summarizes so much of what goes on in contemporary worship. A good deal of preaching seems to specialize in moralizing sermons that concentrate on individual needs—giving good advice instead of Good News. "Evangelical preaching is so obsessed with the need to apply everything that we are shifting into just another moral religion."[18] Flawed theology that allows such human-centered worship explains a large amount of dissatisfaction about sermons that end with lists of *ought*s rather than with God's grace sending worshipers out by Christ in the power of the Spirit.

Paralleling this, worship leaders can also be caught up in *doing their thing*, planning services that generate *feel-good* experiences, deploying marketed styles (with an eye on competition from other churches). Such worship leading inevitably focuses more on benefits for believers than on disclosure and worship of the Triune God. Recently, I received a sermon transcript that ended: "Gonna close with just a couple of songs. And so I'll ask the praise team to come up, . . . we're going to sing three songs. One is a prayer song written within our congregation. . . . Go in grace and *enjoy it*" (italics mine).

Certainly praising God should involve joy and enjoyment of him. But too easily, enjoyment can focus on how *we* feel about the music. So style triumphs over substance, and self-interested worship packages prevail over God-focused trinitarian worship. Thin theology endangers worship at its core, manufacturing a worship event that is muscled by human endeavor and nothing more.

3. Nondirective Use of Scripture

In addition to promoting faulty definitions and thin theology, myopic preaching also fails to see Scripture's vital role in directing worship. While biblical preachers expect Scripture to direct sermons, rarely do they (or worship leaders) appreciate how Scripture also shapes the whole worship event.

Biblical preachers should find in the chosen text not only content for the sermon's message but also guidance for the sermon's purpose. One breakthrough issue in preaching over the last three decades has been the emphasis that Scripture not only *says* things but also *does* things—that it not only has *focus* but also *function*.[19] So preachers are responsible not only for attending to a text's meaning but also for identifying its function. Scripture is not only informational but also transformational (2 Tim. 3:16).

Over the last thirty years, homileticians such as Fred Craddock, Eugene Lowry, David Buttrick, Don Wardlaw, and Thomas Long have called attention to the importance of the shape and genre of Scripture texts for preaching. Mike Graves describes how preachers need to tune into a Scripture text's mood and movement so that they might represent a similar mood and movement in their sermons.[20] Jeffrey Arthurs has drawn attention to the variety of sermons when "re-creating the dynamics of biblical genres."[21] Recent interest in first-person narrative preaching, for example in Kent Edwards's *Effective First-Person Biblical Preaching*, has also emphasized how the literary nature of a Scripture passage influences sermon design.[22] Narrative passages encourage narrative-shaped sermons, parables suggest parabolic sermons, and didactic passages invite systematic teaching. Of course, the shape of particular Scripture texts does not prescribe sermon forms legalistically. Narrative passages, for example, can be legitimately preached in many ways, as can other kinds of texts. But the discipline of "creating sermons in the shape of Scripture" (the subtitle of Don Wardlaw's book *Preaching Biblically*) has become a familiar responsibility to many preachers. Of course this is preaching at its best because we recognize (sadly) that some sermons may have little or no relationship with a text but rather float free at a preacher's whim.

Also at best, many worship leaders try to fit different parts of the worship service around elements of the chosen Scripture text. In fact, the preacher's choice of Scripture text or theme for the next worship service is often the main, sometimes the only, point of contact with worship leaders. So-called contemporary services often commence with praise worship, and at some point the chosen Scripture passage may be carefully read (even with an accompanying Old or New Testament text). More usually the Scripture text is left until immediately preceding the sermon. Music choices around the sermon itself are likely to be chosen with the text's theme in mind, especially following the sermon. Further, some churches may use drama, video, and testimony to support the preaching.

Myopic preachers, however, are unconcerned about the bigger issue of how the Scripture text intentionally influences the *whole* structure of worship. These preachers fit Scripture into a worship structure rather than shape the entire service event around Scripture. It is treated as a bit player rather than the mover and shaker of gathered worship. Indeed, some worship services appear to be a collection of assorted elements lacking any overall purpose. Sally Morgenthaler provocatively describes such services as nonworship services, *worship counterfeits*, because "interaction with God is either nonexistent or so low it cannot be measured."[23] Failure to "worship in the shape of Scripture"[24] aids and abets such low interaction with God.

In order to grow beyond a small picture of worship, both preachers and others who lead worship have a profound responsibility to submit to God's Word together in their respective preparation tasks, with an expectation of Scripture's transformational power impacting worship.

4. Liturgical Amnesia

One pastor commented:

> I find that generally our people have very low expectations of what happens when we gather. By and large, I think that our people are just happy to not be bored to death. If church is fun, they are happy. That drives me crazy. . . . My ministry context expects almost nothing of its worship leaders or preachers when it comes to liturgy. No lectionary, no liturgy, no sweat.

Myopic preaching shows little interest in past worship practices, with low regard for two thousand years of Christian worship. Unaware of best past practices, it therefore expends energy on reinventing the wheel (often in mundane and noncircular ways), churning out ideas without any sense of benefiting from or belonging to a rich past.

Timothy Carson describes how the history of Christian worship ricochets between simplicity and complexity. In repeated cycles, it is drawn back to its biblical roots in simplicity and then builds on tradition as it responds to culture with increasing complexity. "Names such as Luther, Zwingli, Calvin and Knox are all affiliated with not only theological and ecclesial moves but also *liturgical* ones."[25] Their understanding of the nature of church influenced their worship reforms as they built on past worship practice with awareness of what needed to be retained, simplified, or omitted. Carson comments, however, that many Protestants in the Free Church tradition today have engaged in "liturgical borrowing all too frequently . . . without sufficient historical or theological grounding."[26] Wherever liturgical memory is missing, myopic preaching flourishes.

Worship that disregards its past operates pragmatically, living in a historical vacuum, taking cues from other successful worship practices, and likely bouncing from one good idea to another. For example, many evangelical churches now light an Advent wreath yet think little of Advent spirituality, which would greatly enrich what otherwise is likely to be treated as a surface ritual.

Myopic preachers are likely to diminish several key practices from Christian worship's rich history. First, and most important, they downplay the role of baptism and the Lord's Supper. Instead of rating these as essential elements of worship and vital ways of entering community and communing with Christ *on his terms*, they downgrade them to *add-on ordinances* valued far below sermons. Baptism, in both infant and believer's traditions, is treated more as a personal exercise, practiced on the margins of church life. The Lord's Supper occurs infrequently, often at a fast pace, having little connection with sermons and, much more seriously, offering little expectation of encounter and communion with Jesus Christ. Rather than being the crowning act of corporate worship, enabling participation together in obedience to the Head of the church, it shuffles along as an addendum to the sermon that merely delays the end of the service.

Some, like James Torrance and Don Saliers, emphasize how the act of remembering that lies at the heart of worship especially focuses on baptism and the Lord's Supper, which, when properly practiced, powerfully school people in corporate formation. Often, however, evangelical practice has tended to emphasize spiritual formation for individuals and therefore has diminished the corporate aspects of both baptism and the Lord's Supper involving the body of Christ together.

These worship practices deserve great care, precisely because Jesus Christ instituted them. Robert Webber gives a stunning example of myopic treatment of the Lord's Supper. After hearing Webber speak on the importance of the Lord's Supper, a pastor said, "I love what you had to say. We do communion on New Year's Eve, but I don't think my people would tolerate it more often than that. Could you suggest an alternative that would have the same effect?" Webber writes that this is tantamount to saying, "I preach from the Bible once a year, but I don't think my people would tolerate it more often. Can you suggest an alternative? Jesus said there is a way to remember me—it is bread and wine. Why don't we follow the clear teaching of Jesus?"[27]

Why not, indeed?

Second, the *Christian year* structures the pattern and rhythm of seasons that tell Christ's story through twelve months. Rooted in Old Testament practices, the Christian year emerged through the first four centuries of church history to provide a profound framework for preaching, worship, and community formation. While John Calvin rejected this pattern, other Reformers did not. Many contemporary churches, however, have never properly considered its advantages, even when limited to key periods such as preparing for Easter or Christmas. A friend told me that they left a former church because of this problem. For example, time prior to Easter focused on a fifty-day program solving some life issues and "Easter Sunday came like a thief in the night . . . unplanned for and unexpected."

William Willimon observes that without the Christian year, "Many of our services not only lack coherence and direction but are also too much alike in emotional tone and in theological substance. The pastor is going over the same pet themes. . . . The church year with its round of seasons on themes based on the life of Christ, preserves us from this boredom and sameness."[28]

And many others, especially Robert Webber, assert powerful spiritual arguments for continuing its practice. The *lectionary* (already mentioned) is an additional resource supporting the Christian year that is largely ignored by myopic preaching—its advantages and disadvantages receive attention later (see chap. 7).

Third, and of great significance, are *patterns of worship*. Webber is especially associated with reintroducing four movements of worship to an evangelical church that, suffering from liturgical amnesia, had largely forgotten its biblical and historical roots. He sees these four movements as retelling Scripture's story of God's long relationship with humankind—from creation, through its fall to re-creation in Christ.

1. Assembling the people
2. Listening and responding to God's Word
3. Remembering and giving thanks (which may include communion for those churches that regularly practice it)
4. Going forth to love and serve the Lord

Myopic preachers care little about patterns of worship and their constituent parts. Who is bothered by whether elements such as confession, intercession, and dismissal are missing? Indeed, some contemporary worship services seem to lack any thought-through structures. Someone has dubbed them COW churches: *Church Our Way*. But as we will see, some evangelicals are rediscovering how valuable some of these aspects are as they seek to recover more liturgical memory.

5. Feeble Community Formation

While the first four characteristics of myopic preaching tend to focus on acts of gathered worship (though they have wider implications), this fifth aspect has a wider perspective: how worship influences the character of believers together in church community. It is strongly connected with the sixth issue: naivete about culture.

Thin theology resulting in practical unitarianism encourages worshipers to do their own thing. Because of the rampant individualism and selfism endemic to this approach, aided and abetted by contemporary culture, myopic preaching is rendered incapable of forming community. It veers toward building successful organizations with much self-interest and away from creating communities of service toward others. Craig van Gelder helpfully compares the *corporate church* with the *missional church*.[29] He claims that the majority of Christian congregations share one characteristic in common: "At the core of their genetic code is an organizational self-understanding, where the church's primary identity is related to it being responsible to accomplish something."[30] He describes how the corporate church, embedded in the European version of Constantinian Christendom (and therefore representing many churches over the last two centuries), understands itself to exist "as an organization to accomplish something, normally on behalf of God in the world."[31] It is a *doing* church.

On the face of it, a *doing church* sounds attractive and lively. Isn't it better that a church is doing something rather than nothing? And don't we admire churches that have relevant programs, outreaches, and missions that make a difference to others? By putting the focus on human doings, however, the church is more likely to assume that its own energy and vision are what matter most. Challenging *individuals* to commitment and achieving goals becomes all-important. One of the biggest casualties of this corporate church model is its failure to see how God is trying to build his new *community* for the sake of his mission. Myopic preaching is unlikely to grasp this community dimension of worship as God seeks to grow and mature his people together, overcoming sin together through confession, praise, thanksgiving, offering, and communion as the bride prepared for the Lamb. The great claims of 1 Peter 2:9–12 and Ephesians 4:9–12 are not treated as collective possibilities. Instead, individuals are encouraged to believe, behave, and belong to the church as an organization, like any other, to which they choose to go.

Further, within corporate churches, myopic preachers seem to assume that sermons are all that are required to disciple people effectively. Evidence increasingly suggests, however, that preaching alone is failing to shape church communities. As Dallas Willard comments:

> We (evangelicals) have counted on preaching and teaching to form faith in the hearer; and on faith to form the inner life and ordered behavior of the Christian. But, for whatever reason, this strategy has not turned out well. The result is that we have multitudes of professing Christians that may be ready to die, but obviously are not ready to live, and can hardly get along with themselves, much less others.[32]

Some recent worship studies have particularly focused on worship's role to form community. For example, claiming that "it takes a church to raise a Christian," Tod Bolsinger asserts, "Christian transformation comes through the pattern, the personal relationship and the power of God to the believer found in Jesus Christ through the Spirit experienced within the community."[33] How a community worships, over time, impacts belief and behavior in profound ways. Don Saliers argues for reconnecting spirituality with the practices of Christian worship because "worship both forms and expresses the faith-experience of the community. . . . At its best Christian worship presents a vision of life created, sustained, redeemed and held in the mystery of God.

What we do together in acknowledging God 'schools' us in ways of seeing the world and of being in it."[34]

Myopic preaching is baffled by language such as "God schools us." Because such preaching continually addresses *you* in the singular and applies self-help principles to individuals, it fails to challenge hearers about sharing selves in God's community.

In gathered worship, people participate in "God's already preexisting reality through language, ritual and symbol as revealed in history through Scripture."[35] God's community, living his story, oriented to his glory, predates any individual worshiper's experience of truth. So how worshipers come to understand and practice Christian belief partly depends on how the community is forming them. As Marva Dawn sums up:

> Who you are as an individual believer depends greatly upon the character of the community of believers in which you are nurtured. How faithfully does that community incarnate God's Presence and pass on the narratives that reveal God when they assemble together? . . . In a society that values show and appearance more than character and internal integrity, congregations often fail to consider worship's role in nurturing participants' character.[36]

Rather than individuals assuming that they already know truth as they seek more personal experience, worshipers within community are impacted in powerful ways with new language, such as using *we*, and expressing sin's reality and a need for reconciliation. God's people learn together fresh responsibilities to manifest God's holiness before a watching world. Instead of self-centeredness, they grow in God's paradoxical new way of thinking and living through self-denial. "The presenting, remembering, and re-presenting of God through the Word and the Table comes first to the congregation, which then in turn responds. As opposed to contemporary worship, which often begins by coming to God with our self-expressions."[37]

Myopic preaching misses out on worship's collective, transformational qualities "for building up the body of Christ, until all of us come to the unity of the faith and of the knowledge of the Son of God, to maturity, to the measure of the full stature of Christ" (Eph. 4:12–13). By avoiding themes of unity, love, and reconciliation as primary characteristics of being God's people, it utterly fails to appreciate the community-forming potential of worship, and the word *maturity* is missing from its vocabulary.

6. Naivete about Culture

The gospel is complexly linked with culture. As "the Word became flesh" (John 1:14), God's revelation in Christ was plunged into a social, historical, economic, and cultural context. Ever since, the church has wrestled with the relationship of gospel and culture. Cornelius Plantinga and Sue Rozeboom describe three aspects: first, cultural adaptation of worship is *inevitable*. They cite how the four Gospels tell the same story in a variety of contexts—for example, Matthew for a Jewish audience and Luke for a Gentile audience. Second, cultural adaptation of worship is *desirable* because people need to hear the gospel in understandable terms to which they can respond. Third, however, they warn that such adaptation is also *risky* because the desire to be understood is fraught with dangers of compromise. Plantinga and Rozeboom rightly advise that working through these aspects requires much thought and prayer.[38] As David Wells warns, culture is not "neutral and harmless . . . a partner amenable to being co-opted in the cause of celebrating Christian truth."[39]

But myopic preachers are naive about culture. They fail to give it much thought and prayer. Boldly, Marva Dawn asserts that the church has two tasks: "to Praise God and to Nurture Character."[40] She claims that these tasks were easier in the past when elements in Western culture supported the church's goals. She uses the word *culture* both negatively to describe "culture *surrounding* worship" and also positively about the "culture *of* worship" with God at its center. It is culture's negative impact that causes concern, especially through the influence of postmodernity and as society's idolatries have invaded the church and its worship. Seeing these as signs of fallen principalities and powers at work, she protests the idolatries of efficiency, money, vicarious subjectivism, competition, power, and especially success. All of these "dumb down" the church. "We miss the infinitely faceted grandeur of God and destroy the awe and wonder that characterized worship before God became only a 'buddy' ill-conceived and only subjectively experienced."[41]

Naivete fails to see risks and dangers. At the local level, churches are set in neighborhood cultures with specific characteristics. How churches respond varies dramatically. At one extreme, some are so entrenched in their own subculture that they totally fail to connect with neighbors. Their public life makes no connection with nonchurchgoers. At the other extreme, the seeker-sensitive church movement (pioneered by Willow Creek Community Church) arose to make church completely accessible. No stumbling blocks were allowed to remain in order to create maximum comfort for visitors. But critics argue that by removing distinctive characteristics of Christian worship, the resulting experience lacked what Dan Kimball calls "vintage Christianity." In reaction, so-called *post-sensitive-seeker worship* seeks to practice all the vital elements of vintage Christianity and to be passionate about Christ's community and mission.

Responses to culture at the local level occur against the backdrop of changing Western culture. Words such as *Christendom*, *post-Christendom*, and *postmodernity* speak of massive changes affecting church and society. The shift from modernity, with its Enlightenment culture, to more recent expressions of postmodernity has played havoc with assumptions that have affected worship throughout the past two hundred years because modernity shaped the church many of us inherited. Kimball helpfully contrasts the Modern Era with the Post-Christian Era by likening the church to a tree with its atmosphere and nutrients. The Modern Era has a "Judeo-Christian atmosphere" with God as the Judeo-Christian God and "ethics based on the Judeo-Christian worldview learned from family, even if one is not religious." Its nutrients are monotheism, rationalism, religious proposition with truth that is systematic, local, and individualistic. But the Post-Christian Era has a "global, pluralistic atmosphere" in which "all religions are equal, with Christianity having a negative, finger-pointing reputation. Ethics are based on the cultural level of acceptance and personal choice learned from media and peers." Its nutrients are: pluralism, experience, mysticism, narrative with preference that is fluid, global, and communal/tribal.[42] Kimball shows how in the current time of transition, these qualities overlap in a confusing way because many in the younger generations are still modern and some in older generations are postmodern.

Repercussions of this culture shift raise wide issues, many of which lie beyond this book's scope. But two dangers (already evident in the previous section) are obvious: capitulation to popularist aims and narrow focus on individual experience.

First, worship has fed some insidious nutrients into expectations about preaching and worship, so they easily succumb to popularist organizational aims—to grow numbers, satisfy customers, and build bigger barns. In regard to these baseline threes—membership, money, and maintenance (or bodies, budgets, and buildings)—success is measured as in any other secular business. When preaching is driven by market principles instead of keeping God central, it degenerates into keeping customers happy. Secularism has too often baptized successful communication methodologies with power.

Second, as David Fitch has pointed out, personal experience has dominated. Too often "when we plan our worship, we end up pursuing the arousal of emotions and the 'worship experience' as an end in itself."[43] Because most worshipers' character is formed outside church and shaped by contemporary culture rather than God's holiness, "our doctrines may be right when it comes to worship, but our experiences, emotions, and imaginations remain pagan."[44] Further, much contemporary worship assumes that "personal self-expression, freedom in the Spirit and personal experience are the basis for authentic engagement with God."[45] Inevitably influenced by self-centered culture, individual worshipers bring in assumptions that are far removed from the realities of a "holy nation, royal priesthood" vision of God's church.

The most common secular Greek word for worship is *therapeuein* ("to heal"), from which we get the word *therapy*. But *therapeuein* is never used in the New Testament to describe worship and is found only in Acts 17:25, where it is repudiated. It remains tempting to offer therapy instead of God-centered worship. Recently, I saw a church billboard declaring to passersby:

"*You* are the heart of our ministry." Such a people-centered focus readily appeals, and certainly, people need to hear the Good News and to be served. But the church's main purpose is to focus on God in three persons as worshipers are built by Christ (Matt. 16:18), into his body (1 Cor. 12), for worship and service (Eph. 4:12–14). Properly, the poster should read: "God is at the heart of our ministry. Come and join us as we live for him!"

Myopic preachers fail to see their responsibility to think through complex issues of culture. Often desperate for people to attend (and give to) services that *work* for them, they compromise with cultural norms that subtly, or otherwise, shift focus away from God. It is appropriate that we next turn to music.

7. Ambivalence about Music

Though "music only" was mentioned early in this chapter as one way of falsely defining worship, we now consider how it characterizes myopic preaching. Glorious though music is as God's gift—and it is—music should never be allowed to climb too high in importance compared with other heavy-weight issues of theology, Scripture, liturgy, and community formation. We will see how significant music is for gathered worship, but we must never forget how delicate its role is. Because many preachers find music controversial and divisive, they tend to be ambivalent, either treating music as an issue to be delegated (perhaps apart from choosing a closing hymn) or a matter for compromise to avoid further conflict.

Music relates to several issues already treated, especially the relationship between gospel and culture. Today's digital communication gives music visceral immediacy—you need ask only for people's playlists to discover music's influence. Yet this very power requires immense care in helping music to find its appropriate place within worship's big picture. Music, like all art, is neutral, but its use reflects fallen humanity—sometimes gloriously transcendent yet at other times perversely indulgent.

Many, aware of its negative possibilities, have warned about music's ability to dominate. For example, Harold Best, a keen eclectic musician and strong supporter of arts in worship, welcomes a wide range of musical expression but argues that we must remember where it belongs.

> Let the music come. Traditional, contemporary, avant-garde, ethnic, jazz, rock and chant . . . rejoice in it. Dance with David in it. Let Taize ring the changes on the glory of God, and let "Jesus Loves Me" done in a thousand styles become everybody's invocation and benediction. Let the emotions roll and the endorphins break their dikes. But for Jesus Christ's sake, let's get music back where it belongs—as a lisping sign and not a glittering cause, as the response to a commandment and not just a set of tools for influencing people.[46]

Yet others emphasize its gloriously transcendent potential. Martin Luther claimed that music is the ruler of all the heart's emotions, for nothing on earth has more power than music to make joyful the sad, make sad the joyful, or give heart to the downcast. In the electronic culture, few doubt that music has become a preferred mode of artistic expression and that it forms community in new ways.[47] Great care is needed to work through appropriate use of music in worship, but frankly, myopic preachers are often at a loss to know what to do about music. Martin Luther actually insisted that all preachers also learn about music in worship. But disabled by faulty definitions, thin theology, lack of community formation, and entanglement with culture, myopic preachers too frequently end up as confused pragmatists.

One pastor who gently introduced blended worship into his church, seeking to combine contemporary music with traditional, told me about an angry encounter. A strong adherent of traditional worship aggressively thrust Marva Dawn's *Reaching Out without Dumbing Down* into his hand. "That's exactly what you are doing," he exploded. "You're dumbing down!" Yet ironically, Marva Dawn actually encourages blended worship, pleading for spiritual maturity in congregations that seek to place God at the center rather than insist on personal musical preferences. With reactions such as this, it's no wonder that many myopic preachers are frightened of dealing directly with music. But preachers need to deal head-on with music for the sake of big-picture worship.

8. Not Living in God's Narrative

Already we have discussed the potential for worship to enable people to unite together because they learn to belong together within God's story. Some misunderstand this to mean a limited program that subordinates worship to the pattern of the Christian year or focuses on particular kinds of narrative preaching. Properly understood, however, living God's narrative provides the basic structure for church life.

A Christian lay leader recently commented to me about his disappointment in current church life: "Each time I come to church, it is like another in a series of little boxes that are never connected together into a vision of something greater. I don't have any sense of vision of who we are and where we are supposed to be going. We are not going anywhere." Closely linked with feeble community formation, myopic preaching allows a church to mark time on the spot. It has no inkling that God's community should be on the move within God's purposeful narrative from creation to the endtimes. In the Old Testament, from Abram's call onward, God moves his people toward fulfilling his purpose.

While attending a conference called "On the Primacy of the Biblical Narrative,"[48] I was challenged that we should stop letting the world narrate our stories—telling us what life and success is all about (money, sex, and power). Rather, we should live in God's story, which he is still working out with us. Kevin Vanhoozer described this story as a five-act drama:

Act 1: Creation
Act 2: Election of Abraham
Act 3: Incarnation (Mission of Son)
Act 4: Pentecost (Mission of Spirit)
Act 5: Consummation

Presently we live in act 4, awaiting act 5 in the return of Christ. Yet all the preceding acts form our story too. As another conference speaker said, "We are not just people of the Book—we are people of *the* story." God cannot be worshiped apart from his story.

But rather than encouraging congregations to live in God's story in Scripture as community, myopic preachers are likely to break up God's narrative into fragments that are only applied individualistically. Instead of encouraging people to live within God's great narrative of salvation in Scripture as *the story of stories*, from creation to salvation and new creation, each sermon focuses on *doing* something rather than on *being* a new people. Robert Webber's testimony is striking:

> I once understood the gospel as God asking me to let him into my narrative, to find room for him in my heart and life. But now I realized that God bid me to find my place in his narrative. In God's story, he, with his own two hands —the incarnate Word and the Holy Spirit, recapitulated and reversed the human situation so that I can now live in him. Through him I can live in the expectation of a restored world without the presence of evil. Here and now, because God became incarnate and "recapitulated" all things, I live in him, in his narrative, and he lives in my life, which is to be a witness to his narrative for the world.[49]

Living out God's story has become a popular way of describing how worshipers meet with God to engage in his purpose. Cornelius Plantinga and Sue Rozeboom identify three lenses in God's story: covenant renewal, Christ-centeredness, and the span of history from creation to re-creation with eschatological vision. Plantinga summarizes: "A Christian church at worship is gathering strength to obey God's gracious directions for covenant life."[50]

While telling out God's cosmic story, worshipers learn to share their own stories.

> Storytelling creates community. Persons who tell each other stories become friends. And men and women who know the same stories deeply are bound together in special ways. . . . New connections are established between persons

who have heard and identified with the same stories. And the deeper the meaning of the story, the deeper are the relationships that are formed by the sharing.[51]

Myopic preachers remain unconvinced about this bigger picture of participating in God's narrative. Instead, they tolerate (sometimes even encourage) worshipers fitting *worship experiences* into their own personal stories, as a result missing God's big picture.

9. Isolated Preparation

The cumulative effect of these foregoing characteristics is separation between preachers and worship leaders as they prepare for worship services. Over the last couple of years I have met a disturbingly large number of worship leaders whose only contact with the preacher has been to receive the Scripture text, perhaps the sermon title, and occasionally the sermon theme some time before the service.

Myopic preachers inevitably prepare for worship separately, doing their own thing as they construct sermons with minimal interest in how the whole worship service is constructed or how God wants to build his worshiping community. Even in more traditional, liturgical settings, scant thought may be given to shaping the whole act of worship's content and structure. Once myopic preachers have decided how to approach the lectionary readings, they may opt out of involvement in planning the rest of the worship service. Because there is no sense of shared task or vision, preachers and worship leaders see no need to communicate. Isolation rules instead of collaboration.

Over time, the whole round of weekly duties can become increasingly arduous. It reminds me of John Wooten, who pulled a 160,000-ton yacht over seventy feet in a strong-man competition held at Fort Lauderdale Harbor, Florida. He spent forty minutes tugging a rope attached to the ship. Afterward he said, "I don't feel so good. My neck hurts." Doing our own thing in isolation is exhausting!

10. Worshipless Sermons

Worshipless sermons are the sad and inevitable outcome of myopic preaching. Theologically thin, spiritually disconnected, empty of God, silent about his grace, self-satisfied, and self-oriented, such sermons are devoid of worship. This is partly because the preachers themselves lack awe and wonder at their part in God's call and response. Humble dependence in gratitude before God who has given his Word should take place instead of rushing ahead to offer their own words. Karl Barth was asked by a student, "What should I preach about on Sunday?" His reply was, "The question should be, 'How dare I preach on Sunday?'"

Worshipless sermons, while possibly containing plenty of Scripture, have no connection with the contexts of gathered worshipers or, even more tragically, with the great sweep of worship as God calls his people into daily living. Scripture may be explained well, but no immersion of believers into Christ's high call takes place. Baptism and the Lord's Supper, if they occur at all, are limply left on the sidelines. If worship is mentioned, faulty definitions are reinforced. If challenges are given, they resemble to-do lists, utterly failing to offer invitations to respond to God's grace. Resembling little boxes of individualized truth, they "force stale, dry words into our heads rather than telling the stories of Scripture in ways that illuminate our lives. They do not crack the kerygma open and let those stories spill over the real events of our daily lives."[52] Allowing music to take center stage, preachers collude in presenting little boxes week after week with no unified, glorious story to live out. Nothing changes. Individuals walk out as they came in, without any sense of belonging or responsibility to each other, settling for objectives more in line with contemporary culture than gospel calls to repentance, faith, and new behavior by walking in the Spirit. Hearers seem inoculated against any dangers of encountering the real God in three persons.

Bluntly, there's just no encounter with God. William Temple famously defined worship:

To worship is to quicken the conscience by the holiness of God,
To feed the mind with the truth of God,
To purge the imagination by the beauty of God,
To open the heart to the love of God,
To devote the will to the purpose of God.[53]

Worshipful sermons seek to share in this glorious dynamic, sending resounding *amens* beyond four walls. As acts of worship themselves, they are offered to God as sacrifices of praise. Worshipless sermons are flat, bemused by such assessment.

Paradoxically, from church consumers' point of view, they may rate as highly satisfactory—five star; full of Scripture, life, and vitality; drawing crowds; building organizations; and exciting listeners. Worshipless sermons do not have to be dull, nonbiblical, and without application. But viewed before the God of glory, who gifts and calls preachers to do his work, the one before whom prophets and disciples tremble (Isa. 6:5; Luke 5:8) and whose grace both calls us to worship and enables us to offer ourselves (Rom. 12:1–2), they fall far short.

A Health Warning

Hopefully, very few preachers are characterized by all ten failings, but together they spell out great dangers facing the contemporary church. Myopic worship reduces preaching to creating weekly, worshipless sermons, and worship is limited to organizing public services. For both preachers and worship leaders, little lies beyond working up yet another sermon and yet another service. Worship shrivels down to functions and preferences. Shortsighted leaders minister to shortsighted congregations who know no better but who long for something more.

Restricted to times, places, and styles, *good* worship becomes defined by personal preferences, with accompanying defensiveness lest anyone disagree. So worship is stuffed into boxes marked by favorite service patterns, musical accompaniment, hymns, and songs. Any possibility of some panoramic, comprehensive vision of a community belonging to Christ and worshiping the Triune God is lost in weekly routines.

Some may ask whether spending time and effort trying to change such a situation is worthwhile. Isn't myopic preaching an inevitable outcome of busy lives in the twenty-first century? On a practical, realistic level, as long as someone in the church takes responsibility for worship services, why should busy preachers be involved? Why should they need to learn anything fresh about worship? Aren't they under enough pressure already?

But as we will see, worship should not be viewed as the one-hundred-and-second burden to be added to the one-hundred-and-one that already claim attention. Rather, worship should embrace all our activity as the number one priority that puts everything else into perspective. As we worship God, we participate in triune reality that interacts with what yet lies beyond our smaller worldviews. Worship's big picture throws wide open God's community possibilities, drawing preachers and congregations into fresh approaches to life and ministry.

Whenever they are trapped within the preaching dome, myopic preachers are doomed to live perpetually with crippling limitations. Focusing on little, self-important sermon swatches limits the vastness of belonging within God's grace and story. Failing to see their own calling and task as worshipers, they remain closed to worship's awesome dimensions. Unable to preach as worshipers or to worship as preachers, they mislead the entire church. Myopic preaching is not a defect that can be made up for in other areas. It sabotages God's greatest purpose—the call to worship him with our very lives.

With urgency, in part 2 we turn to sketch out a more complete, panoramic view of worship—the bigger picture of worship that is urgently needed for the health of God's church. Successive chapters will seek to counter each of these myopic characteristics, beginning with a fuller definition and deeper theology in the next chapter.

PART 2

Toward a Bigger Picture of Worship

4

A Fuller Definition and Deeper Theology

I didn't know there was a theology of worship.

comment made by a preacher
to John Armstrong

The trinitarian approach to God must always be important for
Christian worship as a safeguard against our worshiping an idol
of our imaginations instead of the true God.

John Baillie

In 1994, I was a guest of the Orthodox Patriarchate in Istanbul as a member of a small group of Baptist leaders. We dialogued with Orthodox bishops and leaders about our different understandings and practice of the Christian faith. Much of interest occurred over the four days, but two incidents particularly struck me. First was the Orthodox delegation's reaction to a paper I presented on Baptist history. Using my thirty minutes as accurately and sensitively as possible, I sketched out the Baptist story beginning in 1609 and tracing subsequent developments. As soon as I finished, however, an Orthodox professor stood up and asked, "Where were you before 1609?" I was dumbfounded. What kind of question was that? Did he not believe that reformation and renewal are possible and that they might lead to authentic developments in the Christian story? Yet as continuing dialogue made clear, he was genuinely puzzled about how much the foundational doctrines of the church, formulated in great councils

63

(some in Istanbul), were part of the Baptist story. Did Baptists just begin in the seventeenth century, or can their theological and spiritual roots be traced back in some ways through the whole church story (including the Orthodox)?

Also memorable and challenging was the lengthy Eucharist service that we shared with its rich, though to us strange, liturgy, including much singing, prayers, and Scripture readings. A Southern Baptist professor standing next to me said in a low voice, "They could really do with brightening this up with a few good Baptist hymns." I am not sure how serious he was, because I felt immersed in a timeless form of worship that had been offered to God from the early days of the Christian church. It was grounded in solid theology, on biblical doctrines articulated by great councils, in worship focused worthily on God—Father, Son, and Holy Spirit. Joined by devout local people, I knew that I was sharing with a Christian body who understood and practiced worship in theologically thoughtful ways.

Whatever else I learned from these incidents, they alerted me to how deep and thoughtful some acts of worship are and how shallow and theologically simplistic some other worship services may be. Yes, reformation and renewal movements can redirect biblical theology and practice, but this should never be at the expense of worship. The first two characteristics of myopic preaching (described in the previous chapter)—*faulty definitions* and *thin theology of worship*—tragically combine to render worship superficial. Unless preachers develop a worthy definition of worship grounded in deeper theology, they remain trapped in small-picture worship.

Toward a Fuller Definition

In order to find a true definition of worship, each faulty definition must be addressed in turn.

Worship Is Bigger than Music

As already noted, music has immense power—for good or ill. On one hand, gloriously transcendent music helps collective thought and emotion soar in praise to almighty God and is attested in Scripture from Moses onward (Exod. 15:1–18). On the other hand, it may (even bitterly) divide people over preferences of style. Music may be wonderfully inclusive or dangerously exclusive. Because of its negative power, as Harold Best concludes his book he urges, "Let's get music back where it belongs,"[1] since it can dominate gathered worship instead of supporting it.

Music occupies such a strategic role in worship that it will require considerable attention in this book. But whatever form gathered worship takes, music should always better enable worshipers to express truth to God together. Therefore, music has a servant rather than a leadership role. Once while visiting a traditional church with a choir, I saw a printed sign in the choir room: "The voice is the *servant* of the music; the music is the *servant* of the text; the text is the *servant* of the meaning." In each line, *servant* was underlined to emphasize how voice, music, and words all serve God's truth. Later I will outline some principles about how music can best fulfill this servant role not only by enabling worshipers to focus praise, prayers, offering, and the Lord's Supper on God but also by building up his community. Worship is always bigger than music.

Worship Is Bigger than Preaching

Those who preach also need to see the servant role of their message. Robert Webber expresses his exasperation:

> Whenever I worship or speak at a church where the pastor is the focal point, I feel dominated and stifled. . . . Any response is often looked at as odd or inappropriate. . . . I feel as though I am not worshiping, . . . rather, the pastor is doing everything for me. I'm simply a receiver, a passive recipient of the actions of one other person.[2]

Worship is bigger than preaching—for at least three reasons.

First, both in Scripture (Acts 2:42) and in church history, Word and sacrament are valued as two complementary ways by which God speaks to his people and they respond to him. The language of *sacrament* has been treated with suspicion by some evangelicals because the word smacks of mechanical ritual or dogmatic content. Rather, they refer to baptism and the Lord's Supper as *ordinances*. A great deal could be written about this controversy. But when sacraments are understood as "the means by which God brings home to us the reality of his redeeming love,"[3] it is at least possible to accept that these rituals commanded by Jesus have *sacramental* significance, as God promises to meet with us in special ways through both actions.

The Reformation reemphasized that Scripture and preachers' words are *verba audibilia*—God's words to the ear. The sacraments of baptism and the Lord's Supper are God's *verba visibilia*—visible words that appeal to the eye. Russell Mitman claims that "the realization that Christ comes to us in both Sacrament *and* Word was the overwhelming discovery of the Reformation in the sixteenth century and of the second Vatican Council in the twentieth."[4] Baptism and the Lord's Supper have always belonged with preaching as ways of proclaiming God's truth and love.

Second, preaching is more than sermonizing—the making and delivery of sermons. Proclamation is much wider than preaching. Russell Mitman reflects on how the New Revised Standard Version prefers to translate the three key Greek words *kerussein*, *euangellisein*, and *kataggallein* as "proclaim" in order to embrace a much wider expression of the Word of God than just the sermon. Actually, it uses *preach* only three times. He comments:

When a whole congregation worships is it not also proclaiming? . . . Worshipers experience the total worship service as an event in which something happens— happens to them individually and happens to the corporate community as God meets them in this event. . . . Everything in corporate worship is Word, because what worship is about ultimately is encountering Jesus the Word.[5]

Proclamation declares the Good News by gathering, hymns, songs, prayers, and offering and joining in the Lord's Supper. Remember the instruction, "For whenever you eat this bread and drink this cup, you *proclaim* the Lord's death until he comes" (1 Cor. 11:26 NIV, italics mine).

P. T. Forsyth memorably broadened preaching to include the entire worshiping community:

The one great preacher in history, I would contend, is the church. And the first business of the individual preacher is to enable the church to preach. . . . He is to preach to the church from the gospel so that with the church he may preach the gospel to the world. He is so to preach to the church that he shall also preach *from* the church.[6]

Such proclamation is never a one-person show but rather God's people together sharing gospel telling and gospel living for the sake of his world.

Third, sermons on their own have dangerous potential to turn hearers into passive recipients rather than active worshipers. Controversially, David Norrington argues that preachers may be beguiled into acting like egotistical prima donnas whose listeners become dependent on them. Instead of helping people develop spiritual maturity, these monologue sermons reinforce passivity and foster immaturity. Indeed, he calls sermons "deskilling agents."[7] While this is an extreme view, it opens our eyes to the worst of practices: preening cults of preachers' personalities and gifts, making listeners into a fan base rather than God's community. I recall a friend saying when moving to a new town, "I've joined a different church where it doesn't all hang on the preacher, and I now realize just how much I used to go to hear a particular preacher rather than to worship God. No longer does everything ride on the success of a preacher!" No matter how gifted preachers may be and how attentive their listeners are, participation in worship through singing and giving, confessing sins and offering prayers for others, communing around the Lord's Table and receiving grace as a community is also vital to gathered worship. Worship is more than listening to good sermons. This need for participation leads neatly into the next issue.

Worship Needs Liturgy

We noted earlier that some may dismiss *liturgy* as a negative catchall for ritualistic disciplines, either above preachers' heads or beyond their interests. But the word *liturgy* deserves rehabilitation as an invaluable, biblical way of describing a congregation's involvement in worship. Originating from the Greek *leitourgia*, meaning "work of the people," it describes what people *do* in corporate worship. "While they were worshiping the Lord [*leitourgia*] and fasting, the Holy Spirit said . . ." (Acts 13:2). Liturgy is inevitable in practice. "Every church has a liturgy, whether it worships with set forms inherited from the ages or whether it worships in the freedom of the moment. The only question is whether we have the best possible liturgy. It is never whether we have a liturgy."[8]

At best, liturgy describes responsible patterning of a congregation's living faith experience so that its members can genuinely engage together in worship. And just as reading a sermon script never equates with being present in person, similarly liturgy is always more than words on paper. It describes live interactions of responsive, worshiping congregations receiving from and giving back their best to God.

Of course, liturgies may be expressed in vastly different ways ranging from highly formal to wildly informal, but all thoughtful patterns deserve respect. I recall someone from an informal church strongly criticizing a worship leader who had read all the prayers in a worship service, including some with congregational responses. "Those prayers didn't come from the heart!" she judged. But careful preparation of congregational prayer and judicious use of great prayers of the past can be offered just as equally from the heart. And frankly, what may be presented as spontaneous, with personal feeling, can sometimes prove bland, verbose, and troublingly individualistic—banal superficiality.

As we will see, undertaking worship design is no lightweight task. Planning gathered worship that enables people to offer their best to God requires spiritual sensitivity and dedicated skills. Authentic liturgy requires thoughtful patterns with a rich range of resources.

Worship Needs Some Pragmatism

Planning such liturgy, therefore, is much more demanding than merely organizing weekly events, but some pragmatism is essential. Practical work, however, must combine with spiritual sensitivity to larger theological and spiritual issues of big-picture worship in order for preachers to avoid sliding down the slippery slope of merely pleasing the human audience. Careful theological reflection and application of worship principles must continually focus on what pleases God and builds his community. Hard work is necessary, but it should flow out of a fuller definition of worship and deeper theology.

Worship Embraces Mission

While some may assert mission's priority over worship, a fuller definition of worship *embraces* mission. Earlier I noted that the New Testament connects worship and mission as unified aspects of God's relationship with man.

Indeed, because worship embraces all of life lived for God, it fulfills the ultimate purpose and largest goal of human life. No higher purpose exists for humans than to be worshipers.

Evangelism, in its objective of winning people to Christ, therefore has the supreme goal of making them worshipers. "The true goal of evangelism is to produce more and better worshipers. . . . The biblical goal of evangelism is to produce worshipers, not just . . . to enlist more recruits."[9] Worship should therefore be seen as the final focus of salvation—we are saved from sin to be worshipers through and through. Congregations worshiping on Sundays do not indulge in some lesser goal but rather seek to "create a taste of heaven on earth,"[10] participating in fellowship with God the Father, Son, and Holy Spirit and being built up as a *royal nation* to fulfill God's purpose.

Yet paradoxically, at the same time that the aim of worship is to bring glory to God rather than influence humans, its very public offering of a community's best to God is likely to be highly persuasive. Marva Dawn's book title expresses it well: *A Royal "Waste" of Time: The Splendor of Worshiping God and Being Church for the World*. She asserts that quality worship centering on God also inevitably impacts those who seek faith. She asks, "What does it mean to be Church for the sake of the world, when we worship, and during the rest of the week?"[11] Since worship services visibly demonstrate who Christians are, who we believe God is, what he requires, and our awe of him, they should speak volumes to a watching world.

> Worship is a display, a performance, commanded by God so that all of creation may see the life-transforming glory of God. . . . Our worship of God either affirms or contradicts our message about God. Unbelievers . . . will draw lasting conclusions about the veracity and uniqueness of our God based on what they see or do not see happening in our weekly church services.[12]

So while worship primarily focuses on God, its celebration secondarily challenges the world. Further, as we will see later, worship has a vital role in forming missional congregations who live differently in the world.

Worship Is Bigger than Sunday Services

Earlier I noted how easily worship can be applied exclusively to services in church. After all, Sunday services are commonly called *worship*. R. Kent Hughes prefers to call them *corporate worship* or *gathered worship* to emphasize that they are only one expression of worship.[13] Indeed, I prefer to use the term *gathered worship*. Not only does this stress how God gathers his people rather than us doing our own thing, but it also suggests a complementary movement as God sends out his church, thereby scattering it.

Too easily worshipers can walk away from church services, thinking, "I've done worship," limiting it to time and place. Rather, they need to say, "That was so good—worshiping with other believers. We now have freshly experienced God's grace, and he will sustain and help us continue worshiping throughout the rest of this week in everything we do," for worship should overflow into every part of life. "We do not go to church to worship. But as continuing worshipers, we gather ourselves together to continue our worship, but now in the company of brothers and sisters."[14] Worship gathers people together to build God's community, and it continues as worshipers scatter into daily living with others.

Russell Mitman suggests that "to be continued" should be printed at the bottom of service sheets to emphasize how worship extends beyond liturgy.[15] Eastern Orthodoxy has a phrase: "the liturgy after the Liturgy." W. E. Sangster called for "service beyond services." Worship services, at their best, are glorious opportunities to bring worship to God as thankful and praising communities. Yet beyond these limited, public, corporate events, worship should flow into mission, work, play, relationships, ethics, and service. Gathered worship opens up public windows to show how Christians should be living for the rest of the week. Switching metaphors, gathered worship is like an iceberg tip—a visible fraction of what really goes on as the church worships throughout the next six days.

Worshipful living is never just a matter of *going* to church; it is *being* the church through daily, nonconforming spiritual worship (Rom. 12:1–2). What happens within four walls in gathered worship should connect with how worshipers live before the watching world. But keeping balance between these two is extraordinarily difficult. Because gathered worship is so important and focused on weekly practicalities, it all too often dominates worship literature as the default position. For example, Robert Webber's book *Worship Is a Verb* claims, "All of life is worship," yet it mostly examines worship within services. This focus seems almost inevitable, and I will conclude in part 3 by outlining a collaborative worship process for gathered worship. But along the way I will also stress the role of worship through missional community living that pushes far beyond four walls. This issue will be addressed more thoroughly in chapters 8 and 9.

Worship Is Bigger

Damagingly, myopic definitions limit worship to single issues and originate from the human point of view—*our* music, *our* worship services, *our* liturgy, *our* pragmatism, or *our* evangelism. They so often frame small-picture worship bounded by prejudice and misunderstanding.

Rather, worship must always begin with God, who reveals his intentions in Scripture that worship be God-centered, God-empowered, all-inclusive, continuous, and focused on his glory. God intends worship to be creation's highest common denominator. True worship *centers on God*, for it only occurs because of God's *worthship*. Remove God's own attributes and actions and worship loses its entire purpose. Worship should never be human-centered. It is all about God on his terms. As Robert Jacks forcefully put it: "there is a God—and you're not it."[16] God is not only the *subject* of worship, who reveals himself in Jesus Christ and is worthy of all honor, glory, and power, but also the *object* of worship, who calls worshipers to make offerings to him.

Two key groups of worship words in Scripture summarize these two aspects of worship. First, God the *subject* of worship invites *prostration*—to bow oneself down (*shachah* in the Old Testament and *proskuneo* in the New Testament—literally "kiss the hand toward"). Representing the largest word group describing worship in Scripture, *prostration* emphasizes how worshipers are totally overwhelmed by God's glory, otherness, and worthiness. "Come, let us bow down in worship, let us kneel before the LORD our Maker; for he is our God" (Ps. 95:6 NIV). Here is awe, mystery, wonder, and joy. "The time is coming and has now come when true worshipers will worship [kiss the hand toward] the Father in spirit and truth, for they are the kind of worshipers the Father seeks" (John 4:23). Such an attitude of worship reveals humble awareness of God's majesty and grandeur, yet we dare approach with confidence through Jesus Christ (Heb. 9:15–16).

Second, however, worship involves service, for God is also the *object* of worship. In the Old Testament, the word *abad* means to labor and to serve, and in the New Testament, *latreuo* refers to a state of servitude. Worshipers are not just knocked prostrate before God's greatness; they are also set up on their feet to serve him. On trial before Felix, the apostle Paul says, "I admit that I worship [*latreuo*] the God of our fathers as a follower of the Way" (Acts 24:14 NIV). We are brought low in wonder yet also are required to offer ourselves as living sacrifices (Rom. 12:1–2). Awe, mystery, wonder, and joy are joined with offering and service. All these responses and more are due almighty God because of who he is and what he has done. Worship throws us down and throws us forward. As Jesus makes clear, true worship of God is both adoration of and obedient love to him, but it is also loving service of one's neighbor (Matt. 22:37–39).

True worship is *God-empowered*. He initiates it by grace, which first gives us ability and resources by which to respond. Giving life in all its fullness, faith in all its wonder, material goods in all their plenty (at least for many of us in the Western church), God grants us everything that matters. He has given us everything we need for life and godliness (2 Pet. 1:3). By his Spirit breathing life, gifting faith, and inspiring generosity, worshipers return their praise and service for God's glory by God's empowering.

True worship is *all-inclusive*. Christian believers belong to a new creation in Christ (2 Cor. 5:17), living with him and for him for eternity. Astonishingly, *new creation* speaks not only of individual, personal completeness in Christ but also of recapitulation of all fallen creation into newness. While death and disintegration came from Adam, by Christ comes life and reintegration of all things (Rom. 5:12–21; 1 Cor. 15:22). Belonging with Christ is not for Sundays only but for Sundays through Saturdays, not just with sermons or music in church but with our friends and enemies at work, in recreation, in zip codes across the world, and in heaven. Worship as a new creation in Christ is *God's greatest idea and our highest activity*. It claims center stage and every other position as well. With worship as his number one priority, God reorders everything else in relationship to worship. Christian worship is as expansive as total Christian living in response to God. Every time we think we have pinned worship down adequately, more dimensions open up beyond.

True worship is therefore *continuous*. Harold Best's *Unceasing Worship* startlingly describes how God intends humankind to be "continuously outpouring." Made in the image of God, who eternally outpours within his triune self, human beings have no option but to worship someone or something continuously. We are built for worship. We reflect this aspect of God's character. "Nobody does not worship. . . . Worship is the continuous outpouring of all that I am, all that I do and all that I can ever become in light of a chosen or choosing god."[17] While all humankind is made to worship something or someone, Christians believe that as a fallen people (Gen. 3) we need redemption through Christ so that through salvation in him our continuous outpouring might be "set aright and urged into the fullness of Christ."[18] Though human rebellion sabotaged the desire to worship and obey, Christ's coming makes new creation possible, thereby enabling deep worship dynamics "in spirit and truth" (John 4:24). By love that sent his Son to save the world (John 3:16), God seeks to reconcile us with himself (Rom. 5:6–11) so that we together, "in heaven and on earth and under the earth," are reunited as a praising, worshiping creation (Phil. 2:9–11).

The word *continuous* emphasizes persistent commitment to God's faithfulness. "We are continually to love God with heart, soul and mind; we are to love our neighbor without let up; we are to forgive endlessly. . . . We are to continue in the truth whether we play or preach." *Outpouring* also implies free-flowing "lavishness and generosity: when I pour something, I give it up; I let it go. . . . The flow is organically and consistently itself."[19] Because we are made as "continuous outpourers," wittingly or unwittingly, we all spend ourselves in praise for something or other that gives us reason for living. Money, sports, family, possessions, and passions all motivate worship (little *w*), but the Triune God is the only worthy cause of Worship (big *W*).

Who or what I worship describes everything significant about me. Some have summed up *modern* thinking by Descartes' dictum, "I think, therefore I am," and *postmodernity* by, "I feel, therefore I am." But the biblical way to express self is, "I worship, therefore I am." Worship involves all that we are—not one activity among others but how we live whole lives. Some call this *habitual recollection*. Stephen Winward quotes William Temple's provocative statement: "In order to serve God properly, there are times where we must forget him." This *forgetting* is not about ceasing to remember but about living in a state of mind that means even unconscious actions keep God central. Winward compares such habitual recollection to a happy marriage. "The devoted husband and wife do not spend all, or even most, of their time thinking about each other; yet they remain 'in the holy estate of matrimony.' Wherever they are, whatever they are doing, their whole existence is a 'being-in-love.'"[20] Of course, sustaining this relationship of being in love requires some conscious communication effort, but the state of *habitual recollection* aptly describes how worship becomes a way of life.

True worship has one ultimate focus—seeking *God's glory*. This goal is famously expressed by the seventeenth-century Westminster Shorter Catechism:

Question: What is the chief end of man?
Answer: Man's chief end is to glorify God and to enjoy him for ever.

To glorify God with celebration that *enjoys* God strikingly sums up worship's goal—joining in with all creation (Rev. 4:11; 5:9–13), we declare his majesty and praise his name. The word *enjoy* may give the misleading impression that this is always spontaneous and easy, but worship requires intentionality of will with disciplined intellect (Mark 12:30). "We must will, determine, to give to the Lord the glory due to his name. We can learn to worship him with, without, or against our feelings, as the case may be. . . . The set of the will (constancy of purpose, regular practice) is itself a costly and precious offering to God."[21]

Giving God glory is therefore the largest purpose in the cosmos. Humans are at their most alive when worshiping our loving Creator God. Two thousand years of Christian theology, spirituality, and practice can only touch the surface of the comprehensive reality that is Christian worship.

Not only do we enjoy and take pleasure in God, but God takes pleasure in us through our worship. In his bestseller, *The Purpose Driven Life*, Rick Warren rightly identifies the number one purpose for living:

You were planned for God's pleasure. . . . Bringing pleasure to God is called "worship." The Bible says, "The Lord is pleased only with those who worship him and trust in his love." Anything that you do that brings pleasure to God is an act of worship.[22]

God in three persons—Father, Son, and Holy Spirit—invites us to live within the biggest story possible, offering the greatest reason, the vastest perspective, and the profoundest resources for living so that, made in the image of God, we can be reconciled through Jesus Christ, to belong with him and live for him in a community of unbreakable love. Grounded in the revelation of Jesus Christ, the Word made flesh, God's story holds everything together that matters for humankind, from creation to the end of time. Father, Son, and Holy Spirit are involved so intimately that we dare to speak of sharing in "the grace of the Lord Jesus Christ, the love of God, and the fellowship of the Holy Spirit" (2 Cor. 13:14 NIV). Worship demands the noblest vocabulary and mind-stretching theology.

Any venture into defining worship more fully by its throw-down, throw-out, love-God, love-neighbor, new-creation-continuousness, give-God-the-glory dimensions opens our eyes to big-picture worship, for nothing lies beyond its scope.

> Worship, in all its grades and kinds, is the response of the creature to the Eternal. . . . There is a sense in which we may think of the whole life of the Universe, seen and unseen, conscious and unconscious, as an act of worship, glorifying its Origin, Sustainer, and end . . . when conscious it is always a subject-object relationship, . . . an acknowledgment of Transcendence; that is to say, of a Reality independent of the worshiper, which is always more or less deeply colored by mystery and which is there first.[23]

"Worship is the proper response of all moral, sentient beings to God, ascribing all honor and worth to their Creator God precisely because he is worthy, delightfully so."[24] "Worship is all of us for all of God."[25] Its scope embraces all creation, all thinking, all relating, and all living.

Just reflect back on the first three chapters of this book and the inadequacy of small-picture worship. Worship is *never* just another aspect or practice of Christian life, jostling alongside doctrine, church, and preaching. Worship is not something humans do on the way to something more important. It's the reason why we are alive in the first place. God made us to worship and to live in harmony with and in obedience to him. Worship embraces all that we are and all that we have—given by God and returning to him in praise and by worshipful living. It is the foundational, purpose-driven *integrator* holding everything else together, *everything* that believers think and do. "The urgent, indeed troubling, message of Scripture is that everything that matters is at stake in worship."[26]

Acting on God's glorious invitation, worshipers celebrate being alive with heads, hearts, and bodies within his community through Christ's grace (Heb. 7:24–25). Christian worship is the outpouring of adoration, praise, thanksgiving, confession, intercession, listening, working, serving, and witnessing by believers who share bread, wine, songs, silence, joy, noise, quiet, and tears, both personally and corporately to God's glory. Filled with wonder, overwhelmed by mystery, loved by gospel grace, worshipers join in fellowship with the Triune God, both when they gather and when they scatter. Seeing worship like this stirs up profound gratitude.

I was pondering these words in my draft manuscript while sitting on a plane waiting for takeoff when suddenly a man's cell phone rang. He was sitting directly in front of me, and in an instant he was transformed. Loudly (far too loudly), he bellowed into the phone, "That's unbelievable. That's extraordinary. It's incredible, Bill. Wow! I just cannot believe that has happened!" He continued in this vein for about a minute. Then, for another two or three minutes, alternately pausing then exploding, he kept exclaiming, "Unbelievable!" A woman across the aisle shot disapproving looks, but he remained utterly impervious, caught up in genuine amazement at what he was hearing. I have no idea what Bill was sharing, but some truth had broken in to knock him over, and he couldn't contain his joy and excitement; he was so thankful for what had happened. I smiled as I thought about the paragraphs I had just written about the throw-down, throw-out, love-God, love-neighbor, new-creation-continuousness, give-God-the-glory dimensions of worship. Yes, worship means genuine amazement and deep thankfulness.

There is no more unbelievable news than the Christian gospel—God in love chooses *us* to share in his life. Wonder and thanks at such grace should stir us to the core, break us out of boxes, smash through domes, and propel us toward the big picture of worship. Such understanding of worship impacts everything, including preaching (as we will see in chap. 5). But closely linked with this bigger understanding of worship is the need for myopic preachers to overcome thin theology.

Toward a Trinitarian Theology

Anyone reading theology in the last twenty years will know about the resurgence of interest in the doctrine of the Trinity.[27] Many evangelicals have responded thoughtfully and enthusiastically to this fresh thinking, especially in writing about worship.[28] For preaching, too, there have been significant stirrings. Michael Pasquarello III grounds his important book *Christian Preaching* entirely in the doctrine of the Trinity.

Many busy pastors may shrug their shoulders at this news because memories of dry, dusty, early church councils make the doctrine of the Trinity seem distant and irrelevant. But whenever Christian living ignores theology, it dumbs down—settling for faulty definitions and taking direction from sheer pragmatism rather than from God's revelation. Theology is *speaking meaningfully about God.*

Sadly, much current preaching and worship seem to speak of God in *fewer* than three persons. We saw this earlier in James Torrance's criticism of "practical unitarianism." Too often the focus has been on Jesus alone, neglecting his relationship with the Father and the Spirit. Some dub this exclusive focus on Jesus *Jesuology* or *Jesuolatry.* Of course, the birth, death, and resurrection of Jesus Christ are central to the Christian faith and to its preaching and worship. "For I decided to know nothing among you except Jesus Christ, and him crucified" (1 Cor. 2:2). Yet Jesus's life and ministry can properly be understood only within his relationship to the Father and to the Spirit because Jesus is sent on the Father's mission to reconcile the world to himself. As Jesus is obedient to his Father's will, so he gives glory to his Father by his ministry. Jesus is the Mediator. Through the Spirit, believers are able to call the Father *Abba*, for "the Spirit himself testifies with our spirit that we are God's children" (Rom. 8:16 NIV).

Jesus is not a stand-alone figure, relegating the Father and Holy Spirit into shadowy, dispensable background roles. Indeed, no part of Jesus's life can be understood apart from his relationships within the Trinity. "Trinity should be related to our other beliefs like hydrogen is related to water. Take the H out of H_2O and you no longer have water. Take the Trinity out of Christian faith and practice and you no longer have Christian faith and practice."[29]

Bruce Ware lists key reasons why the Trinity is important, including: (1) It "is one of the most important distinguishing doctrines of the Christian faith." (2) It is "both central and necessary for the Christian faith; . . . remove the Trinity and the whole Christian faith disintegrates." (3) "Worship of the true and living God consciously acknowledges the relationship and roles of Father, Son and Holy Spirit."[30]

The challenge for preachers to think as trinitarians, therefore, is not an invitation to engage in some time-wasting, intellectual exercise but rather a call to engage with God afresh. God's promise of *renewed intelligence* that enables believers to be transformed and to discover God's will involves deeper spiritual understanding. By renewed thinking, believers "discern what is the will of God—what is good and acceptable and perfect" (Rom. 12:2).

Robin Parry believes that such thinking is vital for those who lead worship too.

> Good theology matters for good worship. . . . [I] used to think that sorting out your doctrine and sorting out your worship were two quite separate things. . . . Now I see that right belief about God is intimately connected to right worship because believing right things about God is an essential component in honoring God appropriately. That is why Christians speak of right belief about God as "orthodoxy" which means right glory.[31]

Preachers believe orthodoxy, "right glory," should express doxology, "glory words." When preachers think as trinitarians, everything changes about worship.

Some treat the doctrine of the Trinity lightly because of the apparent paucity of specific Scripture references. True, it took the early church nearly four centuries to finally articulate this doctrine. But *the Christian God of Scripture cannot be understood without the doctrine of the Trinity.* Early Christians recorded the doctrine from the very beginning (Matt. 28:19; 2 Cor. 13:14). The practice of speaking of God as Father, Son, and Holy Spirit is embedded in the New Testament, though working out the profound theological implications of such practice necessarily took some time. Trying to understand God's DNA, as revealed in Scripture, understandably demanded the best *renewed intelligence* available.

The complex and arduous theological process of formulating the doctrine of the Trinity based on Scripture resulted in the Nicene-Constantinople Creed (AD 381), which emphasized how the eternal relationship between Father and Son is essential to revelation and salvation. In early church debates, different models and terms emerged.[32] By stressing the relationship and participation of God's three persons in human history, the creed laid foundations for a *social Trinity* model of the Trinity that was developed later. This understanding of God's continuing involvement with human action has become highly influential today. One important word associated with this doctrine is *perichoresis.*

To preserve both the unity of the one God and the individuality of the three persons, *perichoresis* describes how the persons of the Trinity do not belong as distinct from each other but dwell inside each other (John 10:38; 14:8–11), mutually inhering and drawing life from one another, and therefore they are only to be experienced because of their relationship to each other. Because of their mutuality, no divine person acts apart from the others. For example, in creation the Father is Creator, but Jesus is involved (John 1:3), as is the Spirit (Ps. 104:30). Or in Ephesians 1:3–14, the Father elects (vv. 4–5, 11), the Son redeems (vv. 3, 7–8), and the Holy Spirit seals the outcome (vv. 13–14).

Obviously, within this book's scope only a brief survey is possible of the many implications that trinitarian theology has for worship. But we must note particular outcomes of *participating* within the life of the Trinity because the *relationships*, *movement*, and *power* of God in three persons all enable worship of radical wonder. Nothing could contrast more with the unitarian one-way movement that puts so much stress on worshipers' energy, responding to God's act in the past. Here worship joins in gloriously with God acting in the present.

Participation is a key word for understanding worship involvement with the Trinity. *Participation* is defined as "the act of taking part, of sharing in something with others." Mutually responsible sharing requires different parties joining to work together so that each relates to the whole. Astoundingly, though the three persons of the Trinity belong together in divine community *apart* from creation, they have freely chosen to involve themselves in the human story, graciously enabling humans to participate, join, and share in communion with them. Stunningly, all human response to God, including preaching and worship, may actually participate in fellowship, in joining in, *with* God in three persons. "Worship is not merely something we present to God; it is our participation in the life of God, in the fellowship of the threeness of God."[33]

"Practical unitarianism" is tragically closed to Christ's continuing work and to the Holy Spirit. As we saw in figure 1, its sole emphasis on what Christ has done on the cross for personal salvation thrusts responsibility for consequent worship and discipleship onto human shoulders alone. The divine dynamic operates only one way, leaving us in charge of the human-Godward movement—everything depends on us. In contrast, trinitarians, seeking to participate with God, know that salvation is not only a matter of Christ's work in the past but also a matter of his person in the present continuing to intercede and mediate so that through him we belong with the Father, by the Holy Spirit. "Our worship is *with* Christ our brother, *in* Christ our priest but always *through* Christ our sacrifice whose death for us is the means of our cleansing, renewing and perfection"[34] (see, for example, Eph. 1:4–5; 2:18; Heb. 2:10–12; 7:25).

The *relationship* between God and humanity is made possible in the person and work of Jesus Christ and by the go-between Holy Spirit. Only as they open up relationship with us is it feasible "that we might participate by the Spirit in Jesus's communion with the Father in a life of intimate communion"[35] (Heb. 10:10–14). This is the wonder of belonging within the church. Though his role is often ignored by practical unitarians, the Holy Spirit enables the mutual inhering of God's three persons (*perichoresis*) to interact, amazingly *with us*. This is the *social model* of the Trinity.

A fifteenth-century icon painted by Andrei Rublev, a Russian monk, has become popular for expressing these trinitarian relationships. Called "The Holy Trinity," it depicts the three visitors to Abraham in Genesis 18:1–15. Under the oak tree at Mamre, three holy persons are seated, each with a halo around his head. On the left is the Father in majestic gold, in the center is Jesus in sacrificial red, and on the right the Holy Spirit is in green, a color of growth. They all seem equal, but as the Father inclines, so too the Son and Holy Spirit incline to the Father, indicating both a clear differentiation yet also togetherness and unity in body language. Around the table, community is expressed by relationships of love, mutuality, and intimacy.

On the table is the cup. Each figure seems to be looking at it, motioning toward it. Jesus, being in the center, seems to be closest to it, as though inviting a response to a new covenant in his blood. But we notice that the fourth side of the table is open as if to make room for many others to join in. This is not a three-sided table but a four-sided one with an invitation. God's love flows outward in hospitality—sharing who he is and what he gives in triune grace.

While practical unitarianism restricts God's action to one-way movement, *perichoresis* involves a glorious double *movement*. Rather than *our* faith or decision making being central, the spiritual, dynamic double movement is all-important: "(a) a God-humanward movement, from (*ek*) the Father, through (*dia*) the Son, in (*en*) the Spirit and (b) a human-Godward movement to the Father through the Son in the Spirit."[36] Jesus Christ mediates from above as well as from below, enabling believers to participate in worship—humanward from the Father in the Spirit, but also human-Godward, moving to the Father in the Spirit.

Torrance explains that this double movement of grace, "which is the heart of the 'dialogue' between God and humanity in worship, is grounded in the very perichoretic being of God, and is fundamental for our understanding of the Triune God's relationship with the world in creation, incarnation and sanctification. What God is toward us in these relationships, he is in his innermost being."[37] By this gracious action, God enables us to belong within his fellowship and participate with the Father, who gives faith and desire, drawing us through his Son, by his Spirit.

Instead of preachers and worshipers relying on their own energy to truly worship, God's initiating *power* alone makes worship possible, and he draws us in. Instead of preachers "doing their own thing," exhorting listeners "to do their thing" (quoting Torrance again), preachers participate within God's double-movement empowerment. Of course, worshipers have a responsibility to offer themselves as acceptable sacrifices (Rom. 12:1), and they can fail in that task. But they are acceptable only because of Christ's work on the cross, his continuing mediation, and the work of the Holy Spirit, who enables confession: "Abba, Father." Such emphasizing of God's empowering challenges do-it-yourself practices of worship and safeguards the mystery of God's involvement in our life together as he prompts worship yet also receives it and seeks to perfect it.

Much more could be written about the practical implications for preaching as trinitarians,[38] and the next chapter draws together more implications of trinitarian theology for worship. Without it, worship continues to be doomed to small-picture thinking and living. John Witvliet describes how congregations need to grow various "Trinitarian worship habits" that mark "communities that fully embrace Trinitarian ways of thinking and living."[39] Such habits include learning to express memory and hope as they remember God's story because God has acted in history. Also, they need to learn about maintaining *trinitarian balance* and *trinitarian integration* to ensure all three persons of the Trinity are celebrated in worship, theology, and the forming of God's community. We will learn more about this later.

Introducing the Question Toolbox

Much of this chapter has pushed us into theological thinking, which some may have found somewhat daunting. Some readers may be asking, "What practical difference is this going to make for me? Can you tell me a significant learning point to remember and act upon?"

At this point I introduce the first in an important series of six questions that will be developed throughout the next four chapters and then applied in part 3. Intended for all those who lead worship, these questions will form a significant resource—a *question toolbox* for worship preparation. Every aspect of gathered worship can be probed by these questions, including choosing hymns and songs, taking up the offering, saying prayers, and communing at the Lord's Table. Together the questions cover all the key issues involved in big-picture worship. They probe and disturb until they are answered. Addressed in first-person plural language, they ask individual worship leaders to work together in focused preparation and provide a means by which these leaders can collaborate enthusiastically for big-picture worship.

Several times during this chapter, I have noted that a fuller understanding of worship and trinitarian theology stir up wonder and joy in the overwhelming mystery of being loved by gospel grace and being invited to join in fellowship with the Triune God. It underlines how worship owes *everything* to God as gift. In three persons he initiates relationship by overwhelming grace through Jesus Christ and bonds us together through the Holy Spirit. Only because of his love and power can we offer ourselves as living sacrifices. Worship is a sheer gift requiring utter gratitude; positive thankfulness is the foundation of gathered worship.

So the first question asks worship leaders about their level of gratitude.

Question Toolbox

1. *Gift*: Are we thankfully receiving this gift of worship from the Triune God of grace?

This question probes how thankful we are. I have heard music leaders and preachers speak of "thanking God for the privilege of worship," yet sadly, authentic gratitude to God seems rare. Perhaps the practical tasks of organizing worship services and writing sermons have dulled them to the Giver and his gift. Humility and gratitude should mark human response. I heard someone comment, "There is no worship, no music, no prayer, no sermon in itself so good that God has to accept it. Just as we are sinners whose life God redeems by grace, we are all mumbling stutterers whose words and music God accepts by grace." Overwhelming our littleness, God lifts us up into the greatest possibilities of living for him. This is grace at a maximum. God is at the center, and Jesus is Mediator of the largest truth that can ever be told and the greatest experience we can ever have.

Worship should flow from doxology. Note the setting for the apostle Paul's plea: "I appeal to you therefore, brothers and sisters, by the mercies of God, to present your bodies as a living sacrifice, holy and acceptable to God, which is your spiritual worship" (Rom. 12:1). Its "therefore" shouts why it is there: tumultuously marking the outcome of the great doctrines of the faith in the preceding chapters and culminating in the doxology (Rom. 11:33–36). Packed with wonder, it rises to crescendo with implicit trinitarianism: "For from him and through him and to him are all things. To him be the glory forever" (v. 36).

Eugene Peterson paraphrases:

> Everything comes from him;
> Everything happens through him;
> Everything ends up in him.
> Always glory! Always praise!
> Yes. Yes. Yes.

> So here's what I want you to do, God helping you: take your everyday, ordinary life—your sleeping, eating, going-to-work, and walking-around life—and place it before God as an offering. Embracing what God does for you is the best thing you can do for him.

> Romans 11:36–12:1 Message

Answering this first question positively sets the tone for every aspect of worship, influencing attitude and approach, as well as content. It drives out presumption, pride in human resources, and casual thoughtlessness. With joy and humility, it acknowledges God alone as the one who calls us to worship and enables us to respond. With praise and adoration from grateful hearts, it expresses wholesome gladness to the Lord, who meets with us in fellowship. We enter corporate worship with thankfulness: "Enter his gates with thanksgiving, and his courts with praise. Give thanks to him, bless his name" (Ps. 100:4), and we continue in our everyday, ordinary lives knowing that "everything ends up in him. Always glory! Always praise!" (Rom. 11:36 Message). Gratitude marks daily worship in our sleeping, eating, going-to-work, and walking-around lives.

Developing the positive power of thankfulness requires space, reflection, and intentionality, all of which are so easily squeezed out by busyness and the pressures of preparing gathered worship. Yet every week the refrain should be "Come ye thankful people, come." There is no more vital place to begin than by thankfully receiving the Triune God's gift of grace.

When I spoke with Karen Roberts about this first question, she said that her response to God's gift actually led to profound confession. Indeed, she wrote this prayer:

A Worship Leader's Prayer of Thanksgiving and Confession

Loving, Heavenly Father,

I thank and praise you for the gift of your Son, for by his sacrifice I have been redeemed. Forgive me when I take for granted the love you have shown me; help me to be ever joyful and mindful of your call on my life.

I thank and praise you for the work of the Holy Spirit to convict, guide, and empower.

Forgive me when I rely on my own thoughts and actions instead of your indwelling presence in my life as I seek to serve you.

I thank and praise you that your Son, Jesus Christ, is continually interceding on my behalf.

Forgive me when I do not enter into prayer for my brothers and sisters and pray that all nations may come to know your love and restoration. Help me to pray as I plan worship and before and during the service that we may encounter you, the living God.

I thank and praise you for the gift of worship, for placing me into a community that joins all creation in unceasing worship.

Forgive me when I am prideful, seeking the approval of others more than pleasing you. Forgive me when I forget that you are our audience. Forgive me when I put the focus on myself or the music instead of Jesus Christ. May I not settle, or ask others to settle, for small-picture worship, but may our worship be a foretaste of the heavenly worship to come.

For your ever-present love I thank and praise you. I thank you for the joy of serving you as your people gather in worship. Thank you for the joy of my salvation. May I not be a stumbling block to others but a vessel that you can use to build your kingdom.

All glory belongs to you, Father, Son, and Holy Spirit. Amen.[40]

5

Preaching in 360-Degree Worship

Make a joyful noise to the LORD all the earth. Worship the LORD with gladness. Come into his presence with singing. Know that the LORD is God.

Psalm 100:1–2

Life may throw out at least a few memorable breakthrough moments. When I was nine or ten years old, my parents gave me a birthday surprise. For children, birthdays often have a special electric quality of delight. You wait with such excitement because everything is focused on you—the presents, the food, the whole day. Even your brother is pleasant to you! Since my birthday falls in the summer, we were often on vacation when my birthday came around. One year on my birthday my parents announced I was going on a mystery tour and needed to be blindfolded.

First we drove a few miles. Then I was helped out of the car, giggling, trying unsuccessfully to see out of the blindfold's sides, and needing to hold on to my parents' hands. I had no idea where we were. At first we walked in the open air, then we entered a building and began climbing up steps. Up and up—I knew it must be a tower. Once or twice people passed by—"Kidnapping him?" they said. We climbed higher. Reaching the top, I could feel the sun and breeze on my face. My mother and father took the blindfold off, and I blinked with happiness at the sight before me. I was at the top of the Cabot Tower in Bristol, England. The city lay below, the river danced beneath, countryside rolled beyond, and the sea glinted in the distance. It was dazzling and brilliant as I stood there with my kid brother and my parents.

Reflecting now on that moment, I am fairly sure it was the first time in my life that I truly experienced being alive. Up until then I had little perception of a world full of beauty, trust, love, purity, and joy. But right then its big picture just couldn't be beaten. Everything was good in deep places of my body, mind, and spirit. Astonishingly good! As I have grown older, I have had a few other experiences like that, and definitely the best times have been in worship when I have known, joining with others, that I belong to God in depths of beauty, trust, love, purity, and joy.

Chapter 4 opened up just such a big vista, seeing worship as God's greatest idea for our highest purpose, participating with and empowered by his triune grace. As in *The Truman Show* movie, the exit door opens onto a much bigger reality beyond. A fuller definition and deeper theology propel us into seeing preaching and worship in new ways.

An Exercise

Over the last four years, some of my most interesting experiences in thinking through worship and preaching have come from formal meetings with preachers and worship leaders. At one such conference in Missouri, I led a session on issues that separate preaching and worship (as in chap. 2) before presenting some of the definitions listed in the appendix. I asked those attending to reflect on and discuss in groups which definitions, words, and phrases struck them as most pertinent for expressing preaching and worship. In a fast-moving follow-up session, they pinpointed six aspects:

1. *Trinity*. Several pastors commented on the strong trinitarian theme running through some of the definitions. For instance, Robin Parry said, "Christian worship is nothing more nor less than the Spirit enabling us to join in with Christ's worship of the Father. Christian prayer is nothing more nor less than the Spirit enabling us to join in with Christ's prayer to the Father." James Torrance commented, "Christian worship is . . . our participation through the Spirit in the Son's communion with the Father, in his vicarious life of worship and intercession. It is our response to our Father for all that he has done for us in Christ." Pastors asked what difference it would make to their practice of preaching and worship if they paid more attention to trinitarian theology. Indeed, several asked to learn more about how Father, Son, and Spirit are involved in preaching and worship.
2. *Gift of love*. "Worship is a gift between lovers who keep on giving to each other" (C. Welton Gaddy). Several pastors chose this definition

because it emphasizes not only the nature of worship as gift but also its interchangeable love that moves backward and forward between God and us. One pastor preferred the analogy of parent-child love rather than "between lovers." He shared a powerful personal story as a parent about when he first heard his child voluntarily declare, "I love you." "What an analogy to worship!" he exclaimed.

3. *Conversation.* "Worship is God's conversation with the people of God and the community's communication with the divine Communicator" (Russell Mitman). The word *conversation* triggered much discussion because of its obvious relationship to the act of preaching itself. Actually, *homiliea*, the Greek word that gives us the English word *homiletics*, means "conversation." Belief in a speaking God, a God who has revealed himself by words (Gen. 1; John 1:1), has huge repercussions for revelation and response. Notice how the story of Abram (Gen. 11:27–12:9), which begins the genealogy of Jesus Christ (Matt. 1:1–2), is initiated by God, who speaks and promises a new future. Abram's response necessarily involves both journeying in obedience and worshiping (Gen. 12:7–8, 20; 13:18; and so on). At the altars Abram joins in worship conversation. One preacher asked just how closely preaching and worship belong together when both participate in God's worship conversation.

4. *Mystery.* Some pastors highlighted Don Saliers's definition because it stresses mystery: "At its best, Christian worship presents a vision of life created, sustained, redeemed, and held in the mystery of God. What we do together in acknowledging God *schools* us in ways of seeing the world and of being in it." They wanted to safeguard mystery at the heart of worship. And one pastor was particularly intrigued about communities being "schooled" in life and character. "What might this 'schooling' mean for preaching?" he asked.

5. *Bridge.* Others were struck by how worship makes spiritual connections. One pastor strongly approved of the definition, "True worship is Spirit touching spirit. Worship happens when the presence of God is bridged with people's felt needs in their life context" (Michael Slaughter). He emphasized worship particularly belonging to a specific people in a definite context. Rather than one size fits all, each congregation's expression of worship is unique. Others spoke about how preachers seek to *incarnate* God's Word by grounding exegesis and interpretation in their pastoral contexts and how the whole act of worship should parallel this process.

6. *Narrative.* One or two commented on how worship involves God's people living out his story line. "Here is the essence of Christian worship. As members of a people whose story line includes creation, sin, and grace, we commune with our Creator and Savior—with God, through Christ, in the power of the Holy Spirit. Worship is narrative engagement with

the Triune God" (Cornelius Plantinga and Sue Rozeboom). God's story in Scripture not only provides the time line for his people but also places each act of worship into sequence: remembering the past, challenging about the present, or anticipating the future. Preachers as proclaimers are therefore storytellers in Christian worship.

In this lively engagement about preaching and worship, it became clear that some had never previously thought about how they relate together. Hopefully, as you read through the appendix, some definitions and expressions will resonate with you too. Do any increase *your* pulse rate? Do any puzzle or trouble you?

Through sharing issues and raising questions, a bigger picture of worship was becoming clearer. Everyone concurred that preaching and worship *are* inextricably linked. Indeed, several pastors expressed surprise at how much some of these worship definitions applied to preaching: both preaching and worship are grounded in trinitarian theology; both can be understood as gift and conversation; both express mystery and contribute to community spiritual formation; and both bridge spiritual connections by sharing and telling out God's story. One pastor repeated how appropriate one definition is for both: "Worship/Preaching is God's conversation with the people of God and the community's communication with the divine Communicator." This reminded me of Martin Luther's daring claim: "There is in the divine Trinity a pulpit: as God the Father is an eternal speaker, so the Son is spoken in eternity, and the Holy Spirit is an eternal listener. God's triune being is an eternal conversation, and since the Holy Spirit tells us what he hears, we are taken into this conversation."[1] This conference proved to be another important staging post on my journey toward big-picture worship.

My Change of Worldview

From the outset I have not hidden how disruptive my journey with worship turned out to be. Far from gently refining my understanding of preaching, adding a fresh insight here and there, it ambushed, roughed up, overwhelmed, and then completely reshaped my previous worldview of ministry and pastoral calling. Arthur F. Holmes says that "a world view is . . . needed as a guide to thought. A world filled with things to be thought about and arrayed with a multitude of ideas and theories on everything under the sun compels us to be selective. . . . We have to set priorities. What then will determine our priorities and guide our selectivity?"[2]

Initially, *preaching* dominated my ministry worldview as all-important and all-sufficient for determining my priorities and guiding selectivity. Yet my worship journey dramatically showed how limited this preaching worldview was. It increasingly exposed my guilt as a myopic preacher and deepened my dissatisfaction about continuing with small-picture worship. I was thrown into a massive worship makeover that took me to depths of beauty, trust, love, purity, and joy.

In *360-Degree Preaching*, I offer a definition: "Christian preaching, at its best, is a biblical speaking/listening/seeing/doing event that God empowers to form Christ-shaped people and communities."[3] I critiqued a popular metaphor of preacher as *bridge builder* that envisages preaching as crossing over a 180-degree arc from Scripture on one side to hearers on the other. I fear this model's implicit theology placed too large a burden on preachers' shoulders, as though making the Bible world relevant to contemporary listeners was *all* their own work. Preaching that is 180 degrees heightens the risk of preachers acting like practical unitarians, burdened by full responsibility for creating relevant messages.

Instead, I proposed a 360-degree model that placed God at the beginning and end of the preaching event. Because God's Word "shall not return to [him] void" (Isa. 55:11 NKJV), I pictured a *circular* dynamic by which the Triune God begins and finishes the process—beginning with God's revelation in Scripture and continuing by Christ's interceding presence and the Spirit's empowering to impact hearers for his grand purpose. As God speaks in Scripture, by his Son, and through his Spirit, so his words continue to accomplish his deeds as they return to him through his proclaimers.

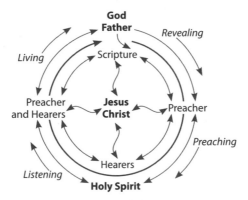

Figure 2. The Spiritual Dynamic of Preaching. Reprinted from Michael Quicke, *360-Degree Preaching* (Grand Rapids: Baker Academic, 2003); used by permission.

In figure 2, the arrow in bold, arching back to God, depicts his Word at work, framing preaching's fundamental theological and spiritual dynamic. Every part of the preaching event is empowered by the Triune God speaking through his Word *and* empowering preachers *and* convicting listeners *and* transforming lives of preachers and listeners. God is at work everywhere. Christ stands with those who gather in his name (Matt. 18:20) and prays for all believers (John 17:20–26), and the Holy Spirit helps them in their weaknesses (Rom. 8:26), actively creating spiritual apprehension (1 Thess. 1:5). "The preaching . . . dynamic, found in God, and driven by God, returns to God as individuals and communities are transformed—all within the grace of the Triune God."[4] Instead of preachers doing their own thing and exhorting listeners to do their thing, preachers participate within God's triune activity. The four quadrants of the circle in figure 2 spell out the spiritual process: Scripture revealing, preachers preaching, hearers listening, and preachers with hearers living.

This preaching worldview, however, virtually excludes worship.[5] It seems to treat preaching as almost an end in itself, operating in a separate box apart from worship. In spite of its trinitarian theology, it endorses myopic preaching. But on my preaching journey, these assumptions have been radically challenged. I was confronted by the absurdity of limiting God's triune involvement to preaching alone. Intent on describing how Father, Son, and Holy Spirit all interact with preaching, I had completely failed to see the bigger picture of how the Trinity is simultaneously involved with worship and all of life. Instead of restricting this model to preaching, I now realize it should be expanded to describe *the theology and dynamics of worship itself*. Without compromising the Christocentric primacy of proclaiming Jesus Christ as lord, who reveals the Father and sends the Spirit, we must see preaching is not the only activity empowered by the trinitarian dynamic, nor does it operate on its own. Rather, the model describes the big picture of God's call and our response in worship, which involves relationships, movement, and power of God's three persons.

It is clear that 360-degree preaching belongs within 360-degree worship. Preaching is not a different kind of activity from worship that is practiced on its own. It works in the same way, for the same purposes, by the grace of the same empowering Triune God. Preaching is "both an act of God in which the hearers are confronted with the Gospel, and also an act of man in which the preacher offers his confession of faith to God."[6] Preaching is an offering made to God by preachers, yet it simultaneously addresses the congregation on behalf of God. Not only is it structurally connected to worship, but everything about it *is* worship. Preachers worship when they preach, hearers worship as they listen, and all participants worship as they respond. Worship is the primary dynamic in which preaching engages—the integrator of preaching within God's big picture.

So a new model is needed to depict this worldview of 360-degree worship. Worship now becomes dominant, though preaching remains significant. Figure 3, therefore, illustrates worship's primary spiritual dynamic—from God back to God—*within* which preachers are called and gifted to preach. Preachers belong within God's triune love, participating in his gracious relationships, movement, and power. Vital though preaching is, it belongs within the glorious work of worship, of God's Word returning to him.

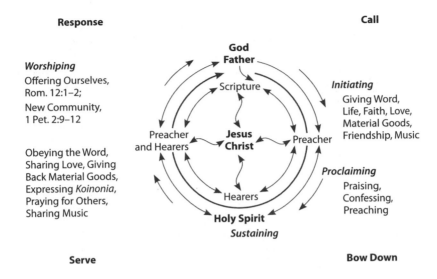

Figure 3. Preaching Included in the Dynamics of 360-Degree Worship. Based on Michael Quicke, *360-Degree Preaching* (Grand Rapids: Baker Academic, 2003); used by permission.

Call and response or *revelation and response* sum up worship's double movement directed both God-humanward and human-Godward. This call and response dynamic emphasizes both aspects of worship—*bow down* and *serve*—reminding us that God is both the subject and the object of worship. God, who is worthy of all praise and glory and before whom we bow down, calls us into fellowship to serve. He has gifted us with Word, life, faith, love, material goods, friendship, and music, and we offer our best back to him. Always his gracious gifts of faith, hope, and love precede worship—"We do not love because we worship; we worship in that we love."[7]

Interestingly, the circular pattern in figure 3 of "God gives—we receive—we respond—God receives" resonates with some writers on worship. Defining worship "as a gift between lovers who keep on giving to each other," C. Welton Gaddy envisages it as circular movement, beginning in the heights and drawing people in by sheer love. "Giving and receiving form a *circular* pattern between God and the people of God, which defies comprehension and lasts for ever" (my italics).[8] God's gifts of faith, material goods, music, and friendship are returned by worshipers through their confession of faith and praise, their tithes and offerings, their music, and their friendship within community. Marva Dawn also emphasizes how worship is a corporate gift: "The gifts of worship flow from God the subject and return to God as the object of our reverence. . . . The sermon is not just the gift of the preacher, nor are choral gifts simply the contribution of the choir, but both involve the offering of themselves by all the members of the congregation."[9]

How dramatically this big sweep of worship's call and response reframes the place of preaching. Preaching remains essential for God's formation of Christ-shaped people and communities because it enables biblical speaking, listening, seeing, and doing like nothing else. Yet it belongs within the breadth of worship's dynamic as God gives—we receive—we respond—God receives. In the totality of worship, God's Word is revealed, proclaimed, and obeyed. By praise, prayer, fellowship, communion, sharing love, returning material goods, and offering daily lives as spiritual sacrifices, Christ's community gives glory to God. Worship embraces everything that is important about preaching and places it within the largest vision of God's greatest purposes for humankind.

While myopic preachers treat sermons as a solo responsibility, this worship model emphasizes how preachers and hearers should be worshiping co-workers through hearing, speaking, and living the Word. Sometimes evangelizing, rebuking, and often challenging about mission through Christ's upside-down kingdom, preaching always belongs resoundingly within the glorious stream of God's returning gift of grace—first hearing from God, and second, obediently seeking to live aright as a new creation. "The members of the congregation share in the act of preaching just as they share in the central act of the Eucharist. Both acts are acts of the body corporate."[10] Tod Bolsinger claims that preaching "must be primarily an expression of the presence of the Triune God with and for the community . . . rather than a solitary experience of hearing a message for living."[11]

Trinitarian theology (admittedly expressed crudely in figure 3 by lines and arrows) grounds preaching in worship. Whenever preachers respond to the doctrine of the Trinity not as some abstract, unpractical theory but rather as an invitation to *participate* in communion with the Triune God, their preaching transforms into worship. They open their minds and hearts to belonging within God's double movement of triune grace. Barriers between others come crashing down. Preachers can no longer consider their task apart from worship nor worship leaders see their role apart from preaching. Rather than both doing their own thing, reinforcing the tragic separation of preaching from worship, they belong *together* within the dynamics of the Triune God's gracious enabling. Preachers once shortsighted about worship now see that worship's big picture includes preaching.

Definitions of preaching must therefore expand. Consider, for example, this carefully crafted definition of preaching by Michael Pasquarello III:

> Christian preaching is a personally involved participatory and embodied form of graced activity that is the Triune God's gift to the church. This is not subject to human mastery and control, but as an expression of doxological speech is gratefully received and offered back to God through the praise and thanksgiving of the Christian community at worship.[12]

Each phrase has significance and is worth considering more closely.

> *Personally involved*: This stresses engagement of heart, soul, strength, and mind (Luke 10:27) of both preacher and hearers. In Romans 12:1, the command to "present your body" involves giving over the whole of ourselves, while "spiritual" (NIV) can be translated "reasonable" to emphasize the engagement of mind and heart. As Thomas Troeger sums up worship: "All of us for all of God."[13]
>
> *Participatory*: This word resonates with worship's double movement as God's three persons actively interact with believers, who share fellowship with the mutual indwelling of Father, Son, and Holy Spirit. It intentionally relates preaching to the economic model of the Trinity, where the doctrine of *perichoresis* explains how believers may interact within the Trinity's powerful dynamic, fellowshiping in the life of the Father, Son, and Holy Spirit. This is God's DNA, building the church and his kingdom.
>
> *Embodied form of graced activity*: This further describes the nature of worship as expressed in the lives of ordinary people living out their responsibilities as a new community that is entirely of God's making.
>
> *That is the Triune God's gift to the church*: This highlights how grace comes as a gift. Utterly undeserving, we belong together as brothers and sisters only by God's will (John 1:12).
>
> *Not subject to human mastery and control*: Preaching is not itself a category of public speaking that is controlled by a human.
>
> *An expression of doxological speech*: Instead, preaching is praising God's glory (*doxa*) because its ultimate purpose is to bring glory to the Father.
>
> *Gratefully received and offered back to God through the praise and thanksgiving of the Christian community at worship*: This final phrase echoes how God's grace both gives and receives in our worship. It is all of him, in three persons, from beginning to end.

Remember, the first toolbox question is, "Gift: Are we thankfully receiving this gift of worship from the Triune God of grace?" What a difference a definition such as Pasquarello's makes to preachers! Instead of beginning with preaching as a discrete activity, it throws preaching into the heart of worship, where it is initiated and offered back to God by the whole worshiping community. Preaching is infused with worship's power and purpose and is offered not only *to* God but *with* God. No longer is preaching solely *about* God's power but *with* God's power; instead of focusing on Christ's *past* action, now it joins in his *continuing* mediation; instead of calling for human responses *to* Christ, it invites responses *with* him, by the Holy Spirit. Preaching as worship truly is "the gift of participation through the Spirit in the incarnate Son's communion with the Father."[14]

But figure 3 is still too restricted. Left on its own, it appears to limit worship's rhythm of call and response to *gathered worship*, integrating elements such as praise, thanks, prayer, proclamation, and the Lord's Supper. With only one reference to community (1 Pet. 2:9–12), it seems to focus on worship inside four walls and damagingly reinforce the faulty worship definition of *Sundays only*. The Christian community at worship should be reaching out far beyond gathered worship.

Beyond Gathered Worship

Offering spiritual sacrifices (Rom. 12:1–2) requires not only gathering to worship but also building community as God's new people to serve the world—your sleeping, eating, going-to-work, and walking-around life. The sacrifices referred to echo Old Testament offerings of unblemished animals on altars and seem a world away from twenty-first-century Christians. With thankfulness we remember that Jesus fulfilled both the role of sacrifice and the role of High Priest once and for all on the cross (Heb. 9:14–15). Yet Romans 12:1 determinedly brings the word *sacrifice* right into worship. Instead of unblemished animals as dead sacrifices, blemished worshipers who have been redeemed by Christ are to be live sacrifices. *Sacrifice* speaks of whole-life commitment of whole people. *Bodies* literally means physical bodies, and *spiritual sacrifice* can be translated "rational or reasonable sacrifice." Worship is fully physical and fully cerebral. God desires all of us to live for him. Richard Foster challenges: "God calls for worship that involves our whole being. The body, mind, spirit and emotions should all be laid on the altar of worship."[15]

Further, worship involves all of us together, in community. When Jesus is asked to identify the greatest commandment, he chooses one about community worship. He sounds out the Hebrew *Shema* from Deuteronomy 6:4.

> The first is, "Hear, O Israel: the Lord our God, the Lord is one; you shall love the Lord your God with all your heart, and with all your soul, and with all your mind and with all your strength." The second is this, "You shall love your neighbor as yourself."
>
> Mark 12:29–31

Romans 12 is addressed to *you* plural, reinforcing how much worship binds worshipers together in community, as brothers and sisters, in new ways of thinking that impact everything they do. "Do not be conformed to this world, but be transformed by the renewing of your minds, so that you may discern what is the will of God—what is good and acceptable and perfect" (Rom. 12:2). There are no vacation days from this transformation. Spiritual worship impacts ethics on a seven-day scale—work, family life, leisure, spending habits, and involvement with neighbors all come into focus. This is worship at its maximum, embracing the whole offering of our lives back to the Creator God who made us and is remaking us in the saving work of Jesus Christ.

Corporate worship changes the way we live and work. Michael Green and Paul Stevens name five marks of acceptable worship that are found in Hebrews 12:28; 13:15–16:5: (1) giving awe and adoration; (2) being radiant with praise; (3) offering fruit of lives and lips that constantly shine for God; (4) doing good in practical ways; and (5) touching our purse. They summarize: "Worship without work is hollow. Work without worship is barren."[16] Worshipers are called to respond in every part of life as God's new community living for his glory.

God calls people to come together in gathered worship, but he also sends them to *be* his people in the world. Gathered worship is complemented by scattered worship—like a city set on a hill that is not hidden, but also like salt savoring the world (Matt. 5:13–14). Christian worship involves both *centripetal* movement drawing believers together as well as *centrifugal* movement in service and mission. In precious corporate quality time, on one day of the week, gathered worship crystallizes what it means to worship God every day. Worship on the one-service scale focuses and nurtures worship on the seven-day scale, cumulatively building into months and years of big-picture worship.

When Tod Bolsinger calls for worship that "lifts us up out of ourselves to participate in the very life and communion of the Godhead, that life and communion for which we were created," he urges that this continue outside church buildings so that the service of Word and sacrament is "completed in small groups that meet in homes on Sunday evening to eat a meal together, review the sermon, study a bit deeper, and support each other as we live out the call of God in the sermon. It is from start to finish a communal event that requires a personal response."[17] As individuals gather to unite their personal responses in corporate worship, they grow as communities to live differently for him and to love and serve others (1 Pet. 2:4–12). Of course in reality, many other commitments too easily fill up time and crowd out opportunities for these kinds of relationships. Yet one of my readers commented:

> We used to share this type of relationship with our friends when we lived next door to them and with other friends farther down the street. We met weekly for Bible study and prayer and saw one another daily, supporting one another as needs arose. We watched one another's children, gardened together, talked over our days, shared our possessions freely, and loved one another dearly.

Sadly, myopic preaching finds this notion of worship helping to form new communities one of the hardest aspects to conceive. Indeed, shortsighted preaching can so focus on individualistic needs that hearers become conditioned to expect personal satisfaction as worship's sum total. Of course worship must involve personal responses, but at its best, it always involves God building his people *together* to live differently for him.

But there seems to be a short supply of people who live differently. In a stinging critique of much of today's worship, Mark Labberton warns about the way we often play it safe in worship because of our desire to keep control, maintain relevance, please worshipers, and provide comfort and familiarity. He claims that such safe worship, under human control and ambition, dangerously domesticates God and diminishes the likelihood of encountering the real God, who wants to change worshipers and change the world. "Worship turns out to be the dangerous act of waking up to God and to the purposes of God in the world, and then living lives that actually show it."[18] When worship becomes domesticated, it is no longer "the often fearful, overwhelmed, convicted, transported, sometimes euphoric response to disruptive Presence."[19] God, the subject and object of worship, is the disrupter and disturber, the one who empowers justice and mercy, the lover of a lost world, and the re-creator of kingdom in Jesus Christ. Lamenting that much current controversy over worship is "just indirect ways of talking about ourselves, not God," Labberton declares the real crisis over worship is this: "Will God's people wake up to worshiping God in such a way that we demonstrate we are awake to loving our neighbor in God's name."[20]

Labberton reminds us that true worship comprises two inseparable loves: love for God and love for neighbors in need. Alongside its rituals for gathering, Old Testament worship sounds out the need for living justly (Isa. 1:12–17; Amos 2:6–16; Mic. 6:8). Jesus commands us to love God and love our neighbor (Mark 12:29–30; Luke 10:25–37), and he demonstrates these twin loves powerfully in word and action. So the call and response of worship focus both on God, whose grace we have tasted, and on neighbors who do not yet know him. "Biblical worship that finds God will also find our neighbor."[21] Worshipers therefore have a responsibility to love neighbors and to break out far beyond safe, closed circles of liturgy offered within four walls. Worship impacts not only individuals' behavior and commitment but also how those individuals intentionally belong to a community and behave in godly ways for the sake of others. Worship *words* need to be accompanied by worship *practices*.

Over the last twenty years, so-called "virtue theologians"[22] have reemphasized how body, mind, and soul need to be shaped and formed toward the truthful purposes of God:

> Christians require character shaped by communities of faith and habits of truth in order to experience truth. . . . True worship leads worshipers into the orientation of God's glory, out of which true experience is birthed, which then produces lives as well as experiences and emotions that are faithful to who we are called to be in Jesus Christ.[23]

What worshipers *do* together by studying, sharing, encouraging, and acting shapes *who* they become together. As people of the Word respond to revelation of the Triune God, they become the people of God *as* they worship.

Already I have sounded a warning that surrounding culture can influence body, mind, and soul for lesser goals instead of higher purposes. Many have observed relationships between culture and behavior. Alasdair MacIntyre, for example, has reemphasized the importance of the good purpose of living—the *telos*. Jonathan Wilson reflects on his complex arguments: "[MacIntyre's] most telling insight is the claim that in our culture we have abandoned most convictions about the *telos* (the 'good,' the created purpose) of human life and human activities. This abandonment of *telos* drains our actions of any real meaning and significance."[24]

In contrast, Christian worship should grasp the *telos* of humankind's purpose as living for God's good, seeking to embody good practices in its community life. Wilson calls such practices "socially embedded activities that incorporate the church into the *telos* determined for it by God."[25] He identifies key practices in gathered worship such as baptism, communion, and foot washing but also widens them to include hospitality, service, justice, and social action. "The church's witness bears testimony not to its own life, but to God's grace in its life."[26] God's grace is therefore attested not only by liturgy but also by practical life and ethical responsibilities of Christian communities. Living for God's ultimate good, such community living demonstrates God's good purposes. Glory and honor are God's due, but so are love, justice, mercy, and kindness. As we will see later (chap. 8), these are the marks of a missional church.

Repercussions of worship beyond services, by loving God *and* neighbors, are wide-ranging and will be given fuller attention in chapters 8 and 9. God desires to build a holy nation and a royal priesthood—a people living differently. Inevitably, such living differently flies in the face of current culture's norms. Homiletician David Schlafer and ethicist Timothy Sedgwick identify some distinct Christian practices that offer worshipers "clear alternatives to those that are prevailing or taken for granted."[27] Describing them as "lenses" by which a community gains moral discernment, they list six: (1) prayer and worship; (2) forgiveness and reconciliation; (3) formation of households as communities of faith; (4) hospitality as the embrace of the stranger and those in need; (5) citizenship and political responsibility; and (6) reverence for creation. While not offering an exhaustive or prescriptive list, they claim these construe the character of ethical Christian life.

More characteristics can be added, but they all add up to the church's responsibility of living in God's story. Earlier I noted how Kevin Vanhoozer's five acts placed the church in act 4. While God has set its end point in consummation (act 5), through the whole story God—Father, Son, and Spirit—seeks to form a new people to live for his good *telos*. And this story has cosmic repercussions, for ultimately all will see God's long-intended plan that "through the church the wisdom of God in its rich variety might now be made known to the rulers and authorities in the heavenly places" (Eph. 3:10, see vv. 8–11).

Somehow in spite of inevitable inadequacies, these wider worship dimensions should be incorporated into 360-degree worship. In a continual formation process, never fully arriving at maturity this side of glory, worship both praises God's transcendent mystery revealed in Christ and also grows his people together as his community. As Marva Dawn succinctly sums up, the church's task is "to praise God and to nurture character."[28]

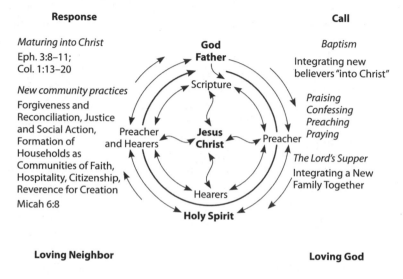

Figure 4. Community Transformation in 360–Degree Worship

In figure 4, some elements mentioned above are included in worship's double movement expressing love to God and to neighbors. It illustrates how the worshiping church belongs within God's vast, purposeful sweep of living out his *telos* before the world. This truly is big-picture worship that opens us up to see the whole of life as worship. "At its best, Christian worship presents a vision of life created, sustained, redeemed, and held in the mystery of grace."[29] This is a cosmic picture of worshipful life as it is intended to be—created by God and lived for God's glory. Figure 4 further underlines the utter inadequacy of myopic preaching's minimalist view. In contrast, big-picture worship involves everything in worshipful living for God.

Big-Picture Preaching

So my depiction of 360-degree preaching (see fig. 2) turned out to be a springboard for a much bigger picture of 360-degree worship. This discovery completely unhinged and reframed my previous thinking about preaching. In the closing minutes of the movie *The Truman Show*, Truman finally steps through the exit door to face a completely new world beyond. Up until now, all his life he has had a limited worldview. In the movie, the show's creator-producer tries to stop him from leaving, arguing that he risks ruining everything by leaving his safe world and stepping out into the unknown.

Myopic preaching similarly lives in a safe world, limited to sermon making. It may seem risky and unnecessary to step out beyond into bigger reality. But figures 3 and 4 describe just such a stepping-out into big-picture worship with its new worldview revolutionizing understanding and practice. When preachers embrace this new worship perspective, everything changes. The Authorized Version of the Bible (King James) uses the word *magnify* to describe worship's exaltation and *enlarging* of God (as in Pss. 35:27; 40:16; 70:4). Such magnification moves beyond small pictures, helping us glimpse the magnificence and grandeur of big-picture worship. Instead of diminishing worship, preachers learn to magnify it in six ways as their worldview changes.

Most obviously, preachers come to see themselves as *worshipers first and foremost*—their highest calling is to worship. They are worshipers before they are preachers. Redeemed by God's grace, called into fellowship with him, they have a primary relationship with God as worshipers. Filled with wonder, overwhelmed by mystery, loved by gospel grace, Christian worshipers join in fellowship with the Triune God, offering the best of themselves to God, who gives life, gifts, faith, and purpose and has the right to claim every minute of their lives, every relationship they share, and every square inch of their influence. And what is true of Christian worship in general applies especially to preachers—once nobodies yet now ennobled "ambassadors for Christ" (2 Cor. 5:20). Preachers now grasp that worship embraces everything that is of primary importance *to God*.

Second, they need to see that *preaching itself is worship*. Preachers recognize they are worshiping not only when singing, praying, hearing Scripture, offering, and sharing the Lord's Supper but also as they preach. Preaching belongs within trinitarian worship—initiated, activated, and motivated by the Triune God as preachers call others to hear and respond afresh to God's Word by renewed living out his story. Preachers should worship when they preach. Delivering sermons belongs within worship's call and response, proclaiming God's truth to his people and focusing their responses of worshipful living. In one of my last conversations with Robert Webber, I shared this insight and excitedly he agreed, urging me into new language. He said, "Don't talk about preaching *and* worship, or preaching *and leading* worship, but preaching *as* worship." Worshipful preaching responds to what God has initiated by his Word in spirit and truth with wonder, mystery, joy, service, and action. Instead of preachers separating themselves from worship, they need to see that worship becomes the primary description of preaching itself.

Third, they need to see that *worship itself proclaims* and that God's call to his whole people should lead to all responding for the sake of God's glory. "The chief end of man is to glorify God and enjoy him for ever."[30] Joining in with all creation (Rev. 4:11; 5:9–13), worshipers declare his majesty, praising his name in word and deed. Ever since God revealed who he is and what he has done for us in Jesus Christ, celebration with resounding joy, praise, and adoration has arced back to the God who alone initiates such worship and who alone is worthy to receive it (Rev. 4:11). Worship reaches far beyond organizing weekly services into full-throated living of a new community for God's glory (1 Pet. 2:9–10).

Fourth, one key way such full-throated living happens is by worshipful preachers helping hearers learn how they belong *in God's unfolding story*. Belonging in act 4 of Vanhoozer's dramatic model, they enact God's purpose in the church's mission. Each time they gather for worship, they are living out God's story, making progress in community growth and purpose.

Fifth, and closely connected with these last two aspects, worshipful preachers actively seek *community transformation*. They help individual believers integrate into church life and learn what it means to belong and mature together in Christ's new community. Worship helps grow quality of life in word and deed by practices such as those identified in figure 4. David Schlafer and Timothy Sedgwick urge preachers to help hearers develop moral discernment in the light of Scripture by centering Christian moral life in key practices that "seek to construe a full sense of the character of the Christian life that Christians share in common . . . witnessed in Scripture and in the ongoing life of the church."[31] These practices are not to be confused with preaching itself but should give a framework to preaching that must arise concretely in the engagement of Scripture with the immediate life of the gathered community. Worship should make a difference—forming community living for God, modeling gospel integrity, offering alternatives, yet remaining in dialogue with its surrounding community.

Sixth, and as a result of all the above, preachers no longer consider their task *apart from worship*, nor can any others involved in leading worship separate themselves from preaching. All must learn to work together within the dynamics of the Triune God's gracious enabling. Properly understood, worship is so much bigger than any roles undertaken by preachers and worship leaders. Rather, big-picture worship integrates everything that is significant for all of us to live for God's glory, gathering and scattering, and it requires thoughtful, open collaboration in leadership (which will be described in part 3).

Preachers who belittle worship miss the whole point. Preachers are worshipers whose sermons are worship and whose task is worshiping. All other descriptions of preaching fall short of God's glory.

Widening Bandwidth

Though I am a dismal technophobe, figures 3 and 4 remind me of an aspect of computer technology—bandwidth. Over recent years I have been regularly bombarded with the wonders of increasing my computer bandwidth. The term *bandwidth* refers to a network's capacity measured by available or consumed data expressed in bits (an abbreviation of *background intelligent transfer service per second*). My old modem dial-up of 56 kilobits allowed 56 thousand bits per second. But going wireless requires 54 megabits with 54 million bits per second, which may be upgraded to 300 megabits, 300 million bits per second. In the big league, Ethernets using gigabits (each one billion bits per second) operate with bandwidths of 10 gigabits and more. And the stakes keep rising.

Bandwidth provides an apt analogy for worship. Myopic preaching operates at the narrowest level, with a thin bandwidth holding sermons in isolation. But big-picture preachers open up to worship's incredibly expanding bandwidth, with capacity measured in billions of spiritual gigabits as preachers and hearers co-worship through hearing, speaking, and living the Word.

Placing preaching within a wider bandwidth in no way diminishes its significance. Let's restate that preaching is God's preferred method of saving and transforming people—it is a critical task in God's kingdom. But rather than see it as an isolated (and superior) element, we must see worshipful preaching as belonging within glorious, harmonious praise as God's people, on earth and in heaven, complemented by myriads of angelic worshipers beyond imagining, live for God's glory. Worship is therefore God's primary *integrative activity* that holds together all that is important about human living. Initiated by God's grace and returning by God's power, worshipful preaching joyfully enters its broad bandwidth. But preachers who continue within a narrow bandwidth are in danger of missing out on God's larger picture for their lives and ministries and, more seriously still, of going astray in God's bigger purpose for the churches they seek to serve.

Magnifying Worship

Throughout this chapter, our understanding of worship has been continually stretched. It is so much more than we once thought, with dimensions reaching far beyond small-picture worship. A second question now needs to be added that emphasizes the riches of broad bandwidth, 360-degree worship.

Question Toolbox

1. *Gift*: Are we thankfully receiving this gift of worship from the Triune God of grace?

2. *Magnification*: Are we expressing its richness toward God?

While the first question asks about fundamental attitudes toward God the Giver, this second question addresses the adequacy of response in the light of worship's extraordinary richness. Earlier I used the older Authorized Version language of "magnify" (2 Sam. 7:26; 1 Chron. 17:24; Ps. 43:3) to express how worshipers should make careful response to the enlarged vision of God that occurs with big-picture worship. I was intrigued to read that one church had appointed a director of magnification, who described her job: "I take care of the programming of the services and have two full-time worship leaders and two technology guys under me." Someone else wrote, "I have been on our church's Magnification Team for several years."[32] Magnification pays attention to the glorious reality of God's presence.

Such language evokes the dimensions and possibilities depicted in figures 3 and 4, as responses are made ever wider and deeper to the Triune God. And it raises the stakes for worthiness in quality of worship as communities offer *their utmost for his highest.* So this question probes how much of worship's extraordinary bandwidth is being used to magnify God. It invites engagement with the extraordinary richness of multisensory, multifaceted, and multidimensional big-picture worship.

Too often myopic preachers settle for patterns of gathered worship that channel responses in predictable ways that diminish God. Those who value extempore, informal style lock into familiar cycles of praise and worship songs, sermon, and prayers, sometimes giving only a marginal place for the Lord's Supper and little room for plentiful liturgical resources such as the Christian year framework. Sensory responses may be restricted to hearing and occasionally seeing when drama or visual images are used. But those committed to liturgical patterns may also be caught up with forms that become too routine, with little opportunity for extempore or fresh, multisensory experiences.

Figures 3 and 4 identify dimensions of worship in which God initiates response not only through Word and sacrament but also by life, faith, love, material goods, friendship, music, and silence. With humble gratitude, worshipers should revel in God's creation and re-creation in Christ with all five senses alive to worship's breadth. Worship's all-inclusiveness embraces all that's best in being alive—intensely personal yet profoundly corporate. Take any element, like music for example, and you face a dazzling range of possibilities, from human to angelic, from past to present, from Gregorian chant to rock, and everything in between. How willing am I to express God's glory in fresh ways?

Of course, emphasizing worship's magnificence encourages dramatically contrasting acts of gathered worship. My own experiences include both Orthodox Eucharist with dignity and reverence as well as charismatic worship at the height of the Toronto blessing in the 1990s. I have shared in:

- simultaneous prayer among thousands in Korea and the stillness of Quaker meetings

- short, set prayers read out of prayer books and lengthy African-American worship with three offerings
- seven-minute homilies and Romanian services in which three sermons lasted all afternoon
- healing services around the Lord's Table and sound-perfect Evensong at Kings College, Cambridge
- infant baptisms for my own grandchildren and believers' baptisms in the River Jordan
- mass choirs and orchestras in Royal Albert Hall, London, and a squeaky harmonium in a valley chapel
- a Billy Graham rally in Budapest and an Easter morning vigil in the Jerusalem Garden Tomb

You will have your own list of rich contrasts: sounds, silence; movement, stillness; listening, speaking out; hearing, seeing; smelling, touching; personal, corporate; controlled, uncontrolled; inside buildings of every kind and shape, outside in widely contrasting settings; praise, lament; adoration, confession; eating, drinking, witnessing, interceding; watching, reflecting.

Within this wide bandwidth of worship, the preached Word itself often exhibits extraordinary variety in content, length, and style. Yet it always belongs within the richness of corporate worship. Yes, preaching remains the primary way by which God reveals himself afresh to his people, but it is one glorious strand within the total worship of the people of God as God's Word is proclaimed. Obeying God's Word involves not only listening to sermons but also responding in baptism, communing around the Lord's Table, sharing love, giving back material goods, expressing *koinonia*, praying for others, offering music to God's glory, and, all the while, forming new community. As new community is created and matures into Christ, so a rich variety of practices develop for the sake of others, including forgiveness and reconciliation, justice and social action, and hospitality. Gathered worship spills out into daily living within the surrounding community because worship that loves God flows outward into loving our neighbor.

Question 2 challenges qualities of preparation and participation. It will not excuse monochrome, flat, routine, unsensory, nonparticipatory forms of worship. It exposes myopic preaching's small picture. God invites us to revel in the richness of belonging to him, and we need to give back our very best.

6

Directive Scripture
with Thoughtful Liturgy

Part 1

What makes Scripture *Scripture* is its capacity to mediate an encounter with the transcendent.

John P. Burgess

Recently, while writing a conference paper on preachers' integrity,[1] I was
intrigued by two contrasting lists of integrity issues. On one hand, a
contemporary list included sexuality, finances, accountability, faithful exegesis,
plagiarism, and manipulation of hearers.[2] No surprises there. On the other
hand, an older list startled me by naming first *liturgical* integrity.

> One of the preacher's main liturgical responsibilities is to enable the people not
> only to be reminded of the history of their salvation but so to be reminded of
> it that they relive it. . . . An act of worship should by its fabric and texture be a
> proclamation of the Gospel; it should involve the worshipers in such a reliving of
> sacred history and such an encounter with their ever-present Lord that at every
> point they are being remade as the people of God. . . . So far as this can lie within
> human power the preacher is so to order worship as to make all this possible.[3]

These two lists show how much has changed. For myopic preachers, the first list makes sense, but most would be surprised to see liturgical integrity on the second list. But unthinking personal preferences so easily lack integrity by dominating and excluding others. Sam Hamstra's honest testimony addresses this issue.

> I accented the centrality of preaching. . . . I am an Evangelical who appreciates the seventeenth century Free Church tradition of England that protested against formal worship. I would rather participate in congregational song or listen to one person speak than engage in a unison reading or responsive reading. Similarly I prefer a personal testimony in word or song over a corporate unison profession with an ancient creed. For years I allowed my personal preferences to shape the worship of God's people. From a marketing vantage point I tried to compete on the "open market" with a generic order of worship. In the end, however, I orchestrated dissonant liturgies for God's people by indiscriminately embracing liturgical practices inconsistent with Scripture.[4]

Let's recapture this integrity issue—it matters how preachers lead worship. Inevitably, personal preferences, practices that are inherited and not thought out, and knee-jerk acceptance of marketing principles all compromise worship. Often such compromise occurs unconsciously because, as noted earlier, many preachers receive little or no training about worship at seminary. Robert Webber lamented, "Many seminaries do not even require worship courses or training," and so myopic preaching rules.

This chapter and the next address defects of myopic preaching insofar as it fails to see Scripture's vital role in directing worship and suffers from liturgical amnesia, disregarding the past and operating entirely pragmatically. Earlier I urged that *liturgy* be rehabilitated as a helpful biblical word. Russell Mitman defines liturgy as "the totality of what happens verbally and nonverbally when the people of God find themselves in dialogue with the Triune God who initiates the conversation and seeks to become enfleshed in the event of Word and Sacrament."[5] Whatever forms gathered worship may take, they all express some kind of liturgy.

Since Scripture's relationship with liturgy covers such wide ground, two chapters will be needed. This chapter focuses on how Scripture directs both general worship structures as well as specific patterns for acts of gathered worship. Chapter 7 examines the relationship between Scripture and liturgy in terms of the Christian year, the lectionary, and other worship resources.

Too often preachers assume that working with Scripture is their territory, as they identify text and theme for others to plan gathered worship. After all, proclaiming what God has to say through sermons is deemed their chief task. The Bible becomes the preacher's book—sometimes literally so. I have attended worship services during which no Scripture is read apart from a few verses when the preacher introduces the sermon. No one else may even refer to Scripture in the service. Bibles placed in pews or chairs are largely left undisturbed, limiting engagement with Scripture to what preachers say about it.

But the influence of Scripture should extend far wider than solely shaping sermons. This should happen in at least three ways: (1) Scripture provides the big picture of worship; its great worship passages open our eyes to marvel at God's commands and promises. (2) Scripture reveals the basic pattern for divine-human encounter that underlies corporate acts of worship. (3) Scripture directs specific outcomes for any particular act of gathered worship. Myopic preachers rarely thrill to Scripture's power of revealing worship's wider dimensions and responsibilities, hawking worshipless sermons, but this chapter revels in Scripture's inspiration.

Scripture's Big-Picture Worship

Worship themes thread gloriously throughout Scripture. The Old Testament emphasizes worship from the outset as patriarchs respond to God's covenant promises (as in Gen. 12:7; 28:18) and a new people is formed by God under Moses's leadership (Exod. 15:1–21). Congregational worship was established with increasingly careful attention paid to tabernacle and temple rituals. In addition to daily morning and evening sacrifices, a calendar of festivals directed community worship throughout each year, with celebrations of Passover and the Day of Atonement as key worship events. Detailed organization of the priesthood and sacrifices fill many chapters of Exodus, Leviticus, and Deuteronomy. King David extravagantly prepared the building of the first temple (1 Chron. 29:20) with attention to every kind of detail of building design and materials, furnishings and fittings, and (of course) musicians. After exile, worship continued in the second temple with the cycle of festivals and praises and laments (psalms) sung from its hymnbook.

As the first church exploded into life at Pentecost, it worshiped: "They devoted themselves to the apostles' teaching and fellowship, to the breaking of bread and the prayers" (Acts 2:42). Worship in temple and homes overflowed into believers' lifestyles. Sharing all things in common, they impacted the surrounding community—"praising God and having the goodwill of all the people" (Acts 2:47). As the church's story develops, so too does its worship. The Christians combine Word and sacrament, develop theology of worship (as in Hebrews), write early Christian hymns (such as Phil. 2:2–11), and learn how to present their bodies as a "living sacrifice" (Rom. 12:1). Worship is everywhere. Scarcely can you turn a chapter in Scripture without some reference to worship.

My colleague Gerald Borchert has mainly taught doctoral students in New Testament studies, but he is currently doctoral thesis director at the Robert E. Webber Institute for Worship Studies in Jacksonville, Florida. In this role, he writes about the concentration of doctoral students on certain key texts: "I really did not need to have Isaiah 6 and John 4 quoted to me much more in their presentations."[6] He also notes, however, that his New Testament students often failed to recognize worship references completely. Myopic preachers share this latter failure. Though certain key texts may suffer overuse, they *are* essential in understanding more clearly God's big picture of worship. Romans 12:1–2 has already received attention, and Isaiah 6 and 1 Peter 2:4–12 will be referenced shortly. Preachers seeking a big picture of worship must spend time in all these texts, including John 4:19–26.

John records the quantum leap that Jesus makes for worship. At the foot of Mt. Gerizim, on which the Samaritan shrine for worship stood, Jesus is questioned by a woman about *where* worship should take place: "Our ancestors worshiped on this mountain, but you say that the place where people must worship is in Jerusalem" (John 4:20). In a devastating response that shatters small-picture worship for all time, Jesus makes it clear that worship is not about *right places* or *where* worship occurs; it is about *right people.*

> Woman, believe me, the hour is coming when you will worship the Father neither on this mountain nor in Jerusalem. . . . But the hour is coming, and is now here, when the true worshipers will worship the Father in spirit and truth, for the Father seeks such as these to worship him. God is spirit, and those who worship him must worship in spirit and in truth.
>
> John 4:21, 23–24

Jesus says "true worshipers" are marked by two vital qualities. First, "worship in spirit" describes a new kind of relationship between worshipers and God, who is Spirit. While past relationships were grounded in material reality, requiring places and times, God opens up the possibility of spiritual participation everywhere and any time. The contrast is striking: "What is born of the flesh is flesh and what is born of the Spirit is spirit" (John 3:6). Being "born from above" (John 3:3) invites a different kind of worship as the Lord, who is Spirit, invades depths of personhood, provoking profound spiritual responses: "Create in me a clean heart, O God; and put a new and right spirit within me" (Ps. 51:10). The apostle Paul contrasts the carnal and the spiritual: "Now we have received not the spirit of the world, but the Spirit that is from God, so that we may understand the gifts bestowed on us by God" (1 Cor. 2:12; see also vv. 6–16). Discerning and confessing Jesus as the Christ (John 4:25–26) opens up spiritual worship. At a stroke, Jesus takes worship out of places and times into belonging to the Father.

Early in learning about computers, I encountered the abbreviation WYSIWYG: "What you see is what you get." Supposedly this puts operators at ease by showing that computers only respond to commands. Worship in Spirit, however, is WYSINWYG: "What you see is *not* what you get." Of course, surface activity is important; worship's structure and ordering matter, but its essence concerns what happens *beneath* the surface, as brothers and sisters join in with Father, Son, and Holy Spirit. A traveler in India supposedly noticed a box on a railway platform with these words written on it: "This box is to be carried bottom uppermost. The top has been labeled 'Bottom' to avoid confusion." Worship testifies to another sort of reality that turns perceptions upside down or, rather, the right way up.

Christian worship *in spirit* contrasts sharply with other kinds of experience: "Do not get drunk with wine, for that is debauchery; but be filled with the Spirit" (Eph. 5:18). Rather than being intoxicated as the world understands it, when believers gather in WYSINWYG, they experience deeper realities of being filled with the Spirit. The passive present imperative tense—"keep on being filled"—emphasizes the critical need for constant infilling by the Holy Spirit, who motivates and sustains harmony in corporate worship. Individuals may have sharp differences, for example, about music. But while Ephesians 5:19 identifies different sorts of music, such as "psalms and hymns and spiritual songs," it also testifies to the work of the Holy Spirit, who enables unity that comes from the heart: "Making melody to the Lord in your hearts."

The quality "in spirit," however, does not stand alone. If worship is primarily a spiritual matter, people may assume that worship concerns only interior emotional responses that can be assessed mainly in affective terms by how people *feel about it*. Contemporary culture especially encourages such self-focused spirituality, and combined with emotion-based, consumerist choices, it easily shrinks spirituality to interior, personal, and subjective experiences.

Second, complementing "in spirit" is the other worship quality: "in truth" (John 4:23–24). Worship in truth grounds responses in the authentic revelation of God in Christ and his Word. Confessing with lips and believing in hearts (Rom. 10:9), worshipers place faith with integrity in the one who is "the way, the truth and the life" (John 14:6). Worshipers in truth say what they mean and mean what they say, seeking to match words with lives in truthful responses, not counterfeits. Jesus reserved his harshest words for hypocrites. He seemed to welcome everyone, except those who pretended in worship—in Matthew 6:5 blisteringly rejecting hypocrites at prayer and in Matthew 5:23–24 insisting on reconciliation before offering worship. Hypocrisy, prejudice, and lack of forgiveness sabotage worship. But when praise, confession, intercession, speaking, and hearing God's Word are authentic and gathering around the Lord's Table focuses worthily on the body of Christ, there is worship in truth as well as in spirit.

Old Testament prophets challenged people not to separate worship into a sacred, religious compartment split from the rest of life, claiming that behavior in matters such as politics, ethics, business, and family life all contribute to the quality of worship (Isa. 1:13–18). Inauthentic worship occurs when gathered worship disconnects from daily living, when we fail to present our bodies "as a living sacrifice" (Rom. 12:1).

To imagine that real worship can be attained through debates over such matters as orders of service, the singing of hymns and songs, preferences in musical style, or dress and vestments, is to be in danger of missing the point altogether . . . for the motive with which worship is offered is always of greater value to God than the manner in which the gift is given. Worship based upon the principles of biblical sacrifice is about obedience and love for God above everything else.[7]

It was in his commentary on John 4 that William Temple wrote his famous definition of worship to which we have already referred:

Worship is the submission of all our nature to God. It is the quickening of conscience by His holiness; the nourishment of mind with His truth; the purifying of imagination by His beauty; the opening of the heart to His love; the surrender of will to His purpose—and all of this gathered up in adoration, the most selfless emotion of which our nature is capable.[8]

"In spirit and in truth" hold together everything that is important about worship.

In my early teens, I had to go to church three times every Sunday—morning service, afternoon Sunday school, and evening service. My father was the minister, but this didn't stop me from being bored. I tried coping with boredom by tracing knots in the wooden pews, counting bricks in the wall, and daydreaming. And then suddenly, exhilaratingly, it all changed. No aspect of the services or Sunday school was altered, but *I* was changed—I had met Jesus Christ as Lord and Savior, and my mind and spirit were invaded by possibilities of living in a new way with brothers and sisters because of God's amazing grace, love, and power. I looked with new eyes and responded with a new heart to what was happening unfamiliarly in a familiar place among familiar people. I thrilled to worship in spirit and in truth—glimpsing something of Scripture's big picture.

Scripture not only reveals worship's big picture but also directs how people worship because of its power to mediate encounters with the Triune God. "When Scripture is read, when it is explicated in preaching, when it is incorporated into prayers of thanksgiving and lament, when it frames the celebration of the Lord's Supper, Scripture becomes a means by which Christians are gathered into the body of the living Lord."[9]

Gathered worship operates on three levels.[10] The bottom level describes standard congregational orders of worship—how a congregation usually worships together throughout the year in basic stable patterns: "This is what our average service looks like." The middle level involves variations from this basic pattern often connected with different seasons of church life: "This is what we normally do leading up to Christmas." The top level describes weekly expressions of gathered worship that necessarily involve changes in choices of Scripture, music, and prayers: "This is what we are doing *this* Sunday."

Scripture proves particularly important for directing both the bottom level of basic worship patterns and the top level of specific acts of gathered worship.

Scripture and Basic Worship Patterns

Sally Morgenthaler expresses despair about many patterns of worship she has encountered. She describes three prototypes of what she calls "nonworship services":

Traditional Community Church (TCC)

- one or two perfunctory hymns
- five to ten minutes of announcements
- fifteen-second prayer; Scripture reading (maybe)
- special music or choir anthem
- testimony or special presentation regarding a church project
- offering (solo)
- message
- dismissal

Comfortably Contemporary Church (CCC)

- borrows TCC format with the message as the centerpiece
- usually features a worship band instead of an organ or piano
- substitutes a "sing-song" for the hymns
- may include a mini-drama (three to five minutes)

Cutting-Edge Community Church (CECC)

- instrumental selection performed by worship band
- two vocal selections performed by band and worship team
- corporate song
- introduction of theme via multimedia presentation
- Scripture reading and explanation
- drama
- solo
- message
- dismissal[11]

While these three prototypes are typical of only one part of church life, they sadly represent the widespread experience of contemporary worship's far removal from its early Christian roots. Early worship was influenced both by synagogue worship and its emphasis on hearing God's Word as well as by the celebration of the Lord's Supper. Within a hundred years of Paul's writings, Justin Martyr described patterns of worship that included readings, discourse, prayer, and a meal, though it is unclear whether unbaptized worshipers could share in communion. By the time Hippolytus wrote *Apostolic Tradition* (about AD 217), the Lord's Supper was allowed only for baptized believers. Throughout the subsequent history of Christian worship, preaching and liturgy often interacted. Sometimes this interaction was positive as reformers sensitive to past church worship practices built on their strengths, but at other times it was negative when churches in renewal lost sight of past best practices.

In the past, liturgists often assumed that this history showed that tradition was largely responsible for developing such patterns. More recently, however, Russell Mitman claims that liturgical scholars have recognized the significance of *Scripture's impact* on patterns of worship. Quoting Gordon Lathrop, one of those scholars, Mitman says, "Start with the Bible. . . . The Bible marks and largely determines Christian corporate worship. . . . Ancient texts are used to speak a new grace. . . . The liturgical pattern is drawn from the Bible. . . . The shape of the liturgy evokes and replicates the deep structure of biblical language."[12]

Scripture's impact on liturgical pattern most obviously relates to its record of interactions between God and human beings. Most famously, this human-divine dynamic is illustrated by God's encounter with Isaiah (Isa. 6) with its to-and-fro rhythm of God's glory, human confession, God's commission, human response, and finally, God's sending out.

Mitman also finds a similar dynamic in various other texts—when God appears to Moses, when God speaks to Mary through an angel, and when Jesus feeds the five thousand. Mitman sums up a common fivefold rhythm this way:

1. A divine interruption of human everydayness calls for human awareness of the extraordinary divine in the midst (Exod. 3:2; Mark 6:31; Luke 1:26–28).
2. A human response wonders and questions the divine (Exod. 3:3, 5–6; Mark 6:37; Luke 1:29) with a *disjuncture* of human reflection that invites penitence.
3. A divine Word is spoken (Exod. 3:1–22; Mark 6:38–39; Luke 1:30).
4. There is human response as eventually Moses obeys (Exod. 5:1) and Mary offers herself (Luke 1:38). Interestingly, as the feeding story results in eating, the divine human interaction shows another dynamic: take, bless, break, and give (Mark 6:41–42), which powerfully influences shaping of the Lord's Supper.
5. There is dismissal or sending (Exod. 4:12; Mark 6:45; Luke 1:38–40).

Mitman believes that a fivefold scriptural pattern therefore lies inherently at the heart of all Christian liturgy: (1) gathering, (2) penitence, (3) Word,

(4) offertory or Eucharist, and (5) sending or dismissal. He argues that this basic worship pattern in Scripture accounts for the

> remarkably similar shape of the denominational liturgies and their historic antecedents . . . so the old argument of liturgical worship versus nonliturgical worship is really moot. All worship that seeks to engage Scripture and allows the Word of Scripture to become recontextualized organically in the life of a worshiping community will be inherently liturgical because the Bible itself is a liturgical book.[13]

Mitman's call for "worship in the shape of Scripture" (the title of his book) partly arises from his conviction that the whole worshiping community is involved in a similar divine-human sequence of actions. Everything within the worship event, from gathering to dismissal, is therefore to be understood as *proclamation*, since it is a "communal enactment" of worship patterned on the Word of God.

But this fivefold pattern seems far too specific to apply comprehensively across such widely ranging styles of gathered worship—from highly liturgical to wildly informal. Mitman interestingly distinguishes between *tennis court* churches, which have proscribed boundaries and are likely to adhere to historical worship patterns, and *open field* churches, which have greater informality. He pleads that *both* kinds of churches need "organic liturgy," holding to Scripture's pattern of divine-human interaction, to ensure that different worship elements flow coherently. Yes, open field churches have greater freedom in worship planning, but such freedom carries a serious warning:

> You are free—if you grasp the essential structure upon which the shaping of liturgy is premised. Worship that is patterned after the four or fivefold movement intrinsic to the nature of the divine-human interaction witnessed to in the Scriptures will provide a freedom for the community to enjoy . . . new liturgical expressions. . . . The opposite, of course, leads to fragmentation in the Christian community and . . . focuses on the worship leader's personality rather than on the God who is the Subject of worship.[14]

Remember the earlier reference to COW—church our way.

Gathered worship therefore has scriptural warrant for its basic pattern. Earlier we noted that Robert Webber reduced the core movements to four that "retell the biblical story of God's initiating a relationship with fallen humanity":

1. Assembling the people
2. Listening and responding to God's Word
3. Remembering and giving thanks (which may include communion for those churches that regularly practice it)
4. Going forth to love and serve the Lord[15]

Of course, the scope of worship structures can be widened much further than Webber's four movements or Mitman's five. Drawing authority from Old Testament covenant renewal patterns, Michael Horton lists certain essential liturgical actions according to the pattern of Old Testament covenant renewal: invocation, God's greeting, the Law, confession and absolution, pastoral prayer, preached Word, ministry of the Lord's Supper, thanksgiving and offerings, and benediction.[16]

William Willimon outlines *eight* actions from *First Apology of Justin Martyr* (around AD 90), claiming these reflect early Christian worship in Acts 2:42 and have since provided the "normal, catholic (i.e., universal) Sunday pattern for the majority of the world's Christians":

1. The church gathers.
2. The church remembers.
3. The church listens and then speaks.
4. The church prays.
5. The church offers.
6. The church gives thanks.
7. The church distributes the gifts of God.
8. The church scatters into the world.[17]

Reformed theology sometimes uses a pattern called guilt, grace, and gratitude: the approach to God; the Word of God; and the response to the Word. With preaching central, such a pattern encourages a rhythm of encounter as God speaks and worshipers respond. Another pattern often endorsed by the evangelical tradition is praise, prayer, and proclamation.

Whether a church is *tennis court* or *open field*, whatever pattern it uses should adequately reflect the scriptural pattern of divine-human interaction. From their different perspectives, preachers need to think carefully through worship patterns. For example, in *Worship by the Book*, three pastors—Anglican, Free Church, and Presbyterian—explain in detail their congregational worship structures. Anglican Mark Ashton extols Cranmer's legacy with the Book of Common Prayer, recognizing that creativity and innovations are possible within its "sound framework of biblical doctrine." Putting a worship pattern through the "Cranmerian tests"—asking if it is biblical, accessible, and balanced—he calls for theological structure that "must begin with God's word to us; we must then respond to God on God's terms (confession and repentance)."[18]

With a Free Church perspective, R. Kent Hughes warns of the "irony of freedom." Free Church tradition began in early-seventeenth-century England with principled protest against compulsory use of the Book of Common Prayer, and initially, "at its best, the corporate worship of the Free Churches was radically biblical, ever more scriptural and authentic." He also notes that in the last 150 years Free Church biblicism has deteriorated into Free

Church pragmatism, accompanied by anthropocentrism, so that much "corporate worship has taken the form of something *done* for an audience as opposed to something done *by* a congregation."[19] Hughes names six distinctives of worship: (1) God-centered, (2) Christ-centered, (3) Word-centered, (4) consecration-centered, (5) wholehearted, and (6) reverent. He outlines the structure for usual worship at his church:

Welcome and silence

Apostles' Creed

Hymn

Congregational prayer

Anthem

God at work: in *families* in baptism, in *missions* (three-minute focus), in *lives* (four-minute testimony)

Reading Scripture

Sermon

Concluding hymn and benediction

Presbyterian minister Timothy J. Keller laments polarization of so-called contemporary worship and historic worship as simplistic. He argues that there are at least nine worship traditions in Protestantism alone and explains his preference for Calvin's corporate worship tradition, which he considers relates well to postmodern culture. He identifies three traits of Reformed corporate worship: (1) its *voice*—simplicity of form because of confidence in God's grace (1 Cor. 2:2–5); (2) its *goal*—transcendence with amazement at God's grace (Exod. 33:18); (3) its *order*—cycles of gospel reenactment for reception of God's grace afresh.[20] He provides three outlines of standard services, one of which brings the sermon earlier in a more strictly Calvinist manner.

Praise Cycle: preparation (Scripture); hymn of praise; responsive call to worship (Scripture); invocation; the Lord's Prayer; doxology; silent adoration.

Renewal Cycle: Scripture (call to renewal); prayer of confession; silent confession; words of encouragement (Scripture); Scripture (before the sermon); sermon.

Commitment Cycle: offering and offertory; community life; prayers of the people; hymn; invitation to the Lord's Table; creed; eucharistic prayer; giving of the bread and cup (hymns and songs); prayer of dedication; hymn; benediction and dismissal.[21]

On my worship journey I have kept copies of many different services I have attended and have noted strengths and weaknesses. I have grown in appreciation for carefully planned worship that centers on God and allows me to respond appropriately with others. Accepting Webber's substitution of "remembering and giving thanks" on those occasions when the Lord's Supper is not observed, I believe a fivefold structure (including confession) provides an essential, organic foundation for worship's corporate dynamic. God calls people to gather to himself, and with praise and thanks they respond. With honesty they confess, and God speaks a fresh Word through Scripture and preacher. With openness the whole community responds in worship with renewed remembering of the past, anticipation of the future, and thankful commitment in the present, as God sends them out into the world to serve.

Worship design, however, can commit sins of both commission and omission. Perhaps it is easiest to ask whether any essential core elements are missing. I have witnessed myopic preachers woefully unconcerned about worship patterns, omitting or sidelining core elements such as confession or, more seriously, the Lord's Supper. Sometimes the conclusion of gathered worship, instead of *sending people forth* to continue worshiping in the world, substitutes a cheery word to enjoy coffee and come back next week. Scripture should have a powerful influence on basic patterns of gathered worship, giving coherence and integrity for this most vital act in all human experience—encountering the Triune God.

Scripture and Specific Outcomes for Particular Gathered Worship Services

At the top level of worship design, Scripture has an obvious determinative role influencing not only sermon content but also choices of music and prayers. Usually preachers communicate texts and themes to others leading worship, but such themes can be very loosely interpreted. Indeed, Mitman warns that "thematic services based . . . on topics that are of the worship leader's preference often are manipulative and designed to have the worshipers experience what the leader wants them to experience." Rather, Mitman seeks worship design "in which all parts work together as an *organic* liturgy. All the individual acts, like the sermon, *grow out* of an engagement with the biblical texts and interact with each other homiletically and liturgically."[22]

Such organic liturgy growing out of Scripture sounds good in theory, but how can it work in practice? How can the whole act of gathered worship have integrity as Scripture shapes its pattern?

Much depends on identifying what directs the *outcomes* not only of sermons but also of the whole act of gathered worship. Obviously, a great variety of outcomes are possible. David Peacock raises a key question: "What do we want to give God the opportunity to accomplish in this service?" The outcomes may be:

praise, understanding, inspiration, spiritual and practical help for the next week, unchurched encouraged to return, confession, communion, heart response to God's love, greater awareness of needs of others, commitment, recommitment, intimacy, the immediacy of God's presence, filling and empowering of the Holy Spirit, healing: physical and spiritual, correction and rebuke, teaching and learning.[23]

He claims that between one and three of these outcomes will usually be appropriate for any particular worship service. But his question focuses attention on the vital issue: How can we best *know* what outcomes we should work for in order for God to accomplish his purpose? Bluntly, how can we ensure worship outcomes are not personal choices? These questions confront preachers and worship leaders whose chief responsibility is planning worship *for God's sake*—to achieve his high purpose. And it raises the critical issue of the role of Scripture in directing top-level acts of worship.

Myopic preaching places Scripture in a box labeled *sermon*, with minimal involvement with the rest of worship. But big-picture preaching expects Scripture to direct not only the sermon but also the whole act of gathered worship.

In chapter 3, I described a breakthrough issue in preaching over the last two or three decades as preachers have realized that Scripture not only *says* things but *does* things. Much of this emphasis on texts *doing things* results from preachers respecting different genres of Scripture texts, for example, recognizing that narrative texts (the majority of Scripture verses) work in different ways than psalms or epistles. A text's form has a vital role alongside its content. Preachers, therefore, need not only to exegete words and their meaning but also to heed forms that words take and their intended outcomes. Scripture is God's living Word; it should never be regarded as flat slabs of information that depend on human energy for elucidation. Just as God's Word was first inspired by the Holy Spirit, today's preachers and hearers continue to hear God's Word by the Holy Spirit. Listening to Scripture is spiritual work; Scripture is spiritually dynamic, sharper than a two-edged sword (Heb. 4:12), and God's Word acts to transform individuals and communities (Isa. 55:11).

Biblical preachers, therefore, need to pay close attention to Scripture's dual action, sometimes described as the text's *focus* and *function*. The focus describes what a text is saying and answers the question: What is the meaning of this text? The function describes what a text is doing and answers the question: What is the purpose of this text? In *360-Degree Preaching*, I urge preachers to investigate the focus and function at two stages of sermon preparation: in the *original* setting of the text as well as in *today's* setting. The first requires serious textual work with concern for authorial intention; the second builds on exegetical work with careful interpretation for the present day. Closely connecting these past and present understandings of the text enables the most faithful hermeneutic. Thomas Long summarizes, "What the biblical text intends to say and do . . . becomes what the preacher hopes to say and do."[24]

Due to preaching's traditional task, the text's focus is more easily understood than the function because the focus concerns a text's meaning. But the text's function has huge implications not only for the outcomes of sermons but for the whole direction of gathered worship. Understanding function indicates whether *this* text of Scripture leads to praise, understanding, inspiration, spiritual and practical help for the next week, encouragement for the unchurched, confession, communion, heart response to God's love, and so on. All these outcomes (and many more) are possible as preachers recognize the text's potential to make things happen. Not only should the sermon say and do what the text says and does, but *worship* should also say and do what the text says and does. "Scripture has the innate capacity to shape, not only the sermon that is a part of the worship event, but also the whole of the liturgical action itself."[25]

Big-picture preachers need to collaborate with all who lead gathered worship in listening to the text(s) so that together they ensure that the whole thrust of worship responds to Scripture's direction. And though this exercise will be new to most preachers and worship leaders (and require extra time and work), understanding its process profoundly deepens worship preparation and worship itself. At the top level of gathered worship, God gives clear directions *through Scripture* about which particular worship outcomes he desires. Directive Scripture should therefore be the single greatest influence on designing big-picture worship.

With inevitable oversimplification of the process, let's briefly examine a sample text in Genesis. (For more detail about exegesis and interpretation, see *360-Degree Preaching*.) Genesis 12:1–9 tells the beginning of Abram's story or, better, God's story with Abram. In the Old Testament, it is vital to keep our perspective set on God's actions, because too easily we can be trapped at the lower level of human stories rather than see God's purposes working out in human stories. "The question must be asked of every biblical passage: What is that God who created the world, who made a people for himself and who now is moving on toward the goal of his kingdom—what is that God doing, according to the words of this particular biblical passage?"[26]

To discover the text's *focus* in the original setting, we may agree that this narrative actually begins in Genesis 11:27, not only setting out necessary family details, but describing an earlier move from Ur to Haran and providing vital information about Sarai's barrenness. All these details throw Genesis 12:1–9 into sharper relief. When God initiated Abram's story, he *spoke* (v. 1), he *disturbed* ("Go from your country"), and essential to the story, he *promised* (vv. 2–8) that Abram would become a great nation to both be blessed and be a blessing. To this, a wordless Abram obediently responded, worshiping at altars in the land God had promised. The focus—what the text meant (its message)—shows an initiating God who spoke, disturbed, and promised and Abram, who trusted and worshiped.

Alongside this, however, we must ask about the text's *function* (its purpose). As narrative it is intended to lay the foundations of the story of the people of God. Eventually this leads to Jesus Christ (as in the genealogy of Matt. 1:1). So part of its function is to tell how God's story began with humankind. Remember that characteristic of myopic preaching—"not living in God's narrative"? Here the narrative is highly significant in understanding God's big story in which we all belong. In Genesis 12, several actions are narrated: God spoke/Abram listened; God disturbed/Abram obeyed; God promised/Abram worshiped. The text speaks of revelation, disturbance, and promise, producing listening, obedience, and worship. All those things (and more) went on in the original story.

Turning to the present day, the *focus* and *function* ask what the text says and does now. Having listened to the Scripture text in its original context, preachers now listen in the present tense to what God is saying to today's congregation. God, who spoke, disturbed, and promised in Abram's story, does similar things today in the story of the people of God. But how does God speak, disturb, and promise today? He *speaks* through Jesus Christ, Scripture, the Holy Spirit, and prayer—especially corporate prayer. God *disturbs*—for his mission always involves movement and transformation. Often such disturbance is uncomfortable because few people like change. God *promises*—a spiritual reality that lies central to his work. "The whole story [of Scripture] hangs together as an account of the promises of God and of how he has kept those promises in the realms of human life."[27]

As these outcomes all jostle for attention, some may be more significant for a particular congregation *at this time*. Perhaps the text is commanding a congregation to enter God's story with wonder at Abram's own obedience and to celebrate and worship the God who integrates us into this story. After all, we are children of Abraham (Gal. 3:15–29). Or maybe there is need for specific spiritual challenges about listening to God's voice—about corporate prayer, for example. Or possibly God is directly challenging people to move out in mission, calling a congregation to move out of a comfort zone (making this a very uncomfortable text to preach). Or perhaps there is some vital promise that God wants to reiterate today for this people, even if it seems a very unlikely promise (like Abram's). Here several different outcomes are possible—celebration of God's story, challenge about spiritual relationships, disturbance by a call to change, and encouragement to respond in faith to God's fresh promise.

Much more could be said about the process of identifying the particular focus and function of a text (for there may be several legitimate focuses and functions, and the task of identifying the appropriate one is a demanding one). In *360-Degree Preaching*, I summarize a text's focus and function by one *main impact sentence* in which the preacher fills in the blanks: "By the grace of God this sermon will *say* . . . and this sermon will *do* . . ." How this sentence is completed depends on many factors. Scripture should be the most important influence, but the *voices* of preacher, congregation, culture, and gathered worship all contribute (in dependency on the Holy Spirit) to the specific way the main impact is written.

I last preached this text to a church congregation for which I was nearing the end of a long period as interim pastor as the new pastor prepared to commence his ministry. I identified a main impact:

> By the grace of God this sermon will *say*: God chooses to speak, disturb, and make stupendous promises, and Abram obeys with amazing faith. And what this sermon will *do* is encourage us to trust and obey the same God who calls us to live *beyond normal*.

The theme of living *beyond normal* emphasized how the God of Abram challenges a church in transition. I allowed the text to challenge individuals about how they belong together in a community for whom God will do new things, echoing the covenant in Exodus 19 and 1 Peter 2. And as I will describe in more detail in part 3, I benefited immensely from collaborating with other worship leaders in undertaking this Bible study. They worked to shape the whole worship service in the light of what this Scripture was saying and doing, choosing hymns, songs, and prayers to emphasize the corporate challenge that God was giving and his promise to his people as they continue to live in his story. I posted blogs about my preparatory work on the text, including the main impact sentence above. (I will share more about blogging later.) Indeed, members of the congregation also responded to postings and became part of the community of worshipers planning and praying together. Every choice about the worship service was directed by *this* Scripture's challenge to God's people at *this* time.

Whether a church practices a formal liturgy (and uses the lectionary) or is informal in structure, Scripture's dynamic can powerfully shape every sermon and worship service. When preachers and worship leaders respond to Scripture text(s) as God *speaking* and God *doing*, then *both* the sermon and the rest of the act of worship belong integrally together. Scripture's function vitally shapes the whole preparation of gathered worship. Mitman sums up the process: "How may the liturgical expression, in a new setting, *be and do* what the text *is and does* in its setting?"[28] He likens the task of worship design to *transposing music* that plays the same tune (stays close to the text and its original meeting) in a different key (interprets for a contemporary context). Leading worship sensitively ensures that the community will have before them the texts, and the transpositions of those texts, which will enable them to be about their worship work and to invite God's Word to happen again in their midst.[29]

The third toolbox question ensures action on this chapter's convictions about Scripture's key role in not only shaping basic structures of worship but also directing specific gathered worship services. Because Scripture expresses both what God is *saying* and what he is *doing* today, it profoundly expresses God's will and purpose for worship today. How willing are we to wrestle with its implications?

Question Toolbox

1. *Gift*: Are we thankfully receiving this gift from the Triune God of grace?

2. *Magnification*: Are we expressing its richness toward God?

3. *Scripture*: Are we allowing Scripture to direct?

When Scripture fails to guide worship, *nonworship* counterfeits may proliferate, such as those prototypes described earlier by Morgenthaler, in which interaction with God is either nonexistent or so low it cannot be measured. In too many cases, such service formats are immune to God's presence, stripped of all but oblique references to Jesus Christ, sanitized from the concept of sin, and consequently excised of anything that remotely resembles confession, repentance, and commitment.[30]

We need to answer this question positively and allow Scripture to direct so that God is gloriously present in three persons and a community worships in spirit and in truth, alive to God's grace—confessing, repenting, and committing to live for his glory.

7

Directive Scripture with Thoughtful Liturgy

Part 2

Novelty may fix our attention not even on the service but on the celebrant. . . . There really is some excuse for the man who said, "I wish they'd remember that the charge to Peter was 'Feed my sheep,' not 'Try experiments on my rats, or even, teach my performing dogs new tricks.'"

C. S. Lewis

One sometimes wonders if we are beginning to worship *worship* rather than worship *God*. . . . It's a bit like those who begin by admiring the sunset and soon begin to admire themselves admiring the sunset.

Donald Carson

One churchgoer commented to me after attending a contemporary service at a new church, "You know, they behaved almost as though they were inventing church. They seemed completely unaware how Christians have worshiped throughout the centuries—there was no participation, no confession, little Scripture, and hardly any prayer. *And they didn't care!*" I can just imagine if the worship leader had overheard her: "How dare she say we don't care when we have worked so hard to prepare all the music and have only repeated our normal pattern, which everyone else enjoys." But I also imagine the churchgoer's reply: "I meant you didn't care about how Christians have worshiped throughout two thousand years."

Some churches, blissfully unaware of best past practices, seem to churn out services without any sense of benefiting from or belonging to a rich past. Operating in a liturgical vacuum, such churches frequently stitch one *good* idea to another in patchwork. Patchwork is fine for quilts but not for worship coherence. Churches like the one above are likely to be not only defensive about their worship structures but also extremely wary about using liturgical resources, thinking they represent old (and dead) practices. As noted earlier, myopic preaching suspects anything liturgical.

Yet patchwork worship sometimes includes potentially significant elements drawn from the past. For example, lighting Advent wreaths on Sundays leading up to Christmas is now common. Though little practiced in nonliturgical churches fifty years ago, often four white, red, or purple candles are lit on successive Sundays, and finally a central candle is lit to mark Christ's birth. But attempting to discover the reasons for lighting them and even for the colors reveals confusion. Visiting a very informal church, I was intrigued to see great care in lighting three purple and one pink candle. In my ignorance, I asked what the pink candle stood for and discovered they had no clue either.

Later I read Laurence Stookey's comment: "Most Protestants have no idea on which Sunday to light the 'pink' candle for the first time, let alone why." Apparently, while purple marks the Advent season, the *rose*-colored candle (not pink) denotes a particular Sunday called *Gaudete*, which allowed an easing of "the intense solemnity of the [preceding] 'violet Sundays.'"[1] This practice has long since been discarded by many historic churches, yet here was a pink candle being lit with minimal understanding of Advent solemnity, let alone the need for easing it. Lighting candles in sequence through Advent, however, can help build spiritual awareness of the need for penitence and preparation, and practicing such Advent spirituality *knowingly* can be of great benefit.

It has been eye-opening to learn from several former patchwork worshipers how they have valued coming to a *knowing* practice of older liturgical resources. As Robert Webber's study of younger evangelicals discovered, many are now committed to strong "restoration of premodern traditions."[2] Some have led congregations to adopt the fivefold pattern of worship, teaching them the value of classic worship structures. Others have told me of the differences made by greater focus on the Lord's Supper and making it integral to gathered worship. A number have engaged in collaborative Bible preparation involving others in listening to what Scripture says and does.

Many more have adopted part (or even most) of the Christian year as the framework for their preaching, expressing wonder at their congregation's eagerness to worship in fresh ways. Both Advent/Christmas and Lent/Easter cycles have been introduced to churches with no previous experience. Indeed, one pastor who introduced a sequence of services before Easter into a church that was highly suspicious of formal liturgy said:

> It will be like a Holy Week, but I won't call it that. We shall begin on Palm Sunday, include a Good Friday service (which the church does not normally have), and move on to Easter. On Good Friday I am thinking of having a series of reminders around the room of what Jesus did—a little like Stations of the Cross, though, again, I cannot call it that. I shall encourage people to participate. Often Easter has been really understated in our tradition. Those who are helping me plan are really excited about participating in this way.

I asked him afterward how worship planning had worked out. He responded enthusiastically, "So many people spoke positively about the way worship prepared them for Easter this year. They want us to develop such services again."

Another church that had never before emphasized worship in the week before Easter opened its doors for midday services each day of Holy Week and was overwhelmed by passersby joining in worship. Others who had never practiced vigils of any kind developed special services before Christmas and Easter.

In this chapter, some of these issues will be developed, focusing on three main areas: the Christian year, the lectionary, and worship resources. Of course, these will be well understood by many preachers, but I have encountered too many myopic preachers for whom they are totally unknown. When Karen Roberts and I developed an online course, "Preaching and Worship through the Christian Year," we asked how many students had previous experience of the Christian year and found that less than half had. But by the end of the course, they all testified to its significance for their preaching and worship.

The Christian Year

The Christian year describes the pattern and rhythm of seasons that tell Christ's story through twelve months. Rooted in Old Testament practices, the Christian year emerged throughout the first four centuries of the church's history to provide an important framework for preaching, worship, and community formation. Since the sixteenth-century Reformation, however, the Christian year calendar has been held at arm's length by some Protestants and continues to be suspect for many.

Of course, mere mention of the calendar can raise blood pressure. A former Lutheran explained to me how thoroughly alienated he was by early years in church, facing a procession of Sundays labeled "fourth after Pentecost," "fifth . . . sixth after Pentecost," and so on. "I was liberated when I stepped out of this straightjacket into the freedom of the informal worshiping community I now belong to." On the other hand, others testify to liberation *by* the Christian year. After years of trying to create coherence and direction through cleverly constructed sermon series or church programs, or by dint of sheer pulpit enthusiasm, they have discovered the power of living in God's story—paced throughout the year. Said one pastor who had newly discovered the calendar, "Practicing the Christian year has given me such a rich framework for preaching the Word of God and keeping my community in God's story. I think I still preach like I used to, but now every sermon belongs within his story that keeps us moving on."

In practice, all churches are influenced by one calendar or another. Norma Malefyt and Howard Vanderwell describe four calendars that sometimes *simultaneously* influence the same church congregation.[3] The *chronological calendar* begins in January and ends in December and emphasizes New Year themes from January 1 with a new *church text* or even a *vision* for the year ahead. The *church program calendar* commonly begins after the summer vacation period with new schedules and new classes in September, running through until late spring. It runs and connects with educational and employment cycles. Churches also invent special months, such as *missions month*, and special days, such as *outreach Sunday*. The *greeting-card calendar* marks other services such as Mother's Day, Father's Day, and in the United States, Memorial Day, Independence Day, and Thanksgiving.

In marked contrast to these culturally driven calendars, the *Christian year* provides a completely different structure, intentionally following Christ's story every Sunday throughout the year. As citizens of God's kingdom, it is vital we focus our lives on God's calendar so that his goals distinguish the countercultural pattern of our lives. Centered on Easter, the Christian year moves on through Pentecost to Advent, Christmas, Epiphany, and Lent. Its high days include Good Friday, Easter Sunday, Pentecost, and Christmas, and it also celebrates Christ's ascension and the Trinity. Preachers need to understand something of its origin, design, and significance for big-picture preaching.

Origin

The gospel was cradled in the Jewish time line. Of course, Jesus's incarnation occurred in history (Luke 1:5; 2:2), with his life and ministry recorded at specific times in particular places (e.g., John 10:2–23). Yet because Jesus was a Jew, his story is told within the Jewish calendar and his whole ministry ties in with the annual cycle of feasts, which celebrated agricultural seasons and, using the lunar calendar, retold the story of God's salvation from year to year and generation to generation. In particular, the three annual pilgrim festivals are important: the Feast of Unleavened Bread or Passover (Exod. 12:1–27), the Feast of Weeks or Harvest (Lev. 22:15–21), and the Feast of Tabernacles or Ingathering (Lev. 23:39–41). As a child, Jesus goes up to Jerusalem to celebrate

Passover (Luke 2:41–52), and throughout his public ministry the connections keep recurring, such as his visit to Jerusalem for the Feast of Tabernacles (John 7:1–14).

Just as continually retelling the Exodus story nourished people of the Old Testament, so retelling and reenacting the Easter story recalls the cross and resurrection heart of the Christian gospel. Indeed, nowhere is the tie between Christian faith and the Jewish calendar more significant (and complex) than at Easter itself. The Synoptic Gospels record that Jesus shared the Passover meal with his disciples on the eve of his death, which had to occur outside the feast itself (for example, see Mark 14:1). The fourth Gospel keeps mentioning the Passover feast as signaling progressive stages of Jesus's story moving ever closer to the cross, seeing Jesus in the role of Passover Lamb. The Jewish feast of Pentecost is also intimately connected with the birth of the church (Acts 2). Jewish religious practice also provided the weekly pattern of seven days (Gen. 2:2; Exod. 20:8–11), and Jesus celebrated Sabbath on the seventh day, which occurred from sunset Friday to sunset Saturday. Of course, controversy breaks out too, especially when he heals the sick on the Sabbath.

But with Christ's resurrection, the first Christians had an entirely new and radical event to celebrate. His resurrection introduced a new dynamic for which the inherited calendar had no equivalent. Christians now had a resurrection day at the core of their faith to celebrate weekly as the Lord's Day (Rev. 1:10). By the end of the first century, this was commonly understood to be the first day of the week. Around the middle of the second century, the word *Sunday* appeared, drawn from pagan worship of the sun but now identified with worship of Jesus, gloriously risen from the dead. In AD 321, Emperor Constantine instructed that Sunday should be a day of rest as well as of worship.

This story of how Sunday developed reveals a complicated relationship between the Jewish lunar calendar, the drama of the resurrection itself, and the Roman calendar controlled by the sun. As the early church began to include festivals that were unique to the Christian faith alongside those that were originally Jewish, the Roman calendar became the norm. For that reason, fixed festivals, such as Christmas on December 25, were set according to the solar calendar in contrast with the moveable feasts, such as Easter, that are determined by the Jewish lunar calendar.

By retelling the story of Jesus year by year, within the comprehensive narrative of God's actions in the world, worshipers grow together in community by sharing story and time. "By continually hearing the stories of God's faithfulness in the past and God's promises for the future, people know to whom they belong and to what they are called . . . from the very beginning, story and time have been inseparable."[4] Each generation of worshipers belongs in a great succession of those who by reenacting the story of Jesus, the Messiah, live out God's continuing purposes.

Design

The Christian year has two key cycles focused on Christ's life and ministry that are set among what are called *ordinary days*—when the church is encouraged to engage in times of reflection. Those unused to practicing the Christian year are often surprised by its pace—slowing down for preparation and then a lengthening of celebration. For example, the approach to Christmas delays celebration until Christmas day, but then the Christian year extends worship of Christ's incarnation afterward. Similarly, the lengthy Lenten approach to Easter results in extended celebration following Easter day.

The Christmas (Incarnation) Cycle includes four weeks of Advent, twelve days of Christmas, and the Epiphany of the Lord. Each week the focus of worship changes. *Advent* is a season that prepares and anticipates the coming of Jesus. Beginning with an emphasis on the second coming, it prepares for the first coming as it reaches the fourth Sunday. *Christmas* joyfully marks Christ's birthday and the mystery of God incarnate. *Epiphany* is a celebration of the revelation of Christ as Savior of the world as the Magi visit and mission outreach of the church is anticipated. This cycle is countercultural to much evangelical church practice that too often locks into the commercial calendar. Rather than prepare spiritually in order to celebrate on December 25 and the days following, many Christians begin the Christmas celebration early and are squeezed into a consumer time frame that often leaves December 25 almost anticlimactic. The wonder of the incarnation is subsequently lost in busy New Year activity.

Returning to the Christian year, *ordinary time* encourages reflection from January 7 through the Tuesday before Ash Wednesday.

The Easter (Resurrection) Cycle begins with forty days of Lent, which invite self-examination and self-discipline, focusing on the realities of human sin that made the cross necessary as God's loving response to our sin. Holy Week begins with Palm Sunday, when Jesus triumphantly entered Jerusalem, and concludes with the so-called *triduum*—Maundy Thursday, Good Friday, and the great vigil of Easter. Easter joy contrasts with all that has gone before as Christians celebrate Christ's resurrection during the fifty days of Easter (sometimes called the *great fifty days*—for obvious reasons). The Easter Cycle ends with the day of Pentecost, which marks the birth of the church as the promised Holy Spirit breathed on his Easter people.

Ordinary time then follows from the Monday after the day of Pentecost through the Saturday before the first Sunday of Advent.

Significance for Big-Picture Worship

The Christian year is significant for big-picture worship in at least four ways: (1) it narrates God's story, (2) it accentuates worship in the present, (3) it provides a source for spirituality in Jesus Christ for community formation, and (4) it gives a practical framework for worship preparation.

It narrates God's story. Obviously, the annual cycles of the Christian year reenact the Christian story. All language about *living in God's story* and *telling out God's narrative* involves congregations moving through the Christian year, with its wide perspective from creation to incarnation through to consummation. "Repeating and overlapping cycles of the feasts and fasts of the church year create patterns of meaning in our lives, giving shape and direction to the events that mark our days."[5] Though cyclical, it is not repetitive, marking time on the same spot. Rather, "like a path going up a mountain, slowly making the ascent to the height, we are to climb the same road at a higher level, and go on until we reach the end, Christ himself."[6] The end point toward which everything is moving is God's *telos*—which finds its consummation in a new heaven and a new earth.

It accentuates worship in the present. Practicing the Christian year heightens awareness of God's actions in the present. Worshipers who are alert to God's grace expressed in the past and extended to the future are even more sensitive to God's power in the present. Two key words for Christian worship are *anamnesis*, a remembrance of the past, and *prolepsis*, an anticipation of the future. *Anamnesis* and *prolepsis* especially occur in the Lord's Supper as worshipers look back with remembrance and look forward in anticipation of fellowship with Christ. Yet being aware of past and future emphasizes all the more the wonder of worshiping Christ in the present.

It provides a source for spirituality in Jesus Christ for community formation. Jesus Christ is the focus of the Christian year and the fount of its spirituality. While the "once for all" Christ event (Heb. 7:27) is grounded in past history, his ministry to us continues (Heb. 7:25). Our lives make sense because of his life. The New Testament claim that believers live *en Christo* means they belong together in him, living by the pattern and power of Christ's life, death, and resurrection every day (Rom. 6:1–14). As we will see in chapter 8, this corporate belonging leads to community formation. When worshipers journey together year after year, living by the pattern and in the power of Jesus's saving life, death, and resurrection, they grow together in spiritual maturity (Eph. 4:13). "Christ is the source of Christian year spirituality. . . . We can experience the power of Christ within the community of the church, through its worship and in our lives twenty-four hours a day, seven days a week."[7] Practicing the Christian year continually reminds worshipers to live together in Jesus's *way of being*.

It gives a practical framework for worship preparation. Norma Malefyt and Howard Vanderwell list ten positive contributions of the Christian year:

1. It improves quality of worship.
2. It gives a sense of direction with an overview of the whole year.
3. It makes possible adequate preparation time for all leaders because short deadlines would prevent wide involvement from others.
4. It allows greater thought and creativity.

5. It makes greater variety possible with different elements during different seasons.
6. It ensures better balance for a range of Scriptures and worship themes.
7. It gives more room for the Holy Spirit to move.
8. It protects against afterthoughts that otherwise you regret missing.
9. It provides greater personal enrichment for worship planners.
10. It avoids a sense of panic with approaching deadlines and inadequate preparation.[8]

Notice their claim that the Christian year gives more room for the Holy Spirit to move while giving plenty of time for planning. The Holy Spirit is not adverse to planning and hard work.

Practicing the Christian year therefore addresses several characteristics of myopic preaching outlined earlier such as liturgical amnesia, feeble community formation, naivete about culture, not living in God's narrative, and isolated preparation. Connecting historically with this centuries-old practice of the worldwide church enables people to grow in community, counter culture's calendars and secular narrative by telling God's big story in Christ, and have a framework for collaborative worship preparation.

> For all Christians there is something valuable about the theological force and architectural completeness of the liturgical year. The lectionaries that nourish it, the prayers that adorn it, the colors and sensory materials that grace it, the temporal and procedural rhythms, the confluences, recurrences and particularities made one with panoramic vista—these and more, whether partially or fully used, can intensify the way a local assembly makes its way through the systematic study of the truth.[9]

Practicing part or all of the Christian year has huge implications that could fill the rest of this book. During the online course I mentioned earlier, Karen and I were almost overwhelmed by the students' energy and application. Many of them were able to develop only limited seasons such as Advent or Holy Week, yet many positive stories spilled out from them and their churches. Several now say they are committed to pursuing Christian year disciplines over the long term in their ministries. Indeed, this week, while I was writing this chapter, a former student contacted me and said, "I honestly think of all the things that have challenged me about leading worship in my church, practicing the Christian year is the most valuable!"

The Lectionary

Closely linked with the Christian year is the *lectionary*. It should be stressed that following the Christian year does not *necessarily* mean adhering to the lectionary, especially when partial practice of the year focuses on major seasons of Christmas, Easter, and Pentecost. For many years my own practice was to follow through preparation and celebration cycles for these major Christian year events with nonlectionary Scripture choices. But at various times in my ministry, I have also found the lectionary structure and choices to be immensely helpful.

The lectionary provides Scripture choices throughout the Christian year, with three readings for each Sunday (as well as a psalm) in cycles of three successive years (referred to as year A, year B, and year C) that focus on a different Synoptic Gospel each year. In the church around the world, the majority of preachers and other worship leaders work within this lectionary structure, planning worship entirely based on its Scripture choices. But a large group of worshipers never use it. Some have had negative, straightjacket experiences, and others are wary of being trapped by imposed texts. For this latter group it is important to see its advantages as well as its disadvantages.

Key Advantages

The lectionary can aid big-picture worship in at least seven ways.

1. Like the Christian year, it connects with the world church—both historically and also across denominations and cultures. Instead of allowing individualistic choices to dominate the local church, lectionary use ensures that a global Christian community reads and belongs to the same texts at the same time in one book. The lectionary acts in a countercultural way to ensure that the Bible is the church's book, giving identity to its world community, ministry, and mission.

2. Closely connected with the first point, the lectionary reinforces practice of the Christian year. Continual retelling of God's narrative in Scripture helps shape community life and develops a *biblical mentality* that safeguards against private entrepreneurship. "Lectionary use bespeaks a new centering, a new mentality in the life of the church—and the Bible is at the core, not as resource but as source."[10] It ensures that other calendars, like the chronological or greeting-card calendars, do not dictate worship patterns.

3. The lectionary "forces the preacher and the community to be engaged by texts which they themselves would not choose,"[11] safeguarding against favoritism or neglect.

4. It surprises preachers by its patterns and connections. For example, Barbara Day Miller comments on the value of Psalm 23 set in contexts, both on the fourth Sunday in Lent of year A, and again on the fourth Sunday after Easter for all three years of the cycle. Such repetition "can give both pause and comfort."[12]

5. It narrows choices for preachers, which enables easier planning, though by providing three Scripture readings (four with the psalm), it also offers some flexibility.

6. It supplies a well-established structure for a year of worship that allows fruitful collaboration between preachers and worship leaders.

7. A vast number of accompanying lectionary aids ensures a wealth of resources at the preacher's fingertips (though these aids should never substitute for personal engagement with the texts).

Some Disadvantages

Interestingly, some regular users of the lectionary are also its severest critics, and the last two criticisms below deserve particular attention.

1. Lectionary choices inhibit other kinds of Scripture selection, such as preaching consecutively through a particular book of the Bible (or a section of a book) or biblical topical preaching. It also rules out development of any sermon series such as a doctrinal series on "What is worship?" or "Who is the Holy Spirit?"

2. Set texts may prove inappropriate for particular situations. Lectionary preachers sometimes testify to serendipitous ways that set texts proved extraordinarily suitable for sudden events, such as an outbreak of war or a major social issue. But many admit struggling to contrive connections between texts and particular situations.

3. Groups of lectionary texts sometimes seem oddly connected, leaving preachers second-guessing their relationship.

4. Lectionary aids are too readily available and discourage preachers' personal engagement with Scripture. While all preachers must resist moving too quickly to commentaries and other aids, the sheer abundance of lectionary study aids makes it even more tempting to rely completely on someone else's work with the text.

5. Some view the lectionary as a "*Christendom* strategy . . . commonly endorsed by denominational authorities, for use among people who were already Christians in greater or lesser degree." Today they argue for a *post-Christendom* strategy. Thomas Bandy calls for an "Uncommon Lectionary" to "integrate Scripture reading and interpretation with the daily lives of ordinary people in diverse contexts, rather than with . . . what is fast becoming an elite minority." Its choices should focus on crucial parts of Scripture for seekers and disciples rather than "investigating the distant corners of the Bible."[13] For example, he commends the "Disciple Cycle," which lasts fifty-two weeks and concentrates on the person of Jesus and is integrated with small group work to coach faith, hope, and lifestyle. This criticism rightly warns about missing the church's mission to win people to Christ.

6. Others critique from the preaching perspective. Eugene Lowry expresses a love-hate relationship with the lectionary. In *Living with the Lectionary*, he begins by listing its liabilities, pointing out that the lectionary has a dual function. On one hand, designed to teach the Christian story, it directly relates

to the preaching task. On the other hand, it also seeks to reenact the drama of salvation—"the lectionary serves as biblical grounding for the continuing rhythmic celebration of the acts of God in Jesus Christ."[14] He claims, however, that lectionary selections are often made for the latter function of praise, with doxology and anamnesis dominating choices.

Such emphasis on doxology may conflict strongly with preaching. When preachers ask, "Are they the kind of selections which will serve well the homiletical goal of proclamation? . . . Often the answer is no—or at least only with difficulty."[15] Text choices sometimes seem better suited to upbeat celebration of God's story rather than to engaging with Scripture on its own terms. Remember that Scripture both *says* and *does*. Lowry expects preachers to find God's challenge, or "trouble in the text," that needs interpretation for the contemporary situation. But instead of helping preachers listen with open minds and hearts to Scripture, many lectionary readings are texts of *closure*. "They represent the end of the line of thought. The lectionary makers love *summaries*. Once the text is read, the matter is closed—and often the resultant sermon has the dynamics of a report."[16]

He notes that to ensure positive closure, the lectionary sometimes omits difficult verses. Lowry cites examples such as the reading of Genesis 15:1–12, 17–18 for the second Sunday of Lent in year C. The missing verses 13–16 give unhappy news that Abram's descendants will be oppressed for four hundred years. Omitting these verses obviously makes for a positive message, yet doesn't the integrity of Scripture demand that preachers deal with the negatives as well? In fact, thorny parts may be essential to understanding the whole. Similarly, the reading selected for the seventh Sunday after Easter, year B, is Revelation 22:12–13, 16–17. You can understand why verse 15 is omitted: "Outside are the dogs and sorcerers and fornicators and murderers and idolaters, and everyone who loves and practices falsehood." But should preachers pick and choose what a text says? Sometimes editing like this seems to occur for the sake of efficiency. The reading for the fourth Sunday in Lent of year C, Luke 15:1–3, 11–32, gives the introduction and then the story of the prodigal son. Does it matter that two stories, verses 4–10, are omitted? Actually, all three stories have a powerful, cumulative effect. Lowry summarizes his concern about these selections: "Texts ought to prompt engagement, not call for the benediction."[17]

Lectionary preachers aware of these disadvantages often practice with flexibility. During *ordinary time* they may preach sermon series while always feeling free to break into set texts when the situation demands. In light of the fifth criticism, they safeguard against "investigating the distant corners of the Bible" at the expense of mission by keeping a strong missional focus (see chap. 8). Responding to Lowry's critique, they work hard to read full lectionary texts in context (see chap. 11).

In the online course "Preaching and Worshiping through the Christian Year," students reveled in applying set texts to shape the whole act of worship.

Their creativity filled several files. For example, one student, a music leader in a church that followed the Christian year and lectionary, commented:

> Often my favorite part of preparing Sunday worship is the creative use of Scripture readings. I have never yet found the lectionary words to be unworkable for Introt and Call to Confession. . . . I have this desire to know that the words I am calling God's people together to speak are not my own . . . words that could not be confused for my own.

He demonstrated this in a service planned for Palm Sunday, with the lectionary texts Psalms 31:9–16; 118:1–2, 19–29; and Philippians 2:5–11 (NIV). Wrestling with the tension between the triumphant entry of Palm Sunday and the imminent grief of Good Friday, he planned a call to worship that reflected this conflict. Starting with Psalm 118:2, 19, he inserted congregational responses: "Crucify him! Crucify him! Crucify him!" The call begins:

Leader: Give thanks to the LORD, for he is good; his love endures forever. Let Israel say: "His love endures forever."
Congregation: Crucify him! Crucify him! Crucify him!
Leader: Open for me the gates of righteousness; I will enter and give thanks to the LORD.
Congregation: Crucify him! Crucify him! Crucify him!

Later, the confession used Psalm 31:9–13 and then Psalm 118 with congregational responses drawn from Philippians 2:9 and Psalm 118:22–23. It begins:

Leader: Hear the grief and sorrow of Jesus our Lord: Be merciful to me, O LORD, for I am in distress; my eyes grow weak with sorrow, my soul and my body with grief. My life is consumed by anguish and my years by groaning; my strength fails because of my affliction, and my bones grow weak.
Congregation: Therefore God exalted him to the highest place and gave him a name that is above every other name.
Leader: Hear the heart of Jesus our Lord: Because of all my enemies, I am the utter contempt of my neighbors; I am a dread to my friends— those who see me on the street flee from me. I am forgotten by them as though I were dead; I have become like broken pottery. For I hear the slander of many; there is terror on every side; they conspire against me and plot to take my life.
Congregation: The stone the builders rejected has become the capstone. The Lord has done this, and it is marvelous in our eyes.

Frequently, I have been challenged by examples like this of worshiping within the framework of the Christian year helped by lectionary readings.

Worship Resources

Mention of worship resources likely conjures up thoughts of practical assets such as instruments, music scores, DVDs, CDs, PowerPoint slides, and possibly even hymnals and songbooks. Or you might think of favorite materials garnered from online sites, journals, books, and conferences. On my first visit to the United States in 1980, I visited First Baptist Church, Houston, a congregation exceeding twelve thousand, and was overwhelmed. The music pastor told me about forty-three different musical ensembles of all ages, sizes, and instrumentation. Seeing the main sanctuary with its magnificent pipe organ and orchestral stage, backed by various rehearsal rooms, choir wardrobes, handbell galleries, and banks of music books and scores, left an indelible impression.

It also raised the critical issue of appropriateness. These Texan worship resources suited their megachurch context well, but would have been artificial and alien back home in small British churches that often have limited musicians and skills. Worship resources must be earthed authentically—real worshipers in context. It is tempting to think worship resources mean *things*. No, first they mean *people*. Nothing matters more than worship leaders' spirituality and their ability to develop the gifts of others within community. Then *their* gathering of fresh material is genuine.

Primacy of Worship Leaders' Spirituality

The most powerful worship resource is the personal spiritual overflow of those set aside to lead. Is your public spirituality an overflow or a cover-up? Do God-qualities "pervade all of our attitudes and our actions"? Are they "simultaneously routine and revolutionary"?[18] Preachers and others who lead worship are catalysts not because they bring good ideas, schemes, and materials garnered from elsewhere, but because they offer themselves with public spirituality that is an overflow of personal worship. Personal encounter with God's holiness and grace gives integrity and authenticity to worship leading. Its absence spells disaster—cover-up worship. The Triune God energizes congregational worship through godly leaders.

Personal prayer is therefore vital. Like others, I confess some difficulty in sustaining vital, regular prayer, and I hesitate to mention my own interior life. But for all its frailty, I recognize it is the mainspring for my public leadership. Gradually, I have learned from many others how to nourish my own prayer life. All kinds of devotional patterns have helped, often including set Scriptures and repetitive prayers. For example, learning to say daily *offices* instituted by St. Benedict, founder of Western monasticism, has provided rich discipline. I have profited from reading Scripture daily (my practice takes two years to read through the whole Bible) and seeing ways of integrating it into personal worship with regular use of the Psalms and other prayers such as the Sanctus—"Holy, holy, holy" (Isa. 6:3; Rev. 4:8). I have benefitted from patterns based on the Lord's Prayer and saying creeds, such as the Apostles' and Nicene Creeds. All kinds of devotional books have provided help, including works by Lancelot Andrewes, William Law, Oswald Chambers, C. H. Spurgeon, and E. Stanley Jones. Of course, hymns and songs are also an immense personal worship resource as well as developing a practice of spiritual journaling to keep myself centered (in spite of being erratic at times). My private time with God has remained a prerequisite because personal worship is the springboard to leading congregational worship. Being schooled by personal devotion precedes schooling others.

Developing personal worship resources therefore lies at the core of leading others. Over the years a couple of my shelves have filled up with prayer books and other worship materials (including hymnals and songbooks), which are also in constant use for preparing public worship. In addition, files containing work designed by members of the worship design team, including drama pieces and visual materials, combine with other resources culled from the Internet and conferences.

Music leaders similarly build up resources out of their core personal worship. Recently, I participated in congregational thanksgiving where each of us wrote down thanks on pieces of paper and brought them to the front while a music video played. The leader's joyful gratitude was evident in his whole demeanor, and the video's words, images, and music combined potently in ways I still recall. I really wanted to give thanks! Talking with the music leader afterward, I realized afresh what a truly thankful person he is, and I learned he had found that video online many months before. Moved by its message but unsure when it might be appropriate, he downloaded it for later use. "Oh," he exclaimed, "there are fantastic worship resources out there!" Yes, fantastic resources, but his transparent thankfulness grounded the whole experience authentically for the rest of us. It was *spiritual overflow*.

Overflowing personal worship should always motivate building other worship resources that widen experience and imagination. For worship based on the Christian year and lectionary, there are many resources, including *The New Handbook of the Christian Year* and *Imaging the Word: An Art and Lectionary Resource*.[19] Other sourcebooks focus on general worship design, such as *Designing Worship Together* and *Contemporary Worship*.[20] Many website resources provide important materials, such as www.worship.calvin. edu/resources/resource-library, www.textweek.com, and www.reformedworship.org. Providing a full list would fill many pages, but how leaders worship personally should always be at the core.

Developing Gifts within the Worshiping Community

I recall a speaker at a conference for small churches, claiming, "God gives to his people all the gifts needed for all *he* wants to do through them." He encouraged even the smallest of churches with seemingly very limited resources that God gives gifts to be identified and released. Whatever the scale of worship—from thousands to a handful—God gifts appropriately.

Second to the importance of the leaders' personal spiritual overflow is the releasing of gifts from worshipers who offer their creativity in music, writing, drama, dance, reading, praying, painting, drawing, sculpting, and even sewing of various kinds. The best resource of all is people gifted and empowered by the Triune God to bring their gifts to worship together.

So much depends on the degree to which preachers and others are willing to allow Scripture to direct gathered worship that is open to this gifting and imagination of the congregation at large. Too often, use of gifts is restricted to a few who can play instruments or sing. It can be surprising what hidden gifts other members of the congregation can bring to gathered worship. Usual elements such as reading Scripture and leading prayer can be enriched. Those gifted artistically can add to worship deeply by creating images and fresh worship spaces, using skills of painting, sewing, lighting, drama, dance, and technology. With Scripture always directing, so much creativity can enable full-sense participation with sight, touch, taste, and even smell added to hearing.

Wider congregational involvement also integrates gathered worship with daily worship in the world, more readily bringing Monday to Saturday before God. Brother Lawrence, a Carmelite monk, coined the expression "practicing the presence of God." Even in the most menial tasks, such as washing up in the monastery, he sought to work for the glory of God. Practicing the presence of God Sunday through Saturday pushes the boundaries of worship into every aspect of life and invites gathered worshipers to see more of God's big picture. When, for example, someone who works in a factory helps to lead intercession for her workplace or another shares a mission activity he is involved in, vital worship connections are made with everyday life.

Openness to Fresh Possibilities

Congregational gifts in music, writing, drama, dance, reading, praying, painting, drawing, technology, and other arts invite many possibilities for gathered worship. Some may hesitate about certain items on the list—especially those whose worship largely occurs through words. Brought up in Presbyterian, Methodist, and Baptist congregations, Thomas Troeger says he often sang, "'Open my eyes that I may see/glimpses of truth Thou hast for me.' But in practice the Presbyterian, Methodist, and Baptist congregations in which I sang these words were never very hospitable to the use of eyes . . .

sometimes there were stained glass windows . . . or an empty cross. . . . The preachers mirrored the austerity of the windows."[21] But concentrating on words alone neglects other senses.

Of course, as with many other worship issues, there is a history of controversy here. Focus on the visual and tactile can make these ends in themselves. Infamously, Aaron's construction of the golden calf substituted a sensual idol for God (Exod. 32). Yet by building an altar to the Lord *in front of* the calf (v. 5), he seemed to want it both ways—to embrace the idol within worship to the true God. So easily idols can develop within worship. I once asked a group of friends about golden calves in today's churches. Quick as a flash they responded: "Marketing for success," said one man. "Yes, the invasion of business principles," said another. A woman commented, "Projects—you know when a preacher just goes on and on about a pet scheme." Someone else chimed in, "Wasn't the golden calf about people feasting and pleasing themselves? I think people pleasing themselves is too important in my church." At the beginning of the chapter, we read Donald Carson's warning: "One sometimes wonders if we are beginning to worship *worship* rather than worship *God*. . . . It's a bit like those who begin by admiring the sunset and soon begin to admire themselves admiring the sunset." It is always vital to keep focused on God and his purpose for his community, as we will see in chapter 8.

Additional dangers arise when using arts in worship. People so easily divide over taste and preference—whether worship expressions are classical and high culture or popular and low culture. Harold Best helpfully suggests that those focusing on artistic content (and I would add "directed by Scripture") should refuse to allow classical and popular to be opposites. Rather, he shows they can belong together at ends of a *positive* continuum. The range from *shallow to deep* reflects that "some art is shallow and some is deep, . . . either kind can be of extremely high quality." *Simple to complex* reflects the paradox that "even though complexity is a deepening of simplicity, true simplicity is often the most difficult thing to explain."[22] *Strange to familiar* also describes how material may change in significance—something said a hundred times before can suddenly take on a *holy strangeness*.

Developing worship resources that touch all five senses and encourage congregational participation opens up a huge area far beyond the bounds of this book. Everything considered so far has repercussions for rich worship participation. For example, trinitarian theology calls for imaginative, multisensory responses. John Witvliet argues for its pervasive influence in words used, especially in the opening acts of gathered worship: congregating, inviting, praising, and praying. Different from any other kind of meeting, it should begin explicitly as "an act of Spirit-forged coming together around the person of Christ for the purpose of addressing God." The call to worship should sound out God's triune invitation, making sure worshipers understand that God "always comes to us before we come to God."[23] Praising should adore

God in three persons, and opening prayer should expectantly seek to worship through the Spirit, whose holy, loving communion is open to us.

In stressing how multisensory worship relies on more than spoken word, Karmen Krahn and Leslie James commend various trinitarian worship designs. They suggest representing trinitarian theology by various symbols of threeness or picturing the outstretched arms of God. They explain how such designs nurture threefold encounter: of mutual abiding in God as Creator, of mutual adoration in Jesus Christ, and of mutual summons in the Holy Spirit.[24]

No wonder it is so important that those who prepare worship ask the second toolbox question. "*Magnification*: Are we expressing its richness toward God?" This challenges creative response to all aspects of big-picture worship from the widest range of people.

8

Toward Community Formation

Who you are as an individual believer depends greatly upon the character of the community of believers in which you are nurtured. How faithfully does that community incarnate God's presence and pass on the narratives that reveal God when they assemble together? . . . How (and whom) we worship nurtures personal character.

Marva Dawn

Worship both forms and expresses the faith-experience of the community.

Don Saliers

Picturing the church as a building runs high risks. Already too many people identify *church* with the place in which they worship. Dan Kimball blames the nursery rhyme (with hand actions): "This is the church, this is the steeple, look inside, and see all the people." Some so strongly equate church with a building that it becomes *my* church, with rank unpleasantness should someone sit in *my* seat and threatened riot should someone suggest even minor alterations. It is surprisingly easy to confuse *going* to a church building with *being* God's church every day. No wonder one service bulletin read: "While our building is located at 1310 North Main Street, First Baptist Wheaton is a community devoted to following Jesus wherever they find themselves on any given day."

Of course, worship places do have great importance because space, architecture, and familiarity profoundly habituate experiences of belonging with

Christ's people. Oftentimes, treasured Christian experiences are intimately connected with contexts. Some of my most significant worship memories are locked into particular worship places, and if I return, those spaces are spiritually evocative. This summer I went back to my first pastorate, which I had revisited only twice in thirty years. Being back in the same church building (virtually unchanged) with some of the same people (rather changed!) took me to deep levels of gratitude and praise. Worship spaces do matter. Yet bricks and mortar must never be confused with the much more demanding vision of God building his people together in community.

Even so, risking dangers of fixating on buildings on Main Street, this chapter dares to develop an often-overlooked metaphor for the church: *God's building* (1 Cor. 3:9, 16; Eph. 2:19–22; and 1 Pet. 2:4–10; with powerful building resonance in Eph. 4:12–19). Inevitably suggesting physical structure and architecture, this picture powerfully expresses the spiritual architecture of community formation. Great architecture implies coherent, elegant design, solid structure, and visible purpose, and it aptly sums up ways by which worship builds God's people corporately in his master design. This chapter therefore develops the concept of the worshiping church as God's building work and integrates it with missional theology before then considering some complex dynamics of community formation.

The Church as God's Building Work

Describing the church as *body* (Rom. 12; 1 Cor. 12; Eph. 4) seems much more popular than describing it as *building* (perhaps because of the risks mentioned above). Memorably, the *body* analogy integrates every part into an organic whole—all members, each with their own gifts, belonging within one body. Further, its warm and personal imagery expresses theology by "the body of Christ" that grows up into Christ its "head" (Eph. 4:15). Understanding church as *body* particularly challenges division, as in Corinth, where spiritual superiority sparked unhealthy competitiveness. "The eye cannot say to the hand, 'I don't need you.' . . . On the contrary those parts of the body that seem to be weaker are indispensable" (1 Cor. 12:21–22). Having different gifts should not separate believers from belonging together.

Picturing the church as *God's building work*, however, highlights other issues. First, in contrast with *body*, which stresses *differences between* believers, God's building emphasizes the *likenesses of* believers who are called to be like "living stones" (1 Pet. 2:4). Rather than highlighting individual gifts, the building picture requires all believers to have the *same* function—to be bonded together in God's construction work. Living stones contrast in size, age, and color, but no big deal is made out of differences. Most importantly, each believer must fit compactly with others by interlocking together to form

God's pattern—a solid structure with a coherent design. Believers resemble piles of bricks or stones ready to be used on God's construction site. Individuality is secondary to strong collective structure.

Second, building requires *God the Designer*. Great architects are revered for designing long-lasting, beautiful buildings, and we have the greatest designer— Father, Son, and Holy Spirit. Jesus's promise to Peter, "on this rock I will build my church" (Matt. 16:18), grounds building church as integral to his ministry, with cosmic repercussions revealing the "manifold wisdom of God . . . to the rulers and authorities in the heavenly realms" (Eph. 3:10). God is at work in every part of the construction process because this building is "in him" and "becomes a dwelling in which he lives by his Spirit" (Eph. 2:22). And his design is pivotal to his big story of creation. Act 4, the story of the church, lies between act 3, the incarnation of Christ, and act 5, the consummation of all things in Christ's return. God constructs living stones through every generation, placing them between those who have gone on before in the story of Israel and the early church and what will happen in the final triumph of Christ. God's design integrates believers into his narrative for the world.

The third issue concerning picturing the church as God's building work is that it stresses *structural unity*. Jesus is described as the "chief cornerstone" in whom "the whole building is joined together" (Eph. 2:20). Most commentators agree that this stone is foundational. Interestingly, a technical building term used for "joined together"—*synarmologoumene*—is found only in Ephesians 2:21 and 4:16. Its meaning "embraces the complicated process of masonry by which stones are fitted together."[1] God does not build his church haphazardly, but integrating living stones with the cornerstone, he skillfully aligns them together in his grand design (Eph. 2:19–20).

The fourth issue is that this building is a work *in progress*—"the whole building rises" (present tense, Eph. 2:21). The church is always in the process of community formation as believers continually join together within God's design, dependent on his direction and strength. Any disruption inevitably impedes progress because building God's household with the Holy Spirit living within requires strong unity. No wonder God's passion for unity and peace is evident throughout the New Testament (as in John 17:20–21; Eph. 2:14; 4:3–4).

Fifth, building implies *intentional leadership*. Early church leaders, apostles, prophets, evangelists, pastors, and teachers are all involved with communicating God's Word to his people. The outcome is "to prepare God's people for works of service so that the body of Christ may be built up" (Eph. 4:12). Later, in verse 16, the technical word for holding masonry together reemerges— *synarmologoumene*. Elsewhere I have described at length how the preacher's role necessarily involves leadership because God's Word has transformational power.[2] In *360-Degree Leadership*, I lament the prevalence of *thin-blooded preaching* that hinders building Christ's body. Because of its individualistic focus, lack of trinitarian theology, and low commitment to missional theology, such preaching fails to form community. In contrast, I urge that *full-blooded preaching* seize leadership responsibilities and proclaim courageously with community focus, trinitarian theology, and high missional commitment. I also urge preachers to exegete Scripture, discerning and applying creative tension *within* biblical texts in order that God build community. I pleaded for preachers to learn leadership skills, such as how to develop teams and enable change process, so they can move beyond delivering cerebral information or individualistic moralizing into church community building.

I believe that preachers have a key role in God's construction project. They, more than anyone else, have a responsibility to preach his Word and, depending on the Holy Spirit, to help lead community formation, urging reconciliation, unity, and mission with realism in dealing with conflict, forgiveness, peacemaking, and service. As masons skillfully join together masonry blocks (Eph. 2:20), so preachers encourage living stones to fit together, keeping community vision alive and confronting ever-present dangers of disunity and conflict with diligence and prayer. Of course, they are not the only leaders, but as proclaimers of God's Word and purpose for community, they have a prime place.

Sixth, and importantly, this building picture describes *worship at its best*. Worship is the most appropriate way to sum up the process and outcome of God's building work. Living stones are being built up into the "royal priesthood" of God's "called-out people," committed to new life together, "offering spiritual sacrifices acceptable to God" (1 Pet. 2:4–10). And coming from a "holy nation," this worship concerns practice in the world: "Abstain from the desires of the flesh. . . . Conduct yourselves honorably among the Gentiles, so that . . . they may see your honorable deeds and glorify God when he comes to judge" (1 Pet. 2:9–12). Worship moves beyond four walls into mission and ethics. God's spiritual architecture builds big-picture worship with the widest of dimensions living out his narrative for the world.

Earlier we noted how myopic preachers have no conception that weekly praise gatherings might cumulatively build community but instead assume such events have short shelf life with few communal expectations. Hearers therefore come and go without growing together. Congregations are composed of individuals who bear little responsibility for one another, let alone for the lost world around them. So, sadly, people's attitudes, love, service, and mission together show little sign of changing for the better. The church marks time on the spot with no visible maturing. In dramatic contrast, big-picture worship creates worshiping communities on the move as living stones humbly commit to be built together, growing into a royal priesthood that glorifies God before the world.

Community formation deserves a higher profile today. At a recent preachers' conference, I asked attendees when they had last preached on 1 Peter 2:4–12 with its big vision of God's worshiping community. Had any of them developed the metaphor of living stones to stress the likeness of believers as building blocks or emphasized how God wants to build people together? Most shook their heads. Afterward the chairman confessed, "I am amazed to realize I have never once preached about the church as God's building or emphasized how worshipers are to be like living stones bonded together. I am going to start preaching that when I get back!"

Missional Theology

Currently, it seems almost impossible to attend any Christian conference without hearing the word *missional*. Recently, a Christian leader said to me rather dismissively, "Missional—it's the latest jargon that everybody is using, yet nobody really understands. Sounds good, though." Though often overused and misunderstood, however, the term *missional church* has emerged out of important insights from the Gospel and Our Culture Network, spearheaded by the work of Lesslie Newbigin.[3] When used rightly, it goes to the heart of describing God's spiritual architecture and his design for new community.

The Western church can be analyzed in many ways. Earlier, when warning against naivete in dealing with culture, I mentioned Dan Kimball's contrast between the church in the Modern Era and in the Post-Christian Era, picturing them as trees, each with a surrounding *atmosphere* fed by *nutrients*. The church/tree in the Modern Era has a Judeo-Christian atmosphere with the Judeo-Christian God and ethics based on the Judeo-Christian worldview learned from family, even if a person is not religious. Its nutrients are monotheism, rationalism, religious proposition with truth that is systematic, local, and individualistic. But the church/tree in the Post-Christian Era has a "global, pluralistic atmosphere" in which all religions are equal, with Christianity suffering a negative reputation for finger-pointing. Its ethics are based on the cultural level of acceptance and personal choice learned from the media and peers. Its nutrients are pluralism, experience, mysticism, narrative with preference that is fluid, global, and communal/tribal.[4] Kimball recognized that in reality these two sets of atmosphere and nutrients often overlap in any one church, with inevitable confusion.

In describing "feeble community formation" (chap. 3), I also used Craig van Gelder's analysis, which contrasts the corporate church with the missional church—the *doing* church with the *being* church.[5] He distinguishes between these two churches based on how they view their own purpose. On one hand, the corporate church, embedded in the European version of Constantinian Christendom, understands itself to exist "as an organization to accomplish something, normally *on behalf of God in the world*."[6] This *doing* church likely focuses on projects and programs that emphasize human vision and energy, fed by nutrients that are rational, systematic, and local.

On the other hand, another church model has arisen because of convergence in missiological circles around a mission theology related to the *Missio Dei* and the kingdom of God. The missional church's self-understanding is "that it is created by the Spirit as a called and sent community to participate fully in God's mission in the world."[7] Rather than focusing on doing things for God, the *being* church sees the world as the horizon, with its parameters depending less on members' energies and more on God's redemptive reign in Christ and empowering by the Holy Spirit. Such an understanding of the church emphasizes how God is forming his new people to join in his triune mission. "God is about a big purpose in and for the whole of creation. . . . A missional church is a community of God's people who live into the imagination that they are, by their very nature, God's missionary people living as a demonstration of what God plans to do in and for all of creation in Jesus Christ."[8]

The *doing* church is marked by thin theology, operating by practical unitarianism, as members fulfill obligations to the church's organizational life. In contrast, the *being* church calls members to grow together in spiritual and missional formation as the body of Christ, in God's building work, maturing into his purposes. It commits to the vision of Ephesians 4:1–12 with worship a long-term, lifelong process that keeps moving toward the goal of glorifying God as his new people come into being—"living as a demonstration of what God plans to do in and for all of creation in Jesus Christ."

The *doing* corporate church all too easily customizes faith into culture, deriving values uncritically without testing them by biblical standards. Such thinking tends to accommodate gospel to society's goals of security, personal happiness, family needs, and social satisfaction, all the while limiting worship to music on Sundays only. The corporate church presumes it lives in an atmosphere of the Judeo-Christian God with ethics largely based on a Judeo-Christian worldview. Strongly fed by individualism, gospel, and a church focus on *me*, it has little notion of being built into community in contrast with the surrounding culture. But the missional church recognizes the vital importance of developing church community with distinctive practices that live out the gospel challenge in its own particular missionary context. It takes 1 Peter 2:4–12 seriously.

In missional theology, Newbigin called for a relationship of true dialogue—a process of new converts (in community) being open to living out the unique implications of the gospel within the particularities of human cultures, living out evangelism in front of others.[9] Every church engaged in such missionary dialogue is changing into something new as part of a continuing process.

Modernity's individualistic creed mocks such a possibility and continues sponsoring the corporate church, encouraging pious consumerism—choosing churches according to preference, convenience, and success. Evangelism is left to the preacher and occasional projects. Numbers matter more than building community. Worshipers are downgraded to attendees, oblivious to mission responsibility for brothers, sisters, and neighbors. "We are more impressed by a church of 4,000 people who have no clue about God's character and His expectations than by a church of 100 deeply committed saints who are serving humankind in quiet but significant ways."[10]

Yet these one hundred deeply committed saints are actively cocreating a Christian culture of big-picture worship. Interestingly, Marva Dawn strongly warns against idolatries of contemporary culture invading the church, but she also uses the word *culture* more positively to describe "the culture of worship." Because Christians are called to be in the world but not of the world, Christian worship must be subversive in the world because it "will turn our values, habits, and ideas upside-down as it forms our character,"[11] yet it must be not of the world, resisting its idolatries. Such subversive worship culture acts negatively in order to be positive.

> God's revelation, conveyed in worship through hymns, sermons and liturgies unmasks our illusions about ourselves. It exposes our pride, our individualism, our self-centeredness—in short our sin. But worship also offers forgiveness, healing, transformation, motivation and courage to work in the world for God's justice and peace—in short, salvation in its largest sense.[12]

Dynamics of Community Formation

Combining the picture of the church as God's building work with living stones and the vision of church as missional community involves complex dynamics (already anticipated in figures 3 and 4). Big-picture worship not only bonds believers together in Christ, empowered by the Spirit as a royal priesthood declaring the praises of God, but also forms a "holy nation," with believers living good lives among neighbors (1 Pet. 2:9, 12). Community formation therefore occurs in several different directions—inwardly and outwardly, backward and forward, personally and corporately, by both verbal and nonverbal means working explicitly and implicitly. And always, God's construction work needs continuous worship.

Continuousness

"And let us consider how to provoke one another to love and good deeds, not neglecting to meet together, as is the habit of some, but encouraging one another" (Heb. 10:24–25). This command is primarily about people growing together in community by regular contact. Strong communities cannot form unless people meet frequently and keep encouraging one another. "In worship we practice the basic skills of our faith. We practice them again and again, so that they become second nature to us, and in becoming second nature, they become the way we see the world and live in it."[13] Continuous practice is essential for developing many aspects, including language, character, countercultural formation, and ethics.

Foreign languages can be learned from teachers and textbooks but also from visiting other countries and interacting with their people. Speaking French comes alive when visiting France. Similarly, the people of God learn the new language of worship not only through teachers and Scripture but also by continuous living among worshipers who speak it. Worship language includes the vocabulary of praise and confession, of God's three persons, of Christ's lordship and kingdom, of sin and grace, and of reconciliation and mission. As members of the baptized community, "we talk funny" because of the "weirdness of the gospel."

> The gospel is not a set of interesting ideas about which we are supposed to make up our minds. The gospel is intrusive news that evokes a new set of practices, a complex of habits, a way of living in the world, discipleship. The gospel means to engender, to evoke, a peculiar experience that we would not have had before we met the gospel.[14]

George Lindbeck's important book *The Nature of Doctrine* triggered considerable theological discussion about language. Claiming that there are three main understandings of religion—cognitive-propositionalist (concerned with objective realities), experiential-expressivist (focused on experience in spiritually symbolic terms), and cultural-linguistic (religion as life and language of the community of faith)—he argues for the last. While not wishing to exclude the other categories, his emphasis on religion as life and language is especially relevant to worship. How worshipers talk about their doctrine and live its consequences help form their understanding. So, for example, expressing language about the trinitarian doctrine of God as three in one shapes the way worshipers live out and think through what it means to participate in God's triune community.

Jonathan Wilson therefore describes "worship as language school" with preachers having a key role in helping communities learn this language of doctrine. First, as grammarians they need to teach and guard the "basic grammar of faith—faith in Jesus Christ, the Trinity, Christology, salvation by grace." Second, as language teachers they must teach others how to use this grammar. "The pastor must put the language of the faith to work, teaching others how to refer their work, their family, their feelings, and their fears to the gospel."[15] And like learning French by immersion with the French language in France, worshipers best learn to speak about who God is and who they are called to be and about sin, grace, forgiveness, reconciliation, and kingdom by interacting continuously within community and abiding in Christ.

Learning Christian grammar by repeating liturgy week after week develops the character of individuals and community. As this chapter's opening quote challenged:

Who you are as an individual believer depends greatly upon the character of the community of believers in which you are nurtured. How faithfully does that community incarnate God's presence and pass on the narratives that reveal God when they assemble together? . . . How (and whom) we worship nurtures personal character.[16]

Tod Bolsinger rightly claims: "Christian transformation comes through the pattern, personal relationship and power of God to the believer found in Jesus Christ through the Spirit experienced within the community."[17] How a community worships impacts belief and behavior profoundly over time, for worship "schools us in ways of seeing the world and of being in it."[18]

As worshipers develop character, they need to *unlearn* usual habits of speech and ways of thinking. Instead of *living of the world* with a language of ingratitude, oblivious to sin and heedless of neighbors, worshipers learn to live thankfully, repentantly, and lovingly *in the world but not of the world*. No longer should they "use the language of politics (we have rights), of psychotherapy (we have complexes), or of economics (we are owed)."[19] Rather, they develop a subversive *culture of worship* as a countercultural community. Such habitual worship works by a process aptly described by the ancient doctrine of *lex orandi, lex credendi* (the law of prayer, the law of belief). This doctrine emphasizes the priority of practicing prayer in the way of Christ. By *doing* prayer, worshipers deepen belief in Jesus Christ. By doing worship together, within his community, worshipers deepen belief and life in God's will.

Repercussions from such alternative community life are far-reaching. Instead of succumbing to popularist organizational aims such as growing numbers, satisfying customers, and building bigger barns, worshiping communities develop as a missionary people seeking to impact society as a holy nation and royal priesthood.

Continuous worship practice also affects ethics. Intriguingly, the term *political worship* has been developed to describe how early Christian congregations constituted a particular social framework as they repeatedly worshiped. Of course, *political* does not refer to political parties or policies or rights. Rather, it expresses the church's "specific, social form of life, a *communio* in which believers find their basic political existence."[20] By worshiping continuously, "men and women have *to attend and participate in it again and again*, so as to practice at the proper place what Barth calls 'the art of correct asking about God's will.' . . . Its ethical knowledge will always be available to it only in the mode of 'being,' embodied in its own praxis."[21]

Through regular worship, believers learn to acquiesce to God's judgment and develop social behavior guided by the "law of the Spirit" (Rom. 8:2). By disengaging from the world's morality, believers can come together, enabling a different kind of acting and judgment. "It is the act of sharing in the praise of God, the consensus in the confession of faith and the entering into God's acts 'for others' which is the mark of ethics springing from worship."[22]

Christian congregations are therefore assemblies of *Christian citizens*, "fellow citizens with the saints" (Eph. 2:19) with their own "political existence" governed by the "law of the Spirit." Bernd Wannenwecht notes several sources of Christian ethics—in Scripture, natural law, and Christian experience—but he claims that worship enables *interaction* of all these:

> In worship we find the core principle, "God is to be worshiped" . . . and the right use of the biblical canon, which was established precisely for the requirements of worship; and in worship both these things—and more—come together in a comprehensive sensory, intellectual, and spiritual experience. This is worship as a form of life.[23]

Many have argued for a strong relationship between worship and ethics. David Stubbs instructively links together three contrasting theologians. Karl Barth envisaged ethics of reconciliation focused on three central *kingdomlike* practices: baptism, the Lord's Prayer, and the Lord's Supper. For example, he claimed that all of human life is to be the "dynamic actualization" of the Lord's Prayer: "He [God] wills that their whole life become invocations of this kind." John Yoder, an Anabaptist theologian, identified five key liturgical practices: baptism, Eucharist, mutual correction, the diversification of gifts and ministry, and open dialogue under the direction of the Holy Spirit. "They are the actions of God, in and with, through and under what men and women do. Where they are happening, the people of God is real in the world." Alexander Schmemann, a Russian Orthodox theologian, challenged individualistic approaches to the Eucharist by asserting that twelve crucial moments occur in the liturgy "in which the patterns of human activity are united to those of God," including assembly and offering. For example, the offering is to be viewed as "a central representative act of the total offering of ourselves to Christ and to each other."[24]

By using new language, developing godly character, shaping countercultural community, and influencing ethics, regular worship helps build *living stones* into God's worshiping community. But several other dynamics also operate.

Both Inward and Outward

Community building pulls in two directions. Moving *inwardly*, building community deepens fellowship. Ever since the first Christians' dazzling commitment, community life has had four hallmarks: teaching, fellowship (*koinonia*), the breaking of bread, and prayer (Acts 2:42–47). These continue as foundational community-building elements of gathered worship. By developing collective awareness of brothers and sisters, such worship expresses love to

God and to one another, not only "loving with words and tongue but with actions and in truth" (1 John 3:18).

Christians are also pulled in another direction to live *outwardly* for God in his world. Early church worship both praised God and enjoyed the favor of all the people (Acts 2:47). As a city on a hill, Christians in worship draw people together into his community, to Christ, the light of the world. Yet as light it shines before the world (Matt. 5:14–15), and as salt it impacts society (Matt. 5:13). "Salt is often preached of as a preservative. But salt is also an agent of change. For instance, spread it on meat and it will change the meat's flavor, color, texture, and shelf-life. . . . Salt is an aggressive instrument of transformation."[25]

These two worship dynamics belong together, just as God's twin command to love him with all of ourselves is inseparable from loving our neighbor as ourselves (Matt. 22:37–38). Some communities, however, opt for only one direction. Often the inner journey seems *safer*, assuming that building fellowship in love is easier than serving and witnessing to others. An older pastor lamented, "What upsets me most about my church is that people like to come together for fellowship and seem to really enjoy being together, but they just don't want to serve others." Such inwardness can downgrade into self-serving fellowship that focuses only on others inside the group. In the opposite direction, however, some churches may be so focused on activities for others that they neglect *koinonia*. So strong is their desire to minister outside the group, they forget to grow together in God's grace.

Can these two worship movements of fellowship and mission develop strongly and simultaneously? Some seem unconvinced. Mark Driscoll, an emergent church leader, asks, "Will your church have a mission of community, or be a community of mission?"[26] This question forces worshipers to choose between *koinonia* and mission. But as God builds living stones into his community, he forms *both* a mission of community, where people grow closer together in Christ, and a community of mission where people serve others for Christ's sake. Both are essential for Christian community formation. The inner journey of developing fellowship matures community for its outer journey of "works of service" (Eph. 4:12).

One church framed its mission statement in terms of "gathering to scatter, and scattering to gather" in order to stress that both movements are complementary. Gathering is the primary movement, leading to scattering and re-gathering. Growing community in both directions simultaneously is no easy task. Developing good relationships across gender, race, age, and social differences is hugely demanding, but so too is the process of worshipers moving out in mission into homes, streets, and places of work. Mark Labberton calls worship "dangerous" because "worship names what matters most; the way human beings are created to reflect God's glory by embodying God's character in lives that seek righteousness and do justice."[27] As a sobering footnote, the church that framed its mission statement about being a gathering-scattering community declined rapidly from 150 to 50 members because many rejected the missional vision; then it slowly rebuilt a community with worshipers who had gained fresh understanding of what it means to be church.

I mentioned this gathering-scattering theme in class, and one student burst out, "Please, let's have a reality check! Just how do we *do* community like this? We glibly talk about growing in community, but honestly, how can it happen?" In response, several students enthused about the role of small groups. Some belonged to churches small enough to develop relationships of accountability and trust, while others described the value of small groups within larger fellowships. Worshiping together on a smaller scale does seem essential for growing deeper fellowship and greater service; living stones only build in close proximity. Indeed some small groups have developed a *new monasticism* in which members covenant together to follow the *rule of life*, exercise disciplined prayer together, and at the same time practice hospitality to the stranger, peacemaking, and reconciliation.[28]

I recall how some of the small worship groups in my Cambridge church worked through both inward and outward directions. In common with other churches, there was much tension over music styles. In one small group with a wide age range, an eighty-year-old, long-term member staunchly opposed contemporary music. Yet as she grew to know and love others (especially younger people), she understood their desire for new music styles. Through honest sharing and praying over differences, she came to realize that *koinonia* is too important to be ruined by music. Indeed, over time she became an ardent supporter of young people and their worship and, importantly, they grew to love and support her (and accept her music too).

Interestingly, that same group faced challenges outwardly. Like others, they wrestled with the right response to the homeless who were sleeping on the church steps and begging for money after church services—a problem I mentioned earlier. Could they help provide shelter and food on church premises? Pushing beyond meeting for gathered worship, could they offer hospitality to these needy neighbors? Through a difficult process of prayer and discussion, group members eventually joined others on the front line of the church community's practical mission to the homeless.

Both Backward and Forward

God's design extends far beyond the story of any particular local church in both directions. He places each group of believers within his world narrative, described earlier by five acts. Belonging to the church story in act 4, worshipers necessarily look backward to God's actions in the past, forming people of the old covenant and creating people of the new covenant in Christ. Gathered worship tells out this story, as "the presenting, remembering, and re-presenting of God through the Word and the Table comes first to the congregation, which then in turn responds."[29]

"Our deepest emotions are intimately linked with how we remember. . . . Without the capacity to remember, we lack a sense of narrative about our lives and our world."[30] *Remembering* focuses on the story of creation, covenant, salvation in Christ, and consummation of God's kingdom. By remembering the Christian story in which we belong, we not only reappropriate God's story as present gift—"This do in remembrance of me" (1 Cor. 11:24–25)—but also grow together as God's people on his journey. Community identity is shaped by ever renewing community memory.

But worshipers also need to look forward. *Prolepsis* anticipates the continuing, unfolding story of God's work through his church in the world. Far beyond immediate agendas is the eschatological dimension that looks not to the things that are seen but to the things that are eternal (2 Cor. 4:18) and beyond the horizon with God's perspective. The church lives in hope that looks into God's future and his promises of glory.

Reenacting God's story week after week, hearing his words in Scripture, and proclaiming him in Word and the Lord's Supper (1 Cor. 11:26) encourage such wide-screen perspective. When churches neglect the past or the future, they lose their sense of place in God's big purposes.

Both Personal and Corporate

Community formation also develops both personally and corporately. On one hand, *individuals* need to be integrated into community, learning how to grow within the church. On the other hand, the church as a *whole community* of nurtured people must learn how to live out God's mission for the world.

The integration of individuals into the church has received considerable attention. For example, Robert Webber commends a four-stage process of spiritual formation, using terms from early church practice, first described by Hippolytus, a third-century Christian leader in Rome. At stage 1, the *seeker* in Christian inquiry enters through a rite of welcome into a process leading to conversion. Stage 2 prepares the *hearer* in discipleship through the rite of enrollment with commitment to become baptized. In stage 3, the *kneeler* moves toward baptism and full membership in the church. At stage 4, the *faithful* actively participates in the church.[31]

Being integrated into a worshiping community has extraordinary repercussions for individuals. Leslie Weatherhead gives a memorable example:

> There is power in belonging. I knew a man who, one Sunday evening in Berlin, was very lonely and very tempted to enter an evil house. Photographs outside allured him. Bodily needs tortured him. He was far from home. No one would know. . . . Suddenly he moved away. (I have often wondered if prayer at that moment was being offered for him at home.) When asked what sudden thought had

moved him out of temptation's power, he said, "I *belong* to a church at home. I couldn't have gone back and faced them if I had let them down. I belong to them."[32]

Perhaps the most potent signs of the importance of belonging are evident when worshipers are dying. Some ask for a bedside communion service, others for favorite Scriptures and the Lord's Prayer. David Watson, the British evangelist who died at the height of his powers at age fifty, said that listening to his church singing brought him the greatest comfort in his last days, preparing him for heaven. My wife, Carol, is a volunteer hospice visitor, and she has witnessed several occasions when friends have come to worship with a dying patient. Sometimes informally, a group has recited Scripture and said prayers around the bedside. Recently, a group of Christian friends joined in worship, saying prayers from memory, clearly connecting with their loved one, and evoking lifelong worship remembrance. "It was inspiring," she said.

But less attention seems to be given to the parallel process. At the same time as believers are being integrated into the community, the *community as a whole* is learning to live missionally. God seeks people who are corporately focused on him in praise and collectively motivated in mission rather than those who are continuing to be caught up with the narcissistic, self-pleasing goals of society. The whole community needs to learn how to be a missionary people, expressing the wide range of mission responsibility, including both evangelism and social action. Rather than leave evangelism to a few, all are willing to witness to the hope that is in us (1 Pet. 3:15). Instead of allowing personal initiatives to go unnoticed, the whole community gives conscious support. "So when one person from the community visits someone in prison, she does so with the prayer support of the community. And that same community participates with her in processing the questions of justice, forgiveness and reconciliation that arise from such ministry in the context of the kingdom of God."[33]

Such spiritual formation of individuals and community does not happen spontaneously. Rather, regular, gathered worship nurtures both individuals into community and community into mission as worshipers not only learn kingdom language but also develop countercultural community with godly ethics. Over the long term, believers learn to be forgiving, show grace, live with integrity, and serve their neighbors because they worship continuously with others who are forgiving, are gracious, have integrity, and model mission. Living stones learn from other living stones to hold fast in God's construction project—a combination of learning to hold fast to God and being held fast by God.

Both Verbal and Nonverbal

Community formation occurs through both *verbal* and *nonverbal* communication. Preachers obviously concentrate on the former, rightly claiming that God's Word effects transformation—inwardly, outwardly, personally, and collectively (Rom. 10:14–15; 2 Cor. 5:20). As they preach God's Word, not only are preachers *language teachers* helping believers speak of God's three persons, of Christ's lordship and kingdom, of sin and grace, and of reconciliation enabling mission, but they are also community builders—especially as they use the plural *we*. Sadly, the plural *you* in Scripture is often lost in translation, allowing individuals to respond individualistically. The Authorized Version of Scripture (King James) contrasts *ye* (when a plural subject) with *thee* (a singular subject), so that community implications are clear (as in Matt. 6:33; 28:19; Luke 24:48; Acts 1:8). Preachers need to counter endemic individualism continually by emphasizing plurality in Scripture. Of course, personal challenges are necessary but should always be heard within community.

Marva Dawn challenges preachers about building community because of the gospel's community implications. They should stress, for example, "that faith is not something we construct by ourselves for our personal use, but rather a gift, into which we are invited, that has been passed on through the community of believers since Sarah and Abraham."[34] Foundational doctrines such as creation in the image of the Triune God have profound importance for communal living. We are made in his image—in community. Further, preachers build community by Scripture's specific instructions "for being hospitable, for carrying the corporate prayers into daily life, for each adult to participate more in the spiritual nurturing of the congregation's children, for more outreach to the neighbors."[35]

But alongside words, Don Saliers suggests that congregations must learn "the *hidden* languages of worship—time, space, sound and silence, the visible, and the bodily gestures belonging to narratives of creation, redemption, and consummation."[36] *Time* involves cycles of days, weeks, and years. Christians live between Sundays and through the Christian year to grow mature habits of identity. *Space* relates to places of worship and what we hear and see within them. *Sound and silence* are both important: "Music and silence must surround the reading and hearing of the Church's corporate memories contained in the Scriptures."[37] Music is especially important for reinforcing the verbal. *Visual gesture and movement* focus on baptism and the Lord's Supper but also include art, drama, poetry, and even dance.

Words and actions combine in profound ways to shape community spirituality. Saliers defines spirituality as "humanity at full stretch before God in relation to the world and to neighbor" and describes how a community's spirituality develops through "a coming alive to the heights and depths as well as the ordinariness of being human before God." He then sums up worship in that definition we have already met: "At its best, Christian worship presents a vision of life created, sustained, redeemed and held in the mystery of grace. What we do together in acknowledging God 'schools' us in ways of seeing the world and of being in it."[38] Such schooling toward new identity occurs through the whole range of verbal and nonverbal communication.

Both Explicit and Implicit

Further, such communication works both *explicitly* and *implicitly*. *Explicit* worship practices include preaching, baptism, the Lord's Supper, singing, praying, offering, and for some, foot washing.[39] These key practices clearly express believers' relationships within the body of Christ.

Less obviously, *implicit* formation occurs through worship's repetitive nature, reinforcing priorities, patterns, and emphases over time—for better or worse. Many testify to the continuing influence of early worship habits. For example, until he was eighteen, Sam Hamstra worshiped with weekly liturgy that included the Ten Commandments. "My liturgical experience led me to conclude that the Decalogue was more important than other aspects of the Christian life, such as the fruit of the Spirit."[40] Yet because he also witnessed his parents' awe and reverence, he acknowledges his debt that, like his parents, he cannot now approach worship without awe and reverence.

By continued practice, worshipers develop capacities that Saliers deems "essential to true humanity." *Recalling and retelling* the story give it human identity. Corporate *praise and thanks* to God expresses profound gratitude and shape a grateful people. "A life devoid of gratitude becomes incapable of receiving gifts and eventually receiving gifts." (Remember the first toolbox question.) *Confession* before God also causes us to encounter truth about ourselves that would not otherwise be known. *Intercession*, praying for the world and its suffering, helps believers identify with the needs of others, forcing issues of ethics and justice onto the agenda. Worship changes people—how they understand God, the world, and themselves. "In recalling who God is and who we are, we identify the world to itself as what it yet shall be under the reign of God."[41]

Many worship dynamics live in tension and complexity as God builds his community inwardly and outwardly, backward and forward, personally and corporately, verbally and nonverbally, and explicitly and implicitly. The next chapter integrates all these into four stages of formation and completes the questions to be posed to worship leaders. One question, however, specifically arises from this chapter regarding who we are addressing in worship.

Question Toolbox

1. *Gift*: Are we thankfully receiving this gift from the Triune God of grace?
2. *Magnification*: Are we expressing its richness toward God?
3. *Scripture*: Are we allowing Scripture to direct?
4. *Audiences*: Are we addressing two audiences?

At first sight, this fourth toolbox question may seem strange. Isn't worship all about addressing God in three persons? Isn't he all-important? We have centered big-picture worship on praising the all-inclusive God, bowing down and serving him to whom all glory, power, and honor is due. Kierkegaard famously pictured worshipers being *onstage* in front of God, who is in the audience. Worshipers should focus on God first and foremost.

Yet even as worship addresses God, it also needs to speak to other worshipers. Because community formation involves growth in different directions—in fellowship with God and in growing together for mission to others—this fourth question necessarily asks about language that builds community for God's sake. Words directed to God should also address his community. This need for a double audience is made explicit in instructions about singing. Christian music expresses both "gratitude in your hearts . . . to God" (Col. 3:16) and "speaking to one another" (Eph. 5:19 NASB). Words in music should both praise God and also teach and affirm one another.

Perhaps you can recall your first experience of singing with a larger group. I remember belonging to a small youth group that was self-conscious about singing, but then I went away to a missionary summer school where several hundred young people sang enthusiastically. The thrill of joining in that first hymn ("How Great Thou Art") not only focused me on God but also awoke me to the wonder of finding how much I belong with others who testify to the same truth. And as these words were directed to God, they also expressed the reality of belonging together as God's new community.

What is true of music also applies to other parts of worship. Whenever we pray, take up an offering, read Scripture, or participate in the Lord's Supper, we are not only doing something for God but also addressing each other as community. Focused primarily on God, worship also challenges worshipers to grow as God's royal priesthood. In order that worship forms community, its leaders must ask, "Are we purposely addressing two audiences?"

9

Integrating Elements of Community Formation

> For so many people today, worship has become dull, intellectual, cold, formal, and alienating; or it has become, consciously or unconsciously, a form of emotional exercise that ultimately has little effect on what goes on in a person's life during the rest of the week.
>
> Robert Webber

As a child I was fascinated by the story of Sir Christopher Wren, and I still recall pages from a children's book describing this remarkable British architect and his masterpiece, St. Paul's Cathedral in London. On my first visit to St. Paul's, I was captivated by its immense flight of steps leading up from the street into soaring dimensions of beauty. Such massive structures combined with delicate features as sunlight filtered in and picked out the architectural details. The organ was playing, which added to the wonder as my eyes were drawn upward to the massive dome at the center with the whispering gallery around. Later I came to know and appreciate other Wren buildings, but nothing compared to that first experience. Much later still I saw that amazing photograph of the cathedral lit up by fire and smoke during a blitz in the Second World War. All around buildings were ablaze and crashing to the ground, yet the cathedral with its majestic dome lit by flames withstood defiantly, riding high above the destruction. It symbolized the indestructibility of spirit and truth.

As I have thought about how big-picture worship involves building God's community, I envisage something similarly grand and indestructible that "the gates of Hades will not prevail against" (Matt. 16:18). And I have wondered whether different aspects of believers growing together might be expressed by a diagram, like an architect's front elevation of a beautiful building, that sums up God's vision of the whole project. Could the process of spiritual formation be represented by a series of stages constructed upon each other that together build up a strong, viable structure?

Tentatively, I sketched out a four-stage design that sought to integrate issues raised in the last chapter. Drawn impressionistically, with broad brushstrokes, the result obviously lacks a draftsman's accuracy but is offered with the hope that it encourages others to explore worship's community dimensions, how different worship elements build together, and what different types of preaching are required (see fig. 5). While Hippolytus's four stages—seeker, hearer, kneeler, and faithful—concern personal formation, this diagram attempts a more expansive vision, including personal development within formation of the whole church community.

Someone criticized this diagram's static appearance: "It ought to be drawn like the 360-degree dynamic cycle, not flattened out in boxes." Another had just seen a 3-D movie and suggested I ought to give out 3-D glasses! Yet another said I ought to devise a mobile hologram so that the whole appears to be moving continuously, which it actually *does* as it belongs within worship's spiritual dynamic (figs. 3 and 4). Yet in spite of the diagram's limitations, each box represents something vital for community formation. Each resembles a building block that when constructed together represents something of the *front elevation* of God's master plan. New believers enter the building process at the bottom, on the left-hand side, at the first stage of personal formation. But as they develop and grow with others upwardly and are continuously joined by newcomers, they learn to be part of God's bigger plan that is ever expanding within his ultimate purposes. Figure 5 describes incessant growth, with new worshipers continually joining stage 1 and growing in community formation. Myopic preaching is content to leave believers in the first box, but big-picture worship pushes believers toward God's grand design.

Four Stages of Community Formation

Figure 5 depicts four stages of formation, beginning with initiation and building sequentially through integration into character formation and missional living. Of course, such divisions oversimplify complex dynamics that often occur simultaneously and cannot be separated out easily. Yet there is a developing *process* by which living stones are built together into a mature construction. Living stones do not spontaneously assemble into mature relationships. At each stage, believers need to grow in both personal and community formation, which is described in the middle two columns.

Figure 5. Four Stages of Worship Formation

Stages	Personal Formation	Community Formation	Types of Preaching
4. *Missional living*	new culture	holy nation, royal priesthood (1 Pet. 2:4–12)	missional, prophetic
3. *Character formation*	new character, new preferences	growing in unity (Eph. 4:1–16)	pastoral leadership through preaching
2. *Integration*—expressing acts of worship as Christ's body	new patterns, new story	the Lord's Supper— corporate belonging (1 Cor. 11:17–33)	liturgical, salvation history
1. *Initiation* into the body of Christ with trinitarian participation	new language, new relationships	baptism—corporate responsibility (Rom. 6:1–11)	evangelistic, doctrinal, celebrative

The last column, "types of preaching," opens up a range of different kinds of preaching that are necessary in order for a community to grow through various stages. This category signals the breadth of preaching required, although separating types of preaching into different stages is inevitably artificial because all kinds of preaching may be appropriate at any stage. For example, at the initial stage, evangelistic preaching declares gospel truth boldly so that individual believers make their faith-response to Christ. Yet *salvation history preaching* that places worshipers within God's story from creation to consummation is necessary from an early stage too, though I place it later in stage 2. At stage 4, as the whole community develops its mission, so missional preaching needs to challenge the church collectively about developing a missionary, subversive culture that confronts the world. It also needs to be prophetic. Listing these types of preaching opens up a challenging range of possibilities for preachers, and all types are necessary for God to build his holy nation and royal priesthood.

First reactions may well regard this as too idealistic a picture that will serve only to increase disappointment when churches inevitably fail. I recognize the need to balance these God-given possibilities to belong together with the realities of our continuing sinfulness. Theologians sometimes contrast the theology of glory with the theology of the cross. Sometimes groups of believers adopt only a theology of glory with supreme confidence in spiritual victory. For example, the church in Corinth (as attested in 1 and 2 Cor.) seems to be so sure of its spiritual gifting that it erroneously believes "everything is permissible" (1 Cor. 10:23 NIV). With scant regard for others within the body of Christ, they denigrate the physical realm as of little consequence. As spiritual optimists, they claim God's glory. The apostle Paul, however, challenges them that Jesus Christ was crucified and that they need to identify with his death and not only his victory. This means realism about sin in their midst and about their vulnerabilities and failures. A theology of the cross allows no cheap grace or easy victory but rather calls for spiritual realism. These four stages are not described with facile optimism but with a theology both of the cross and of glory. Much can go wrong, which only reinforces the need for God's grace at every step.

Each stage will be considered briefly in turn, and at the end of the chapter two additional questions will be posed for worship leaders.

Initiation

So much tumultuously rushes in on new worshipers during this first stage. Hearing the gospel challenge, they are faced by the grace of Christ and his call to "repent, and be baptized" (Acts 2:38). As they respond, the new language of worship opens up: Scripture, sin and grace, kingdom, and community. Singing hymns and songs, offering prayers, and hearing sermons all help them learn this worship language. Speaking in new ways goes hand in hand with thinking theologically, for new worshipers need to understand the lordship of Jesus Christ within the Trinity, with the Father and Holy Spirit. At this formative stage, it is also critical to learn about responsible Christian relationships. Bluntly, will new worshipers stay in the first box of personal formation all their lives?

Two choices face new believers. On one hand, faith in Jesus Christ may be mainly practiced as a commitment to Jesus Christ *without* belonging to a community. Individual spirituality focuses on personal spiritual relationship with God with little sense of entering community with fellow worshipers. Unfortunately, myopic preaching endorses this choice. On the other hand, faith in Jesus Christ may be practiced as involvement in *two* interconnected sets of relationships. First, joined to Jesus as Lord, belonging within the Trinity, worship is received as a gift—"participating through the Holy Spirit in the incarnate Son's communion with the Father and the Son's mission from the Father to the world."[1] Such participation invites wonder, awe, and celebration. (Remember, the first worship question asks how thankfully we respond to God's triune gift of worship.) But second, being joined to Jesus Christ also means integration into his church—his body, his building.

Whichever choice is made highlights the role that baptism plays in community formation. Baptismal theology is complicated by its two practices—infant baptism and believer's baptism—and it is difficult to identify common themes.

The two most important issues, however, relate to whether God's interaction with those baptized is perceived to be weak or strong and whether it is seen as an individual or corporate act. The contrast about how much God is involved is often summarized as the distinction between *sign* or *sacrament*. Baptism as sign testifies primarily to an individual's relationship with Christ with little expectation of God working in the event; baptism as sacrament, however, emphasizes God's present action.

Earlier we cautioned that the word *sacrament* stirs up much resistance from evangelicals because of assumptions that it represents some priestly, impersonal magic. While rejecting outright notions of priestly, impersonal magic, many preachers (including myself) nevertheless see baptism as a rite appointed by Christ himself that marks a high point of a relationship of faith and commitment in which God *does* act in vital ways. From a Reformed perspective, James Torrance quotes the Westminster Confession regarding infant baptism as a "sign and seal of the covenant of grace, immediately instituted by God to represent Christ and his benefits."[2] Seeing this covenant as a unilateral covenant made over nineteen hundred years ago in Christ, its one baptism (Eph. 4:5) is threefold:

1. Christ's baptism is *for us*—supremely by baptism in blood on the cross (Col. 2:11–14).
2. Christ's baptism is *of us* by the Holy Spirit as he continues to baptize, making members of his body.
3. *Incorporation into Christ*—"Christ baptizes us into a life of sonship, of service, of dying, and of rising with him in newness of life (Rom. 6). He baptizes us into that life of communion for which we were created in the image of the Triune God, to be co-lovers."[3]

In believer's baptism, the covenant is not considered unilateral but bilateral, entered into as a seal both of God's grace and of personal faith and commitment. Indeed, everything attributed to faith is also attributed to baptism in Scripture: union with Christ, participation in his death and resurrection, membership in God's family, giving of the Spirit, inheritance of the kingdom, and salvation. Alongside "for by grace you have been saved through faith" (Eph. 2:8) is set, "and baptism . . . now saves you" (1 Pet. 3:21). The Triune God encounters believers in baptism who, baptized "into Christ Jesus" (Rom. 6:3, 11), become integrated with others in Christ's body. The much-used Greek phrase *en Christo* (in Christ) becomes powerful shorthand for believers incorporated into the body of Christ. How dramatically this contrasts with seeing believer's baptism primarily as a matter of personal response. Sadly, much current myopic practice only loosely connects conversion and discipleship, baptism and church membership, private testimony ("Jesus and me") and new relationships ("Jesus and us").

When baptism is recognized as an event in which God acts, it becomes strategic for building living stones. First, baptism (whether infant or believer's) incorporates individuals into Christ and his community. Solitary Christians are impossible because baptism necessarily requires belonging with others—it is God's explicit idea of how new Christian life begins. Second, baptism is viewed as only part of the process of growth. Commonly, three tenses of salvation sum up a believer's journey. Christians *have been* saved, *are being* saved (through continual growth in relationship with God), and *will be* saved at the final appearing of Christ. Baptism has decisive public significance for this salvation journey. For infants, it is a seal of God's prevenient grace that moves them into a process leading to personal confession of faith, confirmation, and discipleship. For believers, it incorporates them into growing together in God's big story (Gal. 3:26–28; Col. 2:11–12) for a lifetime of being built as living stones. Sometimes myopic preaching treats baptism as an isolated event that completes the believer's inner experience, but big-picture worship gives baptism primary importance at the first stage of initiation into God's community. It marks public beginnings of a twofold relationship and long-term process.

Preachers, therefore, have major responsibilities at this stage: they challenge hearers to make faith-responses to Christ and then help new believers grow into congregational life by developing big-picture worship. Obviously, evangelistic preaching is essential so that people hear and respond to the gospel and move from darkness into light. "Once you were not a people, but now you are God's people; once you had not received mercy, but now you have received mercy" (1 Pet. 2:10). Sadly, there is some evidence that evangelistic preaching is not widely practiced today.[4]

But new worshipers also need to hear doctrinal preaching that ensures they learn a new language, "to speak funny" about what it means to belong to Jesus and participate within the Trinity life. Marva Dawn emphasizes how one goal of preaching is to train listeners to be theologians.[5] Theology matters. New believers should understand the theological significance of baptism—initiating them into Christ's body, the church. They also need to know that worship involves a personal relationship with the Triune God *and* a corporate relationship with other members of his church. This does not mean ponderous talk with mini-theological lectures but a willingness to explain worship and church on God's terms.

Additionally, liberating joy and wonder should permeate all preaching, preparing new worshipers for the privileges that lie ahead. The role of celebrative preaching has been well explained within the African-American preaching tradition, which encourages preachers to bring the whole community into holistic experience of the assurance of grace.[6] How vital it is that preachers exult in the sheer amazing grace of God's triune community relationships so generously opened up to newcomers. Celebrating preaching requires a truly celebrative practice of baptism in which the whole community realizes again and again its responsibilities as living stones to help integrate newcomers into God's building project. When one sinner repents, angels rejoice in heaven (Luke 15:7), and when new Christians begin their spiritual journey in public, there should be no-holds-barred celebration as the whole church accepts them into community life. Preachers should encourage the entire congregation to respond to God's gift of new life with wonder, awe, and celebration. Robert Webber criticizes much public worship for its lack of gospel joy, and especially at this initiation stage he says festivity should be enthusiastically prepared for and experienced.[7] How believers begin their public journey with Christ really matters.

Let me illustrate stage 1 from my pastoral experience in Cambridge in my believer's baptism tradition. Concerned that baptism had lost some significance as initiation into the church, we introduced a process by which each candidate preparing for baptism was mentored by an older Christian who helped prepare him or her for public witness and church community responsibility. Working in pairs through a series of Bible studies over many weeks, the candidates learned both the theological significance of their baptism—its trinitarian implications—as well as the spiritual formation that lay ahead in belonging *en Christo* with other believers. On the well-publicized day of baptism, the whole act of gathered worship centered on baptism in testimony, preached Word, and public witness. On this great day for evangelism, I preached *for a verdict* that frequently led to others coming forward in repentance and faith.

But it was stressed that baptism marked not only the candidates' declaration of faith and repentance before Christ and his people but also their fresh encounter with God's grace blessing and integrating them into a new community. After coming up out of the baptismal pool, they changed clothes and later returned for a service of the Lord's Supper. Before receiving bread and wine, they were welcomed into church membership by the laying on of hands and were commissioned as co-ministers in their new community, sharing in its life and mission, "like living stones . . . [being] built into a spiritual house to be a holy priesthood" (1 Pet. 2:5). By intentionally linking baptism with church membership and personal witness with discipleship, no one could escape the formational and community implications of their actions. Further, each new member was immediately placed in a small group with expectations that deeper relationships needed to form.

Stage 1 is very significant because it lays foundations for God's building project as new Christians commit publicly to begin the process of growing in relationship to Jesus Christ and to his church. While myopic preaching suffers from thin theology and treats ordinances as add-ons, big-picture preaching emphasizes how trinitarian theology and an appropriate practice of baptism open up new life in Christ in his new community. The journey of formation commences.

Integration

During stage 2, new believers grow into Christ's new community and learn to share in gathered worship as members of Christ's body. The key word is *learn*, for little of this process of integration comes easily, especially in a culture saturated with endemic self-centeredness. Instead of living by commercial calendars, worshipers learn new patterns of practice that live in God's story through the Christian year. By praise, prayer, bringing offerings, responding to sermons, and especially joining in the Lord's Supper, worshipers continue to be integrated into new community life. Each aspect of worship practice needs to center on God, use Scripture appropriately, employ plural language of community, and emphasize living in God's story.

It seems obvious that adoration and thanks truly need to center on who God is—Father, Son, and Holy Spirit—and to "thank God for what *he* has done, is doing and will do. God's work in Christ is the focus of worship."[8] Unfortunately, sometimes the focus of praise seems marooned in a congregation's *feelings* toward God, centering on emotions of the present instead of addressing God in his holiness and his story. To keep this focus clear, praise needs to include *biblical* testimony to God's worthiness. The book of Psalms provides one obvious resource for praise (as well as lament, confession, and repentance), but other Scripture texts provide shape and content for more adequate adoration and thanks.

As a community learns to center on the Triune God, its members become less individualistic and self-centered. Awareness grows of the need to express praise corporately using a new plural vocabulary—Christian *we*-ness instead of the unholy trinity of *me, myself, and I*. We have noted already that the language of togetherness is writ large in the New Testament—*you* plural dominates. Unity is essential to growth in the body of Christ (Rom. 12:5; 1 Cor. 10:17; Gal. 3:26; Eph. 4:13). While it is permissible to use the first-person singular *I* in corporate worship, learning to say *we* becomes essential for community formation. With plural language, worshipers are no longer able to worship in isolation. Rather, with openness to the Holy Spirit's power to unite (Eph. 4:3) come developing sensitivity to others as well as a vision for God's bigger mission purpose for the world. Living stones join together by learning to express togetherness focused on God.

Prayer takes many forms, including adoration, confession, thanksgiving, petition, and blessing. As with praise (which of course includes prayer), God must be kept center, with Scripture providing rich resources for corporate prayer, which best uses plural language. Confession is particularly significant for personal formation as worshipers show awareness of sin and failure before God and the need for forgiveness and new strength. Omitting confession not only severely restricts personal formation but also damages the entire community's self-awareness and need to depend on God. Further, intercession and petition for one another enable new believers to learn commitment to others in the fellowship and the world. Bluntly, Don Saliers laments, "Our impoverished experience of common prayer for the world is directly traceable to our inability to know and to minister to others in his name."[9] But when worshipers learn to share in prayer for others, they grow in community awareness for both *inner* and *outer* formation journeys.

Offering money as an act of worship must also be learned. Again, as with praise and prayer, it must be emphasized that God is the focus of financial giving, and giving to him is utterly unlike any other donation because it expresses quality of relationship with God. It is a spiritual barometer of gratitude to him. Because he is the giver of all good gifts, worshipers only return what he has first given—giving regularly (1 Cor. 16:2), in proportion to income (Acts 11:29), freely (Matt. 10:8 NIV), generously (Rom. 12:8 NIV), and cheerfully (2 Cor. 9:7). How we give shows how we love. Too often offerings are treated as pragmatic necessities. Budgets, targets, and trajectories are printed in bulletins with warnings that falling finances jeopardize church organization and mission. Of course, drawing up budgets and targets are part of responsible community living, but the primary focus should always be on God (1 Chron. 29:14–20), before whom we joyfully return gifts in love and service. More demanding still, worship also involves how the rest of our money is spent throughout each week.

Responding well to sermons also needs to be learned by new worshipers. In a culture of diminishing attention spans, it is increasingly rare for people to practice the discipline of listening to one person. Hearing God's transforming Word (Rom. 10:8–9; 2 Cor. 5:17) requires practiced willingness. Listeners need to engage with all their faculties even as they seek to love God with all their heart, soul, mind, and strength (Mark 12:30). This requires expectant preparation in prayer and active listening that helps believers participate mentally and spiritually with preachers, discerning what God is saying to his people. Authentic listening leads to practical obedience. Of course, this requires preachers to focus sermons on God and his Word, expressing clearly and relevantly his will for his people in expectation that the Holy Spirit will help worshipers grow in faith and character.

Just as baptism had a vital role at the initiation stage, the Lord's Supper is essential to the process of integration over the long term. The fact that Christ only clearly commanded two rituals—baptism (unrepeatable) and the Lord's Supper (repeatable)—was taken seriously by the early church (Acts 2:42) and in church practice ever since. As with baptism (accompanied by a heavy theological debate), the Lord's Supper can be viewed on a spectrum from sign to sacrament depending on how much God is deemed to be at work in the event. Viewed as a sign, individual believers come to the Table remembering what Jesus has done for *me*. Taking bread and wine provides an opportunity for believers to reflect on personal responses to sin and grace at the cross. Again, while rigorously rejecting any magic connotations of sacrament, when the Lord's Supper is viewed as an act commanded by Christ as his chosen way for believers *together* to encounter him, it becomes an essential place for community growth.

The Lord's Supper is packed with theological significance. David Buttrick lists some of its meanings in theological shorthand: Passover, covenant, Mount Zion, sinners, Cana, feeding of the five thousand, Last Supper, resurrection meals with the risen Jesus, and kingdom parables. "The list suggests that we are not dealing with the story of Israel or stories of Jesus alone, but with a come-together story of God-with-us. Eucharist gathers the time and space of God-with-us, and is crammed with the whole import of the *whole* Gospel."[10] Demonstrating trinitarian theology with God's triune invitation to participate, the Lord's Supper provides the most substantial way for communities to grow together with him. "God, in three persons, creates us in his image not only as humans to be persons in relationship, but also as believers to participate in his community life—especially around the Lord's Table."[11] Remember the earlier reference to Andrei Rublev's icon depicting the persons of the Trinity seated around a table with a chalice, and the fourth side open for others to join in: "The grace of our Lord Jesus Christ, the love of God and the fellowship of the Holy Spirit" (2 Cor. 13:14 NASB).

The Lord's Supper has an explicit corporate dynamic—one loaf, one cup (1 Cor. 10:17)—that necessarily involves members of Christ's community collectively, not only remembering Jesus's death but also rejoicing in his resurrection, ascension, and reign over us. Further, the come-together story of God-with-us anticipates his coming again. Several worship writers underline how the corporate nature of the Lord's Supper emphasizes that Christ is in our midst, continually forming his community as one loaf and sharing one cup—for example, in the fourfold action as Christ takes, blesses, breaks, and shares. When Christ *takes* he challenges participants to offer themselves as living sacrifices to God; when he *blesses* he speaks of responsibility to others—blessed to be a blessing; when he *breaks* he emphasizes how believers should be given for others; and when he *shares* he stresses the mutual life of Christ's community.

James Torrance strikingly claims, "Perhaps we are never more truly human than at the Lord's Table when Christ draws us into his life of communion."[12] This special act of worship has a unique role for community formation—nowhere else is the work of Christ past, present, and future so powerfully expressed by gathered believers. Nothing else can substitute for its experience of grace and power in God's community life. Myopic preaching completely misses its joy. Robert Webber tells how communion was always rather mournful in his earlier worshiping experience as it concentrated on his sin and Jesus's sacrifice. Worship was transformed, however, when he discovered how it also gloriously celebrates the risen Christ, who has overcome sin and created a new people. Recently, a pastor told me, "No matter how many times I celebrate communion, I am excited by it. I cannot help but be joyful—it really is the high point of our church worship!"

Questions about frequency and practice of the Lord's Supper will remain open as believers argue whether it is emphasized better by less or more regular practice. Some Reformers, like John Calvin, insisted it be practiced weekly. Interestingly, several missional church leaders are also emphasizing its weekly practice. Other Christian groups practice it monthly or a few times a year, believing that weekly practice causes it to become too ordinary. But whatever its frequency, it is vitally important that worshipers perceive it to be Christ's appointed method for ensuring continuing togetherness of redeemed brothers and sisters.

At this stage, two types of preaching are significant: liturgical and salvation history. The first likely provokes resistance from myopic preachers because of liturgical amnesia, but earlier I sought to rehabilitate the word *liturgy*. As Russell Mitman says, liturgy is "the totality of what happens verbally and nonverbally when the people of God find themselves in dialogue with the triune God."[13] It involves everything that constitutes gathered worship. Liturgical preaching is therefore concerned about patterns of gathered worship directed by Scripture that enable congregations to participate in the rhythm of worship's call and response. It views baptism and the Lord's Supper as essential elements that are critical ways of entering community and communing with Christ *on his terms*. Liturgical preaching sees sermons as fully integrated into the rest of worship services, with everything influenced by Scripture's outcomes in a fourfold or fivefold structure. All praise, prayer, offering, sermons, as well as the Lord's Supper must keep its focus on God at the center, with effective use of Scripture and deployment of plural language. It is very important that preachers help new worshipers learn the significance of these patterns of worship, especially the Lord's Supper as *the* Christ-ordained place for togetherness. By learning repeatable patterns over time, worshipers become integrated into God's community. And in contrast, how damaging is myopic preaching that allows individuals to miss out on these profoundly collective worship experiences.

The second type of preaching, salvation history, brings worshipers into a larger understanding and experience as they join together in act 4 of God's story for the world. Remember that "not living in God's story" is one of the characteristics of myopic preaching. Preachers need continually to remind congregations of God's past acts and their journey onward in God's future. "Here is the essence of Christian worship. As members of a people whose storyline includes creation, sin, and grace, we commune with our creator and savior—with God, through Christ, in the power of the Holy Spirit. Worship is narrative engagement with the triune God."[14] Such salvation history preaching is also powerfully connected with celebrating the Lord's Supper, with its remembering and anticipation.

Character Formation

Stage 3 identifies the impact Christian commitment has on character right from the beginning as new believers learn to praise, pray, give, listen, and commune together in the power of the Spirit. Sanctification—the moral and spiritual transformation of believers by God's grace—should develop early in the lives of individuals and community (Eph. 5:16; 1 Thess. 4:3). The building metaphor of 1 Corinthians 3:10–14 particularly identifies the need to build on the foundation of Jesus Christ with quality lives because Christ's judgment will reveal whether gold, silver, and costly stones have been used or wood, hay, and straw.

When worshipers belong together, it becomes increasingly appropriate to look for signs of maturing attitudes and deeds expressed by the fruit of the Spirit—"by their fruits you will know them" (Matt. 7:20 NKJV; see also Gal. 5:22). Habitual participation in gathered worship should influence its worshipers for the better. Being surrounded by loving, supportive brothers and sisters should make it easier to become loving and supportive persons. "They were amazed and recognized them as companions of Jesus" (Acts 4:13). As individuals grow in Christlikeness, so too the whole community should mature in expressions of holiness, love, and unity, demonstrating the fruit of the Spirit and learning to defer to others in humility (Phil. 2:1–4).

Quality of character can be evidenced in many ways, such as love and kindness, honesty in conflict, and moral integrity. But nothing reveals a community's level of maturity more than considering how its members exercise their preferences. Before belonging to Christ, people made personal choices based on likes and dislikes "in the spirit of the world." Personal choice reigned; they were consumers disunited. After commitment to Christ, however, believers "received . . . the Spirit that is from God, so that we may understand the gifts bestowed on us by God" (1 Cor. 2:12). Now, in a spiritual community that aspires to "have the mind of Christ" (1 Cor. 2:16), a higher priority determines preferences. Christ's choices reign; the people of God unite. "Let each of you look not to your own interests, but to the interests of others" (Phil. 2:4) as worshipers exhibit the same mind that is in Christ Jesus. The more worship centers on God, learning of him and his ways and participating in fellowship with him, the more believers should learn how to submit their personal preferences within God's community.

Looking not to our own interests but to the interests of others brings us to the critical issue of music in worship. Of course, the role of music for expressing praise has been implicit through stages 1 and 2. "The Christian community sings. . . . Singing is the highest form of human expression. . . . The praise of God which finds its concrete culmination in the singing of the community is one of the indispensable basic forms of the ministry of the community."[15] Music in worship is a glorious gift and will be given special attention in chapter 13. But because music goes deeply into the human psyche and powerfully expresses personal emotion, its very diversity may cause a major conflict of interest. While newer churches likely accept contemporary music as part of their identity, many older churches have experienced considerable tension over music. Indeed, in these churches, how music is chosen has become a litmus test for maturity in Christ.

Maybe tension about music was already surfacing in 1 Corinthians 14:15–16 with fear that "singing praises with the spirit" might preclude singing praise with the mind. Was there concern that pagan influence was seeping in through secular music styles? Throughout church history such anxieties recurred. Today, some argue for *blended worship* as a middle way; others ridicule this as a compromise that fails to recognize how contemporary music is growing churches. But much more is at stake than music. Of course, you may resolve tension by designing different services with contrasting musical styles, but these neatly avoid looking to the interests of others with the same attitude as Jesus Christ. Keeping people happy by offering different music choices in different groups can completely miss the primary purpose of worship that gives God glory by offering lives as a holy nation and royal priesthood, building and maturing his new people in community. Whenever worshipers choose music out of personal preference (whether traditional or contemporary), they are in danger of excluding others and causing disunity.

Marva Dawn is particularly associated with the controversial charge that splitting congregations up by music choices reveals spiritual immaturity.[16] Especially for older congregations, which are often divided over strong preferences for traditional or contemporary worship, stage 3 emphasizes the higher priority of growing together in love, holiness, and unity. Maturing character challenges conflicts of interest that ask how much give-and-take *is* necessary to include brothers and sisters so that they can belong together. Growing into the community for which Jesus Christ died with all barriers down (Gal. 3:28) requires generosity of spirit toward others.

Several authors connect music with community formation. For example, Cornelius Plantinga and Sue Rozeboom suggest how divine relationships within the Trinity "almost say that the persons within God show each other divine *hospitality*. . . . Early Christians called this interchange the mystery of *perichoresis*"—the mutual indwelling of God's three persons. Intriguingly, they continue, "Perhaps we could say that hospitality thrives within the triune life of God and then spreads wonderfully to the creatures of God. The one who spreads it is a mediator, a person who 'works in the middle.'" Applied to leaders of worship, this means they must learn to "speak hospitably," make room for others, and speak of others' worship styles respectfully as they "encourage a congregation's awareness that it is surrounded by the invisible cloud of witnesses that gather with us in worship."[17]

Music's role in community formation is therefore pivotal because it can unite or divide. Again, Keith Getty warns, "It seems to me that if a church splits over music, that music has become more important than togetherness in itself. Music is merely a servant to the body of believers."[18] Myopic preaching too easily settles for self-pleasing music; this division allows music to be the master. One longtime Christian said to me poignantly, "I have always hoped that music in worship would be *inclusive*—that I could find my voice with others. But instead I find that some of the contemporary music services are the most *exclusive*, appropriating one narrow style that forces me away. I feel detached." But I have heard many others complain about traditional music that excludes them. Truly, choosing music by which a community can worship is vital to formation of character.

Stage 3 requires pastoral preaching and leadership through preaching. Unfortunately, pastoral preaching is sometimes limited to problem-solving sermons that address *felt needs*—what Harry Fosdick described as "personal counseling on a group scale."[19] Too often such preaching is individualistic and fits in too easily with the current therapy-oriented culture, rarely challenging hearers with God's purpose of new life in Christ. Pastors as shepherds should give support and comfort, but they also have a responsibility to help the whole community grow in its responsibility to support and care for its members and those outside. Pastoral preaching deals with real-life issues within communities that are growing a corporate identity. James Thompson commends the apostle Paul's pastoral preaching for today's preachers because it formed corporate consciousness by calling new believers to belong together in new support systems in a new family. Paul's instructions in his letters were not intended for individuals to read in their own homes but for congregations that needed to grow in new support systems amid demanding pastoral issues.

> The preacher assists the church in forming a corporate response to our pressing issues. People who live in this community know that the story of Christ's self-giving love is more than their foundational story; it is the norm for community life and a challenge to their own selfishness. They have learned that the lives of others—even those that limit our personal freedom—are more important than our own.[20]

But this also requires leadership through preaching. Elsewhere I have written at length about how preachers are necessarily leaders.[21] Recognizing that certain leadership skills are necessary for preaching, I challenge full-blooded preachers to develop them in exegesis and interpretation of Scripture. At the heart of exegesis, responding to God's Word in context, preachers should identify God's transformation challenge. He always seeks to move us on as better people in Christ, and skill is needed to ensure preaching generates and sustains the text's creative tension. Instead of individualistic and low-compliance treatment of Scripture, preachers need to see its community challenge to big-picture worship of a maturing community living for God. Where there is discord, as with preferences over music, they need to deal with conflict biblically, all the while nurturing God's building project. Not only must they preach great themes of love, forgiveness, reconciliation, and putting other people's interests ahead of our own, but they should also model these practices in relationships and ensure they are ethos givers whose personal practice of grace schools others. "Making every effort to maintain the unity of the Spirit in the bond of peace" (Eph. 4:3) requires intentional leadership that keeps character formation at the fore.

Such community character formation is desperately needed because increasing evidence suggests how poorly many churches are viewed. Researching North American Christianity, David Kinnaman devastatingly summed up his overall findings in his book titled *UnChristian*, which "reflects outsiders' most common reaction to the faith: they think Christians no longer represent what Jesus had in mind." Rather, they come across as hypocritical and insincere, concerned only with getting others saved.[22]

Missional Living

Though positioned as the outcome of worship formation, missional living (stage 4) is intimately connected with all the other stages. Even as personal and community formation occur inwardly by developing congregational fellowship—initiated by baptism, continuously reinvigorated by the Lord's Supper, and characterized by the fruit of the Spirit—so too the whole community should be looking outward. Gathered worship helps believers mature into alternative communities in order that together they will witness and serve (1 Pet. 2:9–12). A new community develops subversive worship culture that attracts and challenges the surrounding culture.

Describing congregations as alternative communities suggests they have a radically different character and agenda. But in reality, myopic preaching all too readily allows churches to accommodate unthinkingly to surrounding culture. Sadly, missional living seems a forlorn possibility. Mark Labberton suggests that two distorted biblical paradigms typify the evangelical church in contemporary US experience: (1) The *exodus paradigm* treats it as an escape to entitlement, and living in the Promised Land, the evangelical church forgets it is blessed to be a blessing to others. So, for example, it spends the most money on itself and gives away only 2 percent of its income and energy to others. (2) Or it sees itself living in the *exile paradigm*, but instead of dwelling in a foreign land and being intent on living like a people who belong to God, the evangelical church has so thoroughly absorbed culture that it has forgotten to seek the welfare of the city. David Fitch calls this "the Great Giveaway" and pleads for "reclaiming the mission of the church from big business, parachurch organizations, psychotherapy, consumer capitalism and other modern maladies."[23] His chapter on worship emphasizes how rarely churches seem concerned to build community for the sake of surrounding culture.

Stage 4 needs missional and prophetic preaching. Missional preaching keeps God's vision for his church as a holy nation and a royal priesthood at the fore. It challenges communities of missionaries to live in the world so that "they [unbelievers] may see your honorable deeds and glorify God when he comes to judge" (1 Pet. 2:12). Such living out its worship before the world presents God's purpose and wisdom (Eph. 3:10); "the church's witness bearing is testimony not to its own life but *to God's grace in its life.*"[24]

Enabling a congregation to grow as a community of missionaries requires preaching that moves worshipers beyond maintenance to missional mode. Milfred Minatrea calls this intentional community building "shaped by God's heart,"[25] which requires missional practices. For example, new members should cross a high threshold for membership that underlines discipleship responsibilities to God and others. (This relates to the initiation stage of formation.) Stress always should be on the *real* rather than the *religious* because disciples need to learn about obeying God in practice so they truly think and behave in different ways from the surrounding culture.

Earlier I identified a number of practices (see fig. 4) that worshipers should develop as "clear alternatives to those that are prevailing or taken for granted."[26] David Schlafer and Timothy Sedgwick are concerned that the contemporary church has lost its moral discernment, harming both its character and its ability to make choices in moral crises and quandaries. Urging "preaching for moral discernment" that connects Scripture with life, they warn that occasional sermons on moral crises do not provide coherence for a larger vision of Christian living. Rather, preachers need to work with an intentional set of practices: (1) prayer and worship; (2) forgiveness and reconciliation; (3) formation of households as communities of faith; (4) hospitality as the embrace of the stranger and those in need; (5) citizenship and political responsibility; and (6) reverence for creation. Together these constitute the character of ethical Christian life that needs to be learned in community and provide six lenses for preaching that helps form community.

Of these, Schlafer and Sedgwick say that the practice of creating Christian households may be considered the "root metaphor for speaking of the Christian life." Households speak of relationships within homes involving every aspect of daily living. They have their own economy and use of money and their usual routines and activities such as "storytelling, meals, daily rituals, play, entertainment, work, child rearing, education and training, and economic exchange."[27] Households, however, are not inward looking but are the "threshold to the larger world"—the place of interaction with wider society as their members learn responsibilities to others. Particularly important is the practice of asceticism: "What disciplines should govern the household?" Negatively, Christian worshipers avoid "most notably patterns of purchase and consumption, including the visual and vocal."[28] Positively, what practices are central to time spent together? For developing such moral discernment, Schlafer and Sedgwick particularly commend preaching the Epistles because they "evidence the distinctive way of life that Christians seek in response to Christ. They bear witness to Christ as they seek to form the household of faith."[29]

Preaching missionally is no easy task; it requires openness to others yet resistance to compromise with cultural forces. Prophetic preaching is associated with courage to stand for God's truth and justice in the world.[30] Stephen Long defines prophetic preaching as "a charisma, divinely inspired, which either seeks to recover a faithful word from within the Christian tradition or to discover a necessary word in new situations that threaten the rule of God."[31] Positively, it proclaims all that God's loving and just kingdom stands for while, negatively, it discerns and confronts all that threatens God's love and justice. Big-picture worship requires preaching that probes, disturbs, and energizes people. "The evoking of an alternative community that knows it is about different things in different ways . . . prophetic ministry seeks to penetrate despair so that new futures can be believed in and embraced by us."[32]

The Question Toolbox

Back in chapter 4, I introduced a series of questions that together make up a *question toolbox* to help leaders prepare worship. Every aspect of gathered worship comes under their questioning as they probe for effective big-picture worship. Now, two additional questions must be added about community and mission.

Of course, community and mission have already been implicit at several points. For example, question 4 about worship's two audiences continually raises issues about whether words and actions directing praise, confession, thanksgiving, and offering to God are accompanied by words and actions that nurture worshipers in personal and community formation. But explicitly, in light of this chapter and its challenges in figure 5, two last questions are required.

Question Toolbox

1. *Gift*: Are we thankfully receiving this gift from the Triune God of grace?
2. *Magnification*: Are we expressing its richness toward God?
3. *Scripture*: Are we allowing Scripture to direct?
4. *Audiences*: Are we addressing two audiences?
5. *Community*: Are we building community by story?
6. *Mission*: Are we enabling community to scatter?

Question 5 asks worship leaders directly about their role in community formation: "Are we building community by story?" It holds together issues in this chapter about new worshipers learning new language, relationships, and patterns *within* the story of God's people and then moving on for him and serving him. If the answer to this question is yes, we will not be able to allow new worshipers to stay in the first box, content in their individualism, and obviously this would involve following patterns of the Christian year. It celebrates baptism as a corporate event by which worshipers are joined in Christ and makes the Lord's Supper a crucial part of building community. By reenacting Christ's story, past, present, and future, it places the church in act 4 within God's continuing purpose. The column in figure 5 marked "personal formation" must be integrated with "community formation" by seeing personal stories in context within God's big story. Answering this question positively pushes worshipers by many different dynamics into belonging to community, developing through the different stages into missional living.

Closely connected with building community, question 6 asks about mission: "Are we enabling community to scatter?" It raises issues of how worshipers will think and act for God, offering daily lives as "a living sacrifice" (Rom. 12:1). This question might easily be asked without reference to worship but instead as a mission challenge focusing on evangelism and social action. But posing it to *worship* leaders ensures that all that is done in gathered worship—singing, praying, offering, listening, and communing—has missionary implications for the way believers think, discern, behave, and act for God in his world. Missional practices necessarily belong within worship, for all who lead big-picture worship must always look beyond building fellowship to helping believers live missionally before their surrounding communities.

This chapter has opened up many complex issues. Inevitably, its rapid survey of different kinds of preaching involved in worship formation fails to give each the attention it deserves. Many implications about community and mission need much more space. For example, just how do preachers address a community that comprises worshipers at different stages? Is it possible to challenge newcomers with gospel basics while nurturing established worshipers into missional living? No easy formulas are likely to emerge, but worship leaders should always be aware of these formation dynamics in their preparation. They have a responsibility to ask whether a Scripture passage relates to one community formation purpose more than another but also to always be confident that God's grace initiates, integrates, forms, and sends out his people in surprising ways. Building living stones is his skill.

PART 3

A New Process

10

Toward a New Pattern for Big-Picture Preaching

Bill has been the worship leader at Cornerstones Community Church for six years. He enjoys working with some gifted musicians and is responsible for organizing two main morning services—a traditional service with a choir and a contemporary service with a praise band. Steve has been the senior pastor for over ten years, and he was keen to appoint Bill since he had heard of his effectiveness at his former church. During the years that Bill has been working, the church has continued to grow, and both services are well attended.

Though the two men are friendly toward each other, Bill finds that Steve has less and less time to spend with him. At the beginning they met every Monday for at least an hour to reflect on the Sunday services and to share ideas for the following Sunday. Bill found it invaluable, providing a clear picture to work with through the rest of the week. Every year there were two or three longer sessions, including a one-day retreat during which they planned six months ahead. But now they never meet together. Steve sends a weekly email with his preaching theme and Scripture text, but it does not arrive until Wednesday (or sometimes later). Bill yearns for some time to be made to share about worship, but Steve seems to be running harder than ever.

Bill and Steve's situation is a jolting reality check to all those high-sounding possibilities in part 2 about building God's worshiping community. Bill and Steve represent countless practitioners who, in principle, may be sympathetic toward big-picture worship but whose busyness hopelessly bogs them down. Weighed down by church expectations and practical demands of planning weekly gathered worship, they have little energy or motivation to do things better. Frankly, myopic preaching reigns; faulty worship definitions have become the norm. Small-picture preaching is endemic, embedded in well-established routines. Inertia keeps worship leaders doing what they have always done with the same results. So new ideas about worship, such as seeking fuller theology and developing community, seem like too much extra hard work that will only add burdens and complicate the status quo.

But reality checks rightly force the issue. If you are a myopic worship leader who wants to stay the same, stop reading now. Let the previous chapters fade as impractical theory. Because taking this challenge seriously and moving from small-picture to big-picture worship demand an entirely new way of thinking and working that is profoundly life changing, ministry altering, and church transforming. My own story told something of my difficult journey as long-held assumptions were roughly overturned and new convictions developed. The only way for Bill and Steve to avoid this worship challenge is to stay safely within a small-picture comfort zone. Depending on your point of view, you may sympathize with Bill as a hardworking music leader who once enjoyed a good relationship with the preacher who has fallen victim to a growing congregation. Or you may sympathize with Steve, who may be seen as even more of a victim, running ever faster to keep up with increasing expectations. But the truth is that *both* Bill and Steve need to view worship differently and open themselves up to fresh ways of working together. And this is not a little matter of adding some fresh surface spice. It requires that both be open to experience anew the radical wonder of being part of God's biggest purpose—living in his triune power to lead his worshiping community.

Karen Roberts once asked Robert Webber whether after describing his big vision of worship in theory he could see it in practice. "Where is this happening? Can you point me to a church that is worshiping as you describe?" Sadly, his answer was no, but he quickly added that it was up to those of us preparing to plan and lead worship to prayerfully figure out the *how-to*.

Part 3 tries to help people figure out the how-to. It describes some practical matters that must be faced by Bill and Steve, as by any other myopic worship leaders, if they are to move forward. Inevitably, limited space allows for only general descriptions with sparse examples drawn from a vast range of possibilities. Yet these next chapters should provide enough guidance for Bill and Steve and others to progress into big-picture worship.

Taking a Bold Step

This book has assumed throughout that preachers (consciously or unconsciously) have a huge influence over how their congregations worship. At

Cornerstones Community Church, unless Steve takes responsibility for initiating big-picture worship, nothing is likely to change. Hopefully, as he shares fresh conviction about worship, others will quickly join him—especially Bill. But Steve must lead. Remember *The Truman Show* analogy when Truman faces the decision about whether to go through the exit door? Having lived all his life within a safe dome, can he now move into a new world beyond? To step out into something new requires honesty, courage, intentionality, time, effort, and above all, spiritual energy.

These qualities are not listed lightly. Honesty is essential because awakening to a new worldview involves admitting myopia. Facing up to my own worship shortsightedness was painful, especially because as a teacher of preachers I was supposed to have thought through the preacher's role. Yet unless preachers confront personal shortsightedness that has contributed to small-picture worship, nothing fresh will happen. Courage is also necessary. I have met several experienced pastors who honestly admitted they were guilty of myopic preaching, but they balked at dealing with inevitable resistance arising from entrenched worship habits. They rejected trying to lead even small breakthroughs because it might prove costly. Steve must lead toward big-picture worship, with Bill (and others in leadership) giving time and effort to sustain momentum for change. With intentionality and determined commitment, they must persist in working out vision, skillfully generating and sustaining creative tension. Unless leaders invest adequate time and effort, little transformation is likely to occur, for major change always requires effort and patience in its early stages.

The most important quality of all, however, is spiritual energy. Expending extra time and effort quickly causes us to run out of steam. We grow impatient with the time lag between initiating something new and actually seeing positive results. Indeed, things often seem to get worse before they get better. Too soon we hear echoes of what an exasperated preacher mentioned earlier: "Why get us more involved in worship? Isn't it enough to produce sermons every week while trying to keep our heads above water among all the pastoral, administrative, and leadership demands?" Yet long-term outcomes of transformational worship will always be worth the commitment.

The secret of big-picture worship lies in its trinitarian theology—the empowering by the Father, Son, and Holy Spirit. Once I limited this empowering to preachers and their work (see fig. 2), but now I see that *everything* in worship belongs within the returning movement of God's grace, which initiates call and response. God gives, directs, inspires, and builds his worshiping community. Preachers as worshipers, therefore, offer all that they are and have to God *working through them*. They are thankful, empowered trinitarians, not self-starting, practical unitarians. God's power, primarily through the Holy Spirit, makes possible all that follows. The stages and steps I describe shortly will accomplish nothing of eternal value unless God is the builder (Ps. 127:1).

Worship Swim

In *360-Degree Preaching*, I use the metaphor *preaching swim* to emphasize how preachers should prepare sermons by immersing themselves within God's living Word rather like swimmers within a flowing river, surrendering their own efforts to God's empowering. But my sole focus on preaching seemed to make preachers swim in a separate stream, disconnected from worship. When I recognized this blunder, I recorded the eureka moment in my prayer journal on January 28, 2008:

> *I suddenly realize my big mistake. All these years I have been teaching my students the "preaching swim" and I have left out worship. I have to reconstruct the swim so that worship leaders can swim with preachers and preachers can swim with worship leaders.*

Big-picture worship prohibits isolationist preaching. Rather, preachers, with everyone else gathered for worship, are immersed in the same spiritual reality of receiving and giving back within the grace and fellowship of God's three persons, growing together as his community. The preaching swim must become the *worship swim*. As Steve prepares to preach, he should recognize that he belongs in the far bigger worship dynamic of God's returning grace, which involves Bill and all other worship leaders.

At this point it is time to deal with the vexed issue about the title *worship leader*. Since the beginning of this book, I have hesitated about the use of that title. Of course, it is such a common term that most of us have grown used to it. Yet every time I use it, I wonder whether there is not a more appropriate title. After all, there is only one worship leader—Jesus Christ—whose participation with Father and Holy Spirit makes worship possible. The Triune God of grace leads worship by offering the call and empowering the response. Calling anyone else *worship leader* claims too much. But what else can we say? One music pastor said to me, "Saying 'worship leader' is so ingrained I find I can't stop myself from using it. But really I want to say 'lead-worshiper'—that makes much more theological sense. Actually, I am trying to retrain myself to use this new title."

Increasingly I have heard the expression *lead-worshiper* employed to stress that God has the primary role in initiating and leading worship and therefore is the only true *worship leader*. In a secondary role, those who plan and direct gathered worship are lead-worshipers with responsibility for setting an example and providing direction for the whole community, helping it respond to God. Unfortunately, the title sounds like a clumsy substitute. In spite of its clumsiness, however, and its having to compete with the ingrained *worship leader* description, from now on I will employ this humbler, more theologically aware term to describe the work of Steve and Bill and all who are willing to engage in the worship swim. At times I will interchange it with *worship planners*. Whenever we see the words *lead-worshiper*, it should remind us of our place in worship's 360-degree dynamic as God—Father, Son, and Holy Spirit—empowers its call and response.

Musician Matt Redman comments:

> As Lead Worshipers, no matter how many years of experience we have, we're just as dependent as the first time we ever led. We might be better singers now, or know a few more chords. . . . But the most vital factor hasn't changed at all—we need the Holy Spirit to help us lead just as much as we ever did. . . . As Lead Worshipers we need to learn to reverence the Holy Spirit—with the Father and the Son He is worshiped and glorified. And we also need to hear His voice—to rely on for the next step as we journey together before His throne.[1]

No longer is it feasible to work solo. The worship swim, therefore, requires new patterns of collaboration. Instead of preachers working through five main stages of sermon preparation on their own,[2] the worship swim integrates preaching into a radically far-reaching new process of lead-worshiping. Goodbye to small-picture preaching; hello to big-picture worship.

Figure 6. Contrast between Preaching Swim and Worship Swim

Preaching Swim	Worship Swim
	Stage 1: Commit to worship
Stage 1: Immerse in Scripture	Stage 2: Let Scripture shape the sermon for gathered worship
Stage 2: Interpret for today	
Stage 3: Design the sermon	Stage 3: Design the sermon
	Stage 4: Help shape gathered worship
Stage 4: Deliver the sermon and lead worship	Stage 5: Deliver the sermon and lead worship
Stage 5: Evaluate the outcomes	Stage 6: Evaluate the outcomes

While the preaching swim comprised five stages, the worship swim needs six, and two of them are new. Stage 1, "commit to worship," involves how teams approach big-picture worship by working through many of the issues identified in part 2. Stage 4 allocates new responsibilities for shaping gathered worship. Collaboration also inevitably modifies other stages, especially stage 2, in which the heightened role for Scripture directs not only sermons but also gathered worship.

Myopic preachers used to solo preparation will likely find these changes complicated and burdensome at first. Is Steve really going to persist in working through the fresh demands of the worship swim? And will Bill cooperate? Does

Steve want Bill to cooperate? Yet I am convinced that big-picture worship is far too important for preachers and other lead-worshipers *not* to engage afresh with its demands. Inevitably, any new thinking demands extra learning and commitment, but this new commitment is not motivated by some short-term goal or clever gimmick. Rather, it is driven by the glorious vision of belonging to God's greatest long-term purpose as his worshiping people, worshiping as God intends, on his terms, with worship that integrates everything that matters into his community and mission, living his story.

A more detailed outline of the worship swim (see fig. 7) shows where collaboration occurs for lead-worshiping. Two columns for preachers and other worship planners contain a series of Xs that mark different responsibilities. This particular list arose from a class exercise in which both preachers and worship planners debated the degree of cooperation. How feasible, some worship planners asked, is it to parallel so much of the preacher's task in stage 2? Should they be expected to read the Scripture text out loud and listen and investigate its meaning? What about interpretation? They came to agree, however, that such work by lead-worshipers alongside preachers greatly benefits worship preparation, though *checking out investigations* (which involves commentary work) and identifying the *main impact* (what the sermon will say and do) was left to the preacher. Similarly, preachers asked how much they needed to collaborate in stage 4. Yet they also appreciated the value of sharing with worship planners. Of course, figure 7 reflects narrow collaboration between preacher and worship planner(s), and (as we will see later) wider participation is to be welcomed whenever possible.

Where would you put your check marks? Perhaps before you answer, it is appropriate to give a brief overview of all six stages. Notice how some of the questions from the toolbox emerge through the collaboration process.

Figure 7. Stages of the Worship Swim Showing Lead-Worshipers' Collaboration

Worship Swim Stages	Preacher	Worship Planner(s)
1. Commit to worship:		
build team(s),	X	X
seek unity of heart and mind	X	X
2. Let Scripture shape the sermon for gathered worship:		
prayerfully read text aloud,	X	X
listen and investigate,	X	X
check out investigations,	X	
interpret for today,	X	
identify *focus* and *function*,	X	X
state *main impact*,	X	X
consider worship opportunity	X	
3. Design the sermon	X	

Worship Swim Stages	Preacher	Worship Planner(s)
4. Help shape gathered worship:		
use the question toolbox,	X	X
shape structure and content,	X	X
delegate responsibilities,		X
ensure planning is complete		X
5. Deliver the sermon and lead gathered worship	X	X
6. Evaluate the outcomes	X	X

Stage 1

This foundational stage involves preachers and worship planners agreeing on worship fundamentals. Together they must consciously commit to work together on big-picture worship.

Much at Cornerstones Community Church depends on Steve's view of worship. Of course, he could argue that success makes change unnecessary. "I am really sorry, Bill, that I only contact you by email nowadays, though I do try to give you as much detail about the sermons as I can. The good old days when we had time to sit down and plan together are now long gone, though we both prayed that the church would take off, didn't we? Now that it has grown, we have to work harder and faster." Small-picture worship continues to reign.

But if Steve is disturbed by myopia's hold over him and glimpses something of big-picture worship, he will urgently meet Bill and insist on the need for change: "I am desperately concerned that how we have been worshiping each week is missing out on what worship really means! I am sorry I have been doing my own thing and you have been doing yours in ways that ignore what God wants to do with us as his worshiping community. Instead of leaving everything about the worship services to you while I get on with sermons and leadership, I now realize *everything* that is important about our lives and ministries is summed up by worship. We have to find ways to work out what this means for us and the whole church. I believe worship is our number one priority. If you are willing to join me, Bill, you and I can have a new beginning. And so will our community."

Worship as the number one priority makes rigorous demands on spirit, mind, and body. Preachers and worship planners need to intentionally share qualities of spirit, especially thankfulness for the gift of worship (remember question 1). They must also honestly examine basic convictions about worship definitions, theology, Scripture, liturgical resources, and community formation. Consciously, they should keep thinking how best to magnify God (question 2). Some big issues are involved, for example, worship structure. Earlier I commended thoughtful, scriptural patterns for worship, noting that the simplest (and oldest) uses a fourfold structure that resonates with the divine-human dynamic found in Scripture. Beginning as early church practice, this has continued ever since: gathering, Word, Lord's Table or thanksgiving, sending out. Worship planners must review such structures for worship.

Throughout this entire process, team building really matters too, and the task of developing and sustaining healthy team relationships is considered at the end of this chapter.

Stage 2

"Let Scripture shape the sermon for gathered worship" places Scripture central to the collaborative process. Toolbox question 3 asks, "Are we allowing Scripture to direct?" Traditionally, working with Scripture has been considered the preacher's task in sermon preparation. Both exegeting the text (listening carefully to its meaning within the original context) and interpreting the text (attending to its relevance to the contemporary situation) are reserved for preachers only. But now the worship swim brings others into this listening process, inviting their response to Scripture too. This provides vital focus throughout collaboration.

Obviously preachers are trained in this task and expect to have check marks alongside each aspect of stage 2. After all, sermon preparation is what they do. But God's Word in Scripture is open to all worshipers, and even at less academic levels, all lead-worshipers should respond as best they can. All lead-worshipers are under the authority of Scripture, and check marks in the second column therefore highlight several new responsibilities. Not only should they prayerfully read the Scripture text aloud, but they also should be encouraged to make some exegetical investigations themselves. They can share in tasks such as asking about authorial intent and how this particular passage of Scripture was intended to function, such as encouraging, rebuking, teaching, or praising God. Such work with Scripture should not compete with the preachers' preparation but instead strengthen mutual understanding. One lead-worshiper reading this said, "This is a *growth* opportunity for worship leaders. I am teaching and mentoring my worship leaders to answer the question, 'What is the text saying and doing?' before thinking about songs, prayers, call to worship, and so on. I want my leaders to *grow*."

Such strengthening is especially significant when seeking to interpret what God is saying now and doing now through this passage. In *360-Degree Preaching*, I suggest that preachers at this stage need to hear five *voices* to aid interpretation—Scripture, preacher, culture, congregation, and worship. Each of these voices speaks within the contemporary situation and may influence how God's Word is communicated. For the worship swim, the order of priority should be changed to: Scripture, worship, congregation, preacher, culture. Scripture's voice remains primary because only God's Word gives authority. Next come the voices of big-picture worship and congregation as God's Word challenges and builds up his community. Instead of seeing worship merely as a context for preaching, big-picture worship sums up the whole purpose of gathering to hear and respond to God's Word. Of course, preachers' own experiences and imagination continue to count, as does the voice of culture that so often contradicts scriptural truth in subtle as well as strident ways. When worship planners prayerfully listen together to all five voices, all kinds of insights and connections tumble out that would never have occurred to the solo preacher. Through such teamwork in interpreting Scripture, worship planners more easily discern specific community and missional implications of God's Word (questions 4, 5, and 6).

Several authors have urged preachers to collaborate in sermon preparation and extolled the value of mutual listening.[3] But the worship swim throws collaboration far wider than sermon making, thrusting Scripture forward as the directing force of all that occurs in gathered worship and beyond in missional living. Already some writers on worship have seen these wider implications, such as Russell Mitman, who argues strongly that preachers should be involved with small groups who help not only prepare but develop liturgy.[4] Tod Bolsinger also pleads for the wider community to be involved in the whole preaching act.[5]

In stage 2, all this work with the text boils down into one *main impact*. After exegeting the text in its original context and listening to it in today's world, preachers need to crystallize what the sermon will be about. They fill in the blanks: By the grace of God, what this *sermon* will *say* is _____ _____, and what this sermon will *do* is _____ _____. In the worship swim, however, this main impact is not restricted to sermons, but instead it affects the whole act of gathered worship. Whatever this Scripture is going to *do* influences worship outcomes such as encouraging, challenging, rebuking, giving pastoral advice, and teaching about God's attributes. Now lead-worshipers should fill in the blanks: By God's grace, what this *gathered worship* will *say* is _____ _____ and *do* is _____ _____.

In the last step in stage 2, "consider worship opportunity," worship planners thoughtfully locate Scripture's main impact within worship structure and content. For example, planners should work sensitively within seasons of the Christian year with awareness about helping communities live within God's story. Because of worship's capacity to build God's people together, worship planners should continually ask on which levels of community formation any act of gathered worship concentrates (see fig. 5). Is it a baptismal service with primary stress on initiation, or the Lord's Supper inviting opportunity for increasing integration? Does the main impact challenge major issues of character formation or missional living?

Stage 2 will be considered in more detail in chapter 12.

Stage 3

While greatly benefitting from working with others in stage 2, preachers obviously have the prime responsibility for designing the sermon. Yet because they have listened to the voice of worship, they now recognize how sermons should be integrated with every other aspect of gathered worship. Sermons remain the vital place for disclosing God's Word, but Scripture's main impact will also be proclaimed through other worship elements such as singing, praying, giving, baptism, and the Lord's Supper. Heard most clearly in preaching, Scripture also impacts everything else that belongs within God's worship dynamic of call and response (figs. 2 and 3) as God's community journeys inwardly in fellowship and outwardly for mission.

Stage 4

"Help shape gathered worship" has always been the primary domain of worship planners. But just as in stage 2 when working with Scripture is opened up beyond preachers, here the worship design is opened up to include preachers. Of course, much depends on church traditions and sizes. In smaller congregations, preachers may already choose orders of service, hymns, and prayers. Larger congregations, however, are likely to involve others in worship planning in a process that sometimes becomes separated from preachers. In Bill and Steve's situation, such separation led to stalemated isolation. Big-picture worship strongly challenges busy preachers who neglect helping shape gathered worship. Worship is so important to God's purpose for his community that no preacher should dare ignore this responsibility.

Notice, however, the necessary modesty—*help* shape—because preachers recognize that worship planners will have greater skills, resources, and (hopefully) time to shape gathered worship. Preachers should at least check the first two steps: "use the question toolbox" and "shape structure and content." Applying the six questions to every part of gathered worship tackles all kinds of practical issues. Of course, question 3, "Are we allowing Scripture to direct?" remains critically important. But many other questions about thankfulness, magnification, audiences, community, and mission all need to be addressed. Worship planners are accountable for working out the details, but preachers need to be engaged in the overall strategy. Stage 4 will be considered in more detail in chapter 13.

Stage 5

"Deliver the sermon and lead gathered worship" visibly involves preachers and worship planners in the outcome of all their work. Since *liturgy* means "work of the people," lead-worshipers should also ensure wider participation not only by inviting others to take part in different ways such as reading, drama, art, and music but also by including everyone responsively in prayer, music, offering, preaching, and the Lord's Supper. Worship should never be something done by a few in front; everyone should participate, joining visibly as the priesthood of believers (1 Pet. 2:5). Here expectations of God building his new community are fleshed out. This stage also raises practical issues about skills of voice and body language that lie beyond the purview of this book.[6]

Stage 6

"Evaluate the outcomes" is often omitted in Christian work, yet big-picture worship expects great things to happen. Assessment is vital to safeguard against wishful piety that just assumes effectiveness. Such evaluation operates at two levels. At the basic level, worship planners assess the outcomes of their own preparation. This is an essential tenet of leadership—any time spent reviewing past activity benefits future planning. Without feedback you keep on doing what you have always done. But evaluation involves another level that dares to ask how effectually the worship swim glorified God by building his community. What outcomes over the long term give evidence of growth in personal and community formation? Are there signs of sound initiation and lively integration? Is maturing character or missional living more evident? This stage will be considered in chapter 14.

Before giving detailed consideration to these stages in the next chapters, two more general issues need attention: team building and widening collaboration.

Team Building

While leading a workshop for some Baptist churches in the Chicago area, I asked the mixed group of preachers, worship planners, and worshipers whether preaching seemed to be separated from the rest of worship in their own churches. The overwhelming response was yes. I wrote down their reasons on a whiteboard:

- Scripture had no role in shaping the service
- lack of time for preparation as choice of text and sermon was made (very) late in the week
- already overcommitted, busy people were involved
- poor teamwork between preacher and others involved with worship
- failure to pattern worship with any order
- little sense of participation for congregation
- sidelining of communion
- omission of pastoral prayer and intercession

Several worshipers said this was the first time they had ever been asked for their opinions about worship, and they were fairly critical of what happened in their own churches. Notice how many of the bullet points identify issues we have already faced and, in particular, how they highlight the failure of leaders to work together.

Dealing properly with effective team building goes way beyond this book's scope. Elsewhere I have challenged preachers to develop the leadership skill of "enabling team learning."[7] Teams are often contrasted with committees. In teams, members have to develop group learning with openness to others' ideas and a collective willingness to see things differently. Committees, however, are often comprised of individuals arguing different points of view over agenda points. Preachers need to develop skills that enable teams to grow close interpersonal relationships for honest and authentic collaboration. Unless they are able to develop effective teams with shared understanding of dialogue and mutual accountability, collaboration along the lines of figure 7 will remain a fantasy—good to dream about but utterly unworkable. Teamwork is essential for anything good to happen, and that is why "build team(s)" is the first step in stage 1. How easily both pastors and musicians can be manipulators, dictators, victims to chaos, and dismissive of each other. Without good working relationships, worship is doomed to live in a small picture spoiled by awkward, territorial, and uncooperative leaders.

Good teams bring obvious benefits. Secular leadership values teamwork because of its creativity and healthy checks and balances that ensure outcomes that are so much richer than the sum of individual contributions. So much is gained by openness to others' ideas in dialogue. Yet considerable skills are needed to build such relationships that lead to honest consensus. Together with agreed-upon guidelines and ground rules for behavior and practice, serious commitments of time, energy, and consistency are required.

Christian teamwork, however, owes its inspiration to sources other than pragmatic organizational leadership practice. Rather, it is demanded by Scripture and trinitarian theology. Scripture abounds with examples of collaboration, as in the work of the temple (1 Chron. 23:3–5) and rebuilding Jerusalem with its worship (Neh. 7; 12). Of course, the *building* metaphor itself necessitates mutual bonding of living stones. But undergirding everything is theological conviction. "The Father, the Son and the Holy Spirit exist and work in relationship with each other. Each has a role to play and unique tasks. Yet their workings . . . are a composite of all three. If the Trinity co-labors in this manner, we can expect that we as God's image-bearers are also called to work together."[8] Teamwork lies at the heart of God's triune nature, and, made in his image, we are created for togetherness.

Since preachers usually occupy the main leadership role, they have greater responsibility for enabling team learning. They must work sensitively to remove obstacles. Based on research among lead-worshipers, Norma Malefyt and Howard Vanderwell identify several such obstacles, rating "incompatible views of worship" the most common and nettlesome.[9] Unless leaders learn to listen with trusting openness, the dangers of competitiveness with personal agendas and tunnel vision will destroy any possibility of agreeing on common goals. Other practical obstacles involve taking insufficient time, failing to plan ahead and to carry out responsibilities willingly for the sake of the team. Further, *any political polling* among members of the congregation that reinforces preferences can sabotage unity.

Only by wise team building that is grounded in gospel love can genuine, mutual openness grow. God's triune grace in action is demonstrated when teams work without competitive spirit and personal agendas. The world marvels when leaders work harmoniously. Of course, many practical details need agreement, such as setting times for regular meetings (preferably weekly) and establishing consistent communication patterns through the Internet. Relationships thrive on good communication, careful use of time, and thoughtfulness. Following through decisions to successful conclusion is also essential, while carefully noting decisions and allocating various responsibilities ensures effective action. Honest evaluation afterward completes the process.

How easy it is to write those last two paragraphs, and how difficult team building is in practice—so much hard work, love, and trust are required. As I have been writing this book, I have asked several leaders in different churches about their worship teams. Whatever the size and style of church and its variety of worship patterns, all have agreed that maintaining good relationships is critically important. A lead-worshiper looking for a new job told me, "The number one priority for my next job is a quality relationship with the senior pastor. I will ask, 'Can we pray and relate together as friends as we prepare for public worship?' Everything depends on that relationship." Quality relationships among lead-worshipers make for quality worship from the congregation.

Bill and Steve at Cornerstones Community Church seemed at first to have a strong personal relationship. But Steve's fresh vision for big-picture worship now means he must make a dramatic recommitment to Bill (and other worship planners) in order to build a genuine team. So much is at stake with big-picture worship. Since I began to write this book, several teams of senior pastors and music pastors have promised that they will try to work through the implications of big-picture worship. I look forward to hearing the outcomes.

Widening Collaboration

Earlier I commented that figure 7 focuses rather narrowly on how preachers and worship planners might collaborate, but wider participation should be welcomed as much as possible. Many models exist for involving others. In my Cambridge ministry, with gathered worship on Sunday mornings and evenings, the worship planners met at the beginning of each month to plan for the month ahead. Because three music groups undertook responsibility for different worship services, time only allowed for general issues and outlining possible worship resources as each team was allocated specific services. Following this meeting, however, the different groups worked out the details, all the time keeping in touch with me and other preachers and drawing in others to help in a wide variety of ways.

More recently, the advent of the Internet has revolutionized participation. In November 2007, I launched a weblog (blog), www.michaelquicke.blogspot.com, to encourage maximum involvement while I was interim preacher at Calvary Memorial Church in Oak Park, Illinois. Blogs are easily begun and much less easily sustained because energy levels quickly flag. A blog posts entries in chronological order with the most recent appearing at the top. Publicizing my blog to the whole congregation, I posted details about future texts and sermons, inviting readers to write comments, which could be viewed by all. When readers needed to write confidentially, they used my personal email address.

Many preachers apparently value this process. Ken Gosnall lists several ways that blogs can change preaching and sermon preparation. For example, blogs "bridge the gap" between preacher and hearers, enabling interaction before the sermon, while "increasing accountability" and "enhancing the preacher's transparency."[10] Learning from others' insights and stories, preachers are less likely to deal with general issues but instead focus on specific areas of spiritual growth and development.

In the light of big-picture worship, however, the greatest value of blogging lies in its wide-open communication that allows not only preachers, church leaders, and designated lead-worshipers to work together but any member of the worshiping community willing to get involved. When I started experimenting with blogging, I wondered how many would respond. On Sunday mornings we have a traditional service with organ and robed choir followed by two contemporary services. A music pastor is responsible for coordinating the traditional service, and many worship groups take responsibility for the contemporary services.

I was stunned by the quality and number of responses. I began blogging with a sermon series on God's promises. (The church does not use the lectionary, though it practices parts of the Christian year.) First, I met with a small church group of fifteen to twenty people who promised to support my sermon preparation. I posted our first night's discussion so that anyone else in the church (indeed from anywhere) could share from that point on.

Blogging God's Promises

Saturday, December 1, 2007

Last night I met with a great group of friends who worship at Calvary Memorial Church, Oak Park, a Chicago suburb. My wife and I have met with them regularly over many months, but this meeting was different. Before we met I had asked them to pray and think about

> *God's promises out of their personal and collective experiences. Be-*
> *cause I guessed many of their reflections might be confidential (and*
> *several were!), they used my personal email address.*
>
> *Why did I ask for their help? Because I am going to preach a series*
> *on God's promises from January through March 2008, and I needed*
> *their collaboration as representatives of the wider church fellowship.*
> *I really want others to be involved in some twenty-first-century story-*
> *telling of God's promises.*
>
> *Discussion was lively and insightful. Immediate enthusiasm for*
> *taking hold of God's great promises was followed by more sober re-*
> *flection. One person shared how these promises sounded good but*
> *had been heard so often (with little impact) that they didn't seem to*
> *relate to him. But if he could really trust them, they would turn his life*
> *around. Another warned how easily they can be corrupted by "name*
> *it and claim it" misuse, while someone else sensed that many feel*
> *they are not good enough for the promises to work for them. Another*
> *spoke eloquently about his religious background in which the prom-*
> *ises were heard but didn't work, until his own engagement with Jesus.*
> *He said, "To act on God's promise you must respond to 'Follow me.'"*
> *Others spoke of the personal nature of many promises—like those of*
> *overcoming temptation, touching on issues such as health, relation-*
> *ships, and money.*
>
> *In addition, several personal stories have come by email. Told*
> *with honesty, they describe how God's promises have impacted their*
> *lives—of joys, sorrows, and conflicts. Sometimes one Scripture text*
> *or perhaps several texts have held them tight over years. Several wrote*
> *of God's promises holding good in times of ill health and trouble. Yet*
> *another raised profound questions about genuine willingness to act on*
> *the promises.*
>
> *I value this group of friends for their honest spirituality as it con-*
> *tinued last night. This is only the beginning of my sermon journey. I*
> *invite anyone else in the fellowship at Calvary to share comments on*
> *this blog. Indeed, it's open to anyone, anywhere. I will let you know*
> *how the preaching develops. Of course, there are limits to the time I*
> *can spend, and I will not be able to use everyone's story, but I promise*
> *confidentiality. If yours is a more personal word, then please use my*
> *seminary email: mquicke@seminary.edu.*

Not only did additional stories quickly emerge, but another group in the church committed to work on a banner to place over the main church doors as well as design publicity handouts. Out of thirteen different slogans, this group eventually chose: God's Promises. Does He Deliver? Not only did this unexpected enthusiasm create publicity that actually attracted newcomers, but it also provided the overall theme for my sermons.

Ultimately, texts for a series of eight sermons were chosen from the many responses I received. I presented overviews of all eight texts to key church leaders and set to work week by week sharing my preparation for successive worship services. My blog enabled everybody (with computer access) to participate in unfolding preparation. Admittedly, it was an abbreviated form of the process in figure 7, but many became involved.

The second sermon, for example, focused on God's promise of happiness. A group member, Jane, shared a powerful story of how Psalm 1 had played a significant role throughout her life. Focusing on this psalm, I began to exegete and interpret it, inviting worship planners and others to share how this psalm might direct the structure of gathered worship with its hymns and prayers. As momentum grew, others became involved in dramatizing and filming Psalm 1 and Jane's story. In spite of a short time frame, widening collaboration brought about an extraordinary fusion of love, skill, and energy. In another blog, I reflected on the difference this made to the whole act of gathered worship.

Blogging God's Promises

Sunday, January 13, 2008

Collaboration—*when Jane (a church member) told me her story many weeks ago about how Psalm 1 had been God's promise to her over many years, I longed for her to share it. Others suggested making a video testimony, and a gifted member of the congregation, Donny (who is a professional), wrote a script (working with Jane) and then filmed and edited a four-minute, seven-second video. Involving many different voices and scenes, developing the image of trees (at the heart of the psalm), it ended imaginatively with different church members on the lawn outside! I was overwhelmed when I first saw it. Oh, what can happen when people share their best to tell out God's Word, and how it enriched me as preacher to have all these friends collaborating with me!*

Realism—*Jane told her story briefly but with honest highs and lows that registered directly. One person said, "That was so real. The failed marriage, the difficulties of trying to start again. That's me." Many conversations and prayers were sparked within the community.*

God's Word now—*the personal realism provided a vehicle through which to declare God's promise of Psalm 1 today. I preached three aspects to claiming God's promise of happiness in Psalm 1:*

- *Discern when to say no to the ungodly—verse 1*
- *Delight to say yes to God—verses 2–3*
- *Grow together in joy—verses 5–6*

Several commented especially on the last part, the picture of Calvary Memorial as an *arboretum*, seeing the plurals of the NRSV translation: "Happy are those who do not follow the advice of the wicked; . . . their delight is in the law of the LORD. . . . They are like trees planted by streams of water, . . . the *congregation* of the righteous" (Ps. 1:1–3, 5, italics mine). What a vision of growing together in God's promises: some silver birches, spruces, giant redwoods, oaks, and others all helping each other to discern when to say no and when to delight in the yeses.

The sermon and video clip were posted on the church website, and responses to the whole act of worship continued throughout the next days. Later, I posted a follow-up including this:

Psalm Surprise

Tuesday, January 15, 2008

One of the surprises about preaching on Psalm 1 was the number of people who claimed it was their "special" psalm too. One shared how significant it had been to them. A mother told me her children were memorizing it. Another said it was their grandfather's favorite.

I recognize the privilege of belonging to a church community that has the resources to undertake such imaginative worship participation. This particular service developed in ways I never envisaged, and the video testimony has since developed a life of its own. I am also aware that computer access to blogs is not possible for everyone and that some may feel excluded. Yet when I stressed how keen I was to receive responses in any form, spoken or written, several congregational members also participated in these other ways. I treasure the honest participation from so many. For example, a worship service on stress and anxiety sparked many responses. Even before preparation, someone wrote, "I can't wait for next week. . . . It's about worry, isn't it? Few of us have got anxiety licked!" A man sent me his story, beginning, "Here's my problem. I suffer from stress and anxiety." Sharing his efforts about trying to cope with financial demands, family concerns, and health worries, he said God's promises of peace often left him as anxious as ever. With permission, I used his story to take us to deeper places with 1 Peter 5:7. I could tell so many more stories like this.

I believe that *whatever* the size of the church community, higher degrees of partnership and collaboration are possible when worshipers trust that *God gives to his people all the gifts needed for all he wants to do through them.* Widening participation enables more and more people to magnify God, to share in the magnificence of big-picture worship, and to be real in their own spiritual growth. What an adventure when others are allowed to join in big-picture worship!

11

Beginning Well

Worship Swim Stage 1

How I would love it if once, just once, the senior pastor seemed to be even interested in opening up to me about worship.

comment from a music pastor

That remains one of the saddest comments I have heard on my worship journey. What a tragedy that two leaders could fail even to converse about worship. What alarming evidence of myopia! Earlier I emphasized that our Triune God uses godly leaders whose integrity helps them develop worship that is "inspired by the Spirit, empowered by the Spirit, directed by the Spirit, purified by the Spirit, and bears the fruit of the Spirit."[1] Personal spiritual overflow from lead-worshipers is the most powerful human worship resource.

Stage 1 of the worship swim therefore requires not only effective team building (as described in the last chapter) but also deeper unity of heart, mind, and practice. The closer lead-worshipers grow together in spirit and in truth, sharing character, understanding, and experience, the more effective they will be in directing big-picture worship. On one hand, they reach toward the wide horizons of big-picture worship, thrilling to trinitarian theology, embracing thoughtful liturgical practice, and committing to community formation. Throwing themselves with wonder and joy into God's call and response (figs. 2 and 3), they affirm that nothing is more important than worship that holds together all they are and all they do. On the other hand, while always aware of God's biggest worship purposes, they must focus on planning weekly acts of congregational worship. Therefore, "commit to worship" (stage 1) requires agreement of heart, mind, and practice for the long-term vision as well as for the immediate worship needs.

Out of twenty-five years of worship experience, Norma Malefyt and Howard Vanderwell classify these agreements as qualifications of heart, head, and hands.[2] In spite of a somewhat artificial division, their lists of qualifications are valuable. (The lists follow under the three headings of heart, head, and hands qualifications.) Of course, listing these qualities should not disguise the difficulties of developing some of them. This chapter's opening quotation starkly warns how relationships can sour. Christians should be painfully aware of sinfulness and frailty in human relationships and be realistic about the need for the theology of the cross before exulting in Christ's resurrection power. Developing qualifications of heart, head, and hands involves much struggle and much grace from God.

Heart Qualifications

Malefyt and Vanderwell identify five heart qualifications:

1. sense of the holiness of God
2. sense of priestlike leadership
3. growing spiritual life
4. love for the church
5. pastoral sensitivity[3]

To these I add a sixth qualification: thankfulness. Together they contribute to reverential wonder for planning and leading public worship. I have summarized each qualification by a single word, and we will consider each in turn.

Thankfulness

It has already become clear that thankfulness is *the* foundational worship response. Remember, the first toolbox question is, "Gift: Are we thankfully receiving this gift of worship from the Triune God of grace?" To this question lead-worshipers must frequently and resoundingly answer yes. Thankfulness is the springboard for authentic worship; positive thankfulness leads to positive worship. Even in prison, the apostle Paul continually luxuriated in the gifts of God's grace, viewing everything with a thankful heart (for example, Col. 1:3; 3:17). Recognizing that worship is a gift and receiving it by God's grace *always* lead to gratitude. Thankful hearts are therefore prerequisite for lead-worshipers who, regretfully, can all too easily find themselves trapped in the grind of professional duties rather than the liberation of gratitude. Each time leaders gather together in worship planning, the meeting should begin with a heartfelt prayer of thanks and continue in gratefulness.

Awe

In Scripture every encounter with God is marked by awe, which expresses wonder before God's total, overwhelming holiness. Moses kicks off his sandals in the presence of God's holiness and "hid his face because he was afraid to look at God" (Exod. 3:5–6 NIV); Isaiah is overwhelmed in the temple (Isa. 6:3–7); neither Simon nor Saul can bear Jesus's power (Luke 5:8; Acts 9:3–6). God's holiness always provokes incredulous wonder and a sense of inadequacy by revealing both God's attributes of power and righteousness and also his deeds in creation, salvation, and wisdom (Prov. 1:7).

Sadly, awe seems in short supply today. Too often worship casually saunters into God's presence. In a sermon about God confronting Elijah in a cave (1 Kings 19:9–18), Eugene Lowry remarked that "some preachers seemed to have missed out on the seminary course titled: Transcendence 101. They think that there is no big deal about preaching. For them it is just a little word about Jesus. . . . They have no conception of God's mystery beyond all mysteries."[4] Confidence to enter worship comes only through Christ's sacrifice—"we have confidence to enter the Most Holy Place by the blood of Jesus" (Heb. 10:19 NIV). Swagger, carelessness, and self-reliance are utterly out of place. So too is the all-too-personal welcome. Marva Dawn warns, "I fear the subtle replacement of the mystery of the Trinity with the pastor's personality in initiating worship . . . almost as if the priest invites us into his living room instead of God welcoming us into his presence."[5] No one should be blasé about encountering God. "Instead of putting off our shoes from our feet because the place where we stand is holy ground, we are taking nice photographs of the burning bush from suitable angles."[6]

Humility

Priestlike leadership is expressed as humility. Some may object to *priestlike* language because Christ is the only High Priest and Mediator necessary for worship. True, but his mediation does not dispense with the need for lead-worshipers who humbly stand before the people, speaking on God's behalf and helping them respond together. Humility is essential, for any public role is susceptible to hubris, and worship leading is no exception. Tragically, human egos can too easily shine at the expense of divine glory.

Preachers should know this well. Gerard Sloyan warns them about "upstaging Scripture" and looking for congratulations, as when people more than occasionally say, "That was a powerful message." Such comments sadly reveal that the sermon "has taken on a life of its own. . . . By some kind of fission it has come apart from the parent body, the worship service. It stands alone in splendor or in shame as a good performance or a bad one."[7] He also warns about the "hazard of fluency" when words come too easily. "The bitterest complaint against pulpit practitioners is that they speak too long. This invariably means that they use more time than there are thoughts to match. . . . There is a thoughtful, prayerful, cultivated you that lies deep. There is also a surface you that is immediately available. The latter your people can have at any time. To preach well is to go in search of the former."[8]

Sloyan's challenge to preachers applies equally to any who lead public worship. Performance so easily becomes ego-driven, competitive, and shallow. The current popular refrain, "It's not about me," often rings hollow as immodest spirits parade with little evidence of weakness, fear, and trembling (1 Cor. 2:3). Yet humble leaders who submit their egos for the sake of God's glory can provide priestlike leadership to worship teams and worshipers.

Prayerfulness

A growing spiritual life is characterized by prayerfulness. Prayer *joins* us in a relationship that God has *already* invited us into as Jesus intercedes at the right hand of the Father (Rom. 8:34; Heb. 7:25) and the Holy Spirit helps us in weakness (Rom. 8:26). Indeed, because prayer expresses such profound participation with God, some describe preaching itself as prayer. Sloyan suggests that "our preaching is part of the one, prayerful thing we do publicly." As God speaks to us in Scripture, so a preacher's sermon is a "continuation of the conversation. It is Spirit-invested but not, like the Bible, Spirit-inspired."[9]

We have already stressed the importance of lead-worshipers' own prayer lives overflowing into public worship. Worship teams should have deep prayer lives before they dare lead others in thankfulness, awe, and humility. Yet sadly, when worship teams meet they often neglect prayer together. Pressures of working up sermons and planning worship services squeeze prayer into perfunctory routine or even omit it completely. One worship planner, after sharing prayer with a preacher in just such a team session, said, "Oh that was so wonderful! I wish all service planning began with prayer." Oh yes! Nothing substitutes for authentic joining-in-with-God prayer.

Love

Another obvious heart qualification is love. Yet again, it can be disturbingly absent. "Countless books have been written about worship but few, if any, speak of love. . . . We have convinced ourselves that we will discover more effective worship if we only get a better preacher, a more creative liturgy, etc. But love is the greatest."[10] God's grace works by love. Only by God's love can preachers, musicians, and other lead-worshipers bond together and communities of living stones be built up. Malefyt and Vanderwell therefore call lead-worshipers to be "deeply and passionately in love with the congregation."[11] Failure to love renders worship empty noise (1 Cor. 13:1). Love must focus not only inwardly by developing fellowship but also outwardly by serving others as missional communities who love their neighbors. Lead-worshipers need to love in both directions too.

Care

Pastoral sensitivity to others is expressed through care for them. Worship planners should model this in their team relationships, always listening well and acting compassionately. Indeed, mature pastoral leadership helps school whole congregations in Christian behavior and relationships. Further, those planning liturgy as the *work of the people* should take care to include as many participants as possible in meaningful ways; sensitive involvement of many living stones strengthens church unity (Eph. 4:1–16). Again, as with love, pastoral care not only nurtures fellowship life but also embraces others beyond.

Reverential Wonder

When these six heart qualifications combine, they produce a remarkable characteristic: *reverential wonder*. Unfortunately, the word *reverence* has received bad press in some quarters, caricatured in pompous preachers with holy tones and churchy piety. But reverence properly understood reveals lead-worshipers' thankfulness, awe, humility, and prayerfulness before God and their love and care for others. Reverential wonder is not a manufactured appearance; instead, it overflows from authentic relationship with God. Sometimes this quality has been referred to as *presidential style*, as described by Thomas Long:

> If the leaders genuinely believe that worship is being conducted in the presence of God, it shows, and what is more, that belief is contagious. Whether the leaders are eloquent or prosaic, formal or informal, experienced or novice, when they perceive that worship occurs in the context of holy mystery everything changes—voice, posture, language, gesture.[12]

I have witnessed reverential wonder in dramatically contrasting situations, from leaders in formal robes in pulpits to others casually dressed in T-shirts and jeans. But sadly, I have also observed leaders who unwittingly display self-importance and overconfidence. William Willimon warns that contemporary culture so admires media moguls, and "pastors unconsciously take on the mannerisms and style of the television preacher, particularly in their leadership of public worship. The pastor as performer, as grinning personality, supersedes the roles of pastor as teacher, priest, and leader of the congregation."[13]

Reverential wonder testifies to continual dependence on God's spiritual fruit-growing (Gal. 5:25). But such dependence is constantly tested by professional pride in performance and sabotaged by prayerlessness. Lead-worshipers need to grow closer together in sharing heart qualifications. I still recall the shock waves when my own leadership team committed to study Dietrich Bonhoeffer's *Life Together*. It made very slow reading because page after page its challenge to live as Christ's community exposed our shallow relationships. Bonhoeffer warns against "confusing Christian brotherhood with some wishful idea of religious fellowship" as though we think it possible to construct some deep social experience just by devoutly longing to be together. No, "Christian brotherhood is not an ideal, but a *divine reality*."[14] Only by belonging together in Christ can communities be formed that share heart qualifications.

Head Qualifications

Malefyt and Vanderwell also identify seven head qualifications:

1. a theology of worship
2. primacy of worship
3. individual's submission for the sake of the whole
4. compatible relationships
5. understanding of the planner's role
6. ability to communicate
7. knowledge of the congregation[15]

The last five qualifications in particular relate to working in teams, and since they were discussed in detail in the previous chapter, we will not address them further here. But the first two—a theology of worship and the primacy of worship—are very significant issues that require agreement. In addition, Scripture's role in directing worship, liturgical structure, community formation, and music choices must be considered.

Brainstorming is a term commonly used to describe synergetic, open-ended discussion that inspires new connections and fresh possibilities. But when worship planners discuss together, a better term might be *soul-storming*. For them, seeking agreement involves spiritual commitment open to the mind of Christ (1 Cor. 2:16). These head qualifications are part of loving the Lord with heart, soul, strength, and mind (Luke 10:27). The stronger myopic preaching's hold on worship planners, with its false definitions and small picture, the tougher is this process of soul-storming. Rethinking long-held views on worship is often painful and always demanding.

Theology

Malefyt and Vanderwell rightly placed this first on the list.[16] Inadequate theology imperils any hope of developing big-picture worship. Lead-worshipers must reflect on their current understanding in light of the challenge given in James Torrance's "Existential Experience Model" (fig. 2) and the contrasting opportunities within trinitarian worship. Do they exhibit any signs of practical unitarianism? Are demands consistently made of worshipers' self-effort rather than inviting them to join in and participate in God's work? Has the language of gathered worship generally encouraged thin theology—perhaps directed to Jesus only? How easily do worshipers think of gathered worship in terms of forming a maturing church community instead of meeting merely individual needs? Asking questions like these may touch raw nerves, but thinking and acting as trinitarians bring about dramatic new perspectives.

Primacy of Worship

It is important to think through the implications of giving worship first place. Doing so rebukes all lesser assessments such as music only, preaching only, liturgics only, pragmatics only, maintenance only, or Sunday services only. Rather, it embraces big-picture worship that offers up all Christian life to God's glory for his grandest purposes. It takes seriously the models presented in figures 3 and 4, placing everything within the trinitarian call and response of God, and recognizes that community formation of God's people (fig. 5) expresses the whole point of being church and, ultimately, of being alive in the first place.

Such commitment to big-picture worship rarely comes easily to worship teams used to working along narrow tracks. Indeed, we noted that Malefyt and Vanderwell rated "incompatible views of worship" as the most serious obstacle to developing a team. Yet dismantling deficient understandings and replacing them with new must begin with worship planners. If, for example, *Sunday services only* has predominated (common in many churches), leaders need to reenvision worship for themselves and their congregations in ways that embrace all of life and all the community. When reconceptualizing God's bigger purposes through soul-storming, lead-worshipers define big-picture worship in their own contexts. Lead-worshipers who together think hard about the primacy of worship can help congregations grow more deeply.

Scripture's Role in Directing Worship

Obviously, agreement among lead-worshipers is required to move away from confining Scripture to the preachers' territory and to develop a true understanding of how it directs all worship. Because Scripture not only *says* things that have to be proclaimed but also *does* things that have to be experienced, it should have a major impact on weekly collaboration. Worship teams need to work through mutual responsibilities for listening to Scripture (stage 2 of the worship swim in fig. 7). Do they agree with the check marks? Are preachers willing to open up their work with Scripture to others, and are worship planners willing to collaborate?

Liturgical Structure

Earlier we noted that planning worship services operates at three levels. At the bottom level, normal patterns of worship structure remain stable in well-established practice. Whether a pattern has developed over three years or three hundred years, any change is likely to provoke resistance. Yet with heart qualifications of prayerfulness, love, and care, lead-worshipers need to think through the strengths and weaknesses of inherited worship patterns.

Russell Mitman contrasted *tennis court* churches that possess clear limits regulated by inherited worship traditions with *open field* churches that have greater freedom. He urged both kinds of churches to heed the scriptural dynamic of God's call and response, which is reflected in a fivefold pattern:

Gathering

Confession

Word

Response to God's Word in Table or thanksgiving

Sending forth

Worship planners must think through the implications of this challenge. Does Scripture characterize worship patterns of revelation and response in ways that warrant a fivefold structure? Would any refinements or changes encourage more worthy worship?

Refining structures is easier than introducing changes. Worship planners should carefully examine each element. For example, the *gathering* is often enthusiastically practiced yet can focus too narrowly on the pastor's warm welcome. I recall one pastor who began, "We are privileged that you have chosen to worship with us today, and we hope you will really find this a great church." He sounded like an airline pilot welcoming customers on board. Gathering to worship God, however, is not about customers invited by lead-worshipers to have a good time with them. Gathered worship is entirely God's idea, and it is he who calls us together. Sam Hamstra quotes a former professor's forceful reaction to such a welcome: "Who are you to welcome me to worship? It's not your service."[17]

So after warm greetings, a *call to worship* should be sounded out from God, before whom the congregation comes with reverence and awe (Heb. 12:28). Given in the name of Jesus Christ or threefold name of our Triune God, this call best uses Scripture verses to emphasize how God, not us, initiates worship. To safeguard against further presumption, traditionally *prayers of invocation* invite the Holy Spirit to work with us and through us. Similarly, *prayers of illumination*, including the familiar prayer, "May the words of our lips and the meditations of our hearts be acceptable," help focus on God's work with us and for us. Open field churches may resist using formal prayers, but they should make efforts to ensure similar prayers are offered. Of course, gathering hymns and songs also should praise God in three persons, always emphasizing his triune wonder and what he has done.

Looking at other elements of the fivefold structure may be more complicated. Some parts may be completely missing from the inherited worship pattern. For example, *confession* may be omitted so that a congregation never collectively acknowledges sin, repents in sorrow, or receives God's pardon. Lead-worshipers need to think through the implications of neglecting confession. Does it matter that there is little space for the community to admit failure and receive God's restorative forgiveness?

The fourth element—*responding to God's Word in Table or thanksgiving*—also raises important questions. Scripture not only *says* things that have to be proclaimed but also *does* things that have to be experienced. How will the worship planners ensure that worshipers can begin to respond after hearing God's Word? Of course, the Lord's Supper provides the ideal place for deliberative response, but what about other occasions? For congregations that practice the Lord's Supper less frequently, Robert Webber suggests that a time of thanksgiving should allow worshipers to respond, to rejoice that God has spoken to them in his story and commit to walk in his ways. Sadly, this vital time for congregational commitment can be lost. Instead of providing critical space for making responses such as prayer, confession, stillness, and music, some worship services end with abrupt dismissals that cut short thoughtful obedience and commitment.

Such failure to provide adequate time for response can be compounded by a gravely devalued *sending forth*. Instead of worshipers being sent out with high motives as God's people to continue worship in the world, final words can miss the point entirely. God's last word to his gathered people should powerfully sound out his challenge and grace to live for him the rest of the week. Sent out by God's authority and in his name, worshipers should continue living for God in the world. That's why benedictions should not be trivialized. "As a matter of fact, when the pastor pronounces the Trinitarian benediction at the close of worship, a promise is made that all three persons of the Trinity will continue to co-labor on behalf of God's children throughout the week ahead."[18]

Gathered worship should never end with trite invitations to enjoy coffee afterward or to come again next week. No, the last part should be planned as the vital transition from gathered worship into scattered worship for God's glory. Worship in spirit and in truth is a big deal!

The middle level of planning liturgical structure relates to seasonal patterns and requires lead-worshipers to think through the critical issue of which calendar they will follow. Earlier we noted that all churches follow one calendar or another, whether it is chronology, church programs, greeting card, or the Christian year. In open field churches in which lead-worshipers have followed other calendars, can they agree that following the Christian year, even for its

main seasons of Lent/Easter and Advent/Epiphany, has immense value for helping congregations live in God's story? How may different spiritual emphases
be developed through the seasons? Can Christmas and Easter be celebrated
more worthily? Might the lectionary also prove valuable in providing content
and direction? These and many other questions have great importance for
building community awareness about living in God's big story.

Thinking through the bottom and middle levels of worship planning lays
foundations for designing weekly acts of congregational worship at the top
level. Hearts and minds that agree on worship's long-term purposes are better
prepared to plan specific worship services along the way. The next chapters
will provide more detail for such top-level planning.

Community Formation

Probably the most formidable challenge confronting worship planners is
community formation. Contemporary worship is so ingrained with people
doing their own thing that any bigger vision of worship involving building
community seems highly idealistic. Endemic individualism runs counter to
thoughts of community formation. Big-picture worship, however, demands
revolutionary rethinking of worship's role as it not only praises God but also
integrates worshipers into communities that grow together with increasing
maturity in order to witness to surrounding culture. Few worship planners
escape huge intellectual adjustments when facing implications of the four
stages of community formation (see fig. 5). Reflecting honestly on their own
situations, they need to spend much time asking about strengths and weaknesses. Just how should they help worshipers through initiation and integration
and then into character formation and missional living? In a discussion about
figure 5 with a group of lead-worshipers, several commented that they had
never thought of worship beyond the levels of initiation and integration, and
even these were sketchily practiced. "The idea of building toward character
formation and missional living has never entered my head when I plan worship," said one. Such ideas need to enter our heads!

At the initiation stage, lead-worshipers must ask how well worship encourages individuals to learn about their relationship to Jesus Christ within the
Trinity as well as what it means to belong with other members of his church.
Is baptism planned as a corporate event for the whole church community,
with congregational participation marked by wonder, awe, celebration, and
festivity? With integration, believers learn to use the language *we* as they grow
in responsibility for each other and gain knowledge of what it means to live
through the Christian year. Again, critical questions have to be asked about
whether the Lord's Supper is being adequately celebrated as a vital focus of
corporate worship. Does it offer community encounter with God, with explicit challenges about belonging to his story in the past, present, and future?

Whenever the Lord's Supper is squeezed onto the sidelines, this essential spiritual event is tragically diminished.

Character formation, though denoted as the third stage, should begin at initiation. Yet as believers mature, their attitudes and actions should demonstrate greater sensitivity in behavior and preferences. Indeed, the whole community learns to express greater unity in words and deeds. Lead-worshipers must continually ask how best they can encourage such spiritual growth in holiness, love, and unity. How can congregations be led to deeper understanding about divisive issues such as music choices in worship? Community spiritual formation also occurs as leaders help school worshipers by modeling in their own team relationships the responsibilities of being the people of God.

Missional living crowns community formation by expressing countercultural living in behavior and witness. The most demanding of all the stages, it describes how worshiping communities should demonstrate signs of Christ's kingdom, such as forgiveness and reconciliation, justice and social action. How contrary to contemporary culture and how utterly dependent on God's grace! Only by participating in his triune love and power can such communities flourish. Courageous worship leadership must continuously keep this big picture of belonging to God's kingdom witnessing to the world at the fore.

Throughout the process of community formation, many complex and sometimes conflicting dynamics combine. As we have seen, both verbal and nonverbal forms of communication are involved, working implicitly and explicitly. But worship planners should recognize how much lies beyond their control; community building is God's own work. Christ is the Cornerstone, whose church is built by the power of the Spirit to the Father's glory. Formation is not shaped by clever management and leadership techniques; it remains an act of the Triune God from beginning to end. Yet lead-worshipers can sabotage it and blunt growth unless they keep alert.

Music Choices

Earlier I placed the issue of how to deal with different music preferences into the larger concern of community character formation. Music choices well illustrate the need for believers to deal maturely with their preferences for the sake of the whole community. Sadly, as we have noted, in some churches music preferences have ripped people apart. Worship planners must understand tensions in their own team as well as in the congregation in order to encourage maturing openness among worshipers as part of community formation.

Undeniably, music evokes strong preferences. Thomas Troeger claims that each of us has a *sonic culture*—musical memories that "run deep in the blood and they can exercise a hidden power over people's responses to worship."[19] Indelibly molded by experiences of sound from an early age, each worshiper's sonic culture likely includes music associated with church worship. But multigenerational and multicultural global Christian worship possesses an extraordinary range of music, creating a wide range of sonic cultures. In light of this rich diversity, Troeger suggests an exercise to identify different sonic cultures represented in congregations. "Identifying the Sonic Culture I Bring to Worship" has five steps.

> Step 1: Each person lists three favorite pieces of music for worship, of any form and style. Pieces that "thrill your heart, that lift you into a state of prayer, that give you a sense of the presence of the Spirit, that strengthen your faith, that bring a lump to the throat or tears to the eyes."[20]
>
> Step 2: Respondents are asked to say, if possible, how and where they learned each piece and any particular memory or association it has for them.
>
> Step 3: Each person is asked to step outside of personal experience and take the role of one who is to plan and lead worship for the whole congregation, asking what the strengths and weaknesses are in the pieces identified in step 1.
>
> Step 4: Respondents are asked to compare selections, associations, and evaluations with those of two other people from the congregation. How similar or different are they? Are they compatible or in conflict?

These steps help worshipers understand who they are and what expectations they bring into worship. While steps 1–4 focus on the present reality, an additional question is necessary in light of community formation.

> Step 5: They are then asked, "What different kinds of music would you be willing to share for the sake of God's wider fellowship? In order to meet with brothers and sisters, are there musical forms that you would be willing to accept?"

For the sake of God and other people, how willing are worshipers to forego personal preferences? Though intended for wider congregational use, Troeger's exercise can be usefully employed by the lead-worshipers themselves who at step 3 need to think through community implications of choices they make.

Of course, music involves much more complex issues when churches actually divide congregations according to music choices: traditional, contemporary, or blended. Sometimes congregations outgrow worship sanctuaries and therefore need to divide. But at other times, music choices drive separation. I think of one church sanctuary large enough to cope adequately with 500 worshipers that houses two services—traditional and contemporary—with less than 250 worshipers in each. Whether separate services are forced by growth or by music choices, lead-worshipers face the same critical question: How important is it for the church community as a whole, even though it meets at different times (and sometimes in different places), to have the same worship ethos for all its services? Is a commonality of music and liturgy somehow significant for belonging to community? Or since two or three different communities are forming anyway, does it matter if they focus on their own kinds of music and liturgy?

This is a large and contentious issue. In answer to the last question, some say it does not matter. Since different congregations become two church communities anyway, why not let them have separate music styles? A pastor friend who inherited a church with parallel traditional and contemporary worship services wrote about his situation. He warmly commended the different services because they allow people to relax into their chosen styles and therefore offer their best to God in their separate ways.

> Some of the congregation worry about being a "divided church." I'm not sure what that really means. Division can't be cured by putting everyone in the same room and singing the same songs! Community can't simply be created by worshiping together. Unity and community have to be about something much deeper—shared values, purpose and mission. . . . Both congregations have grown in size. Links between people grow not through the worship but through shared ministry and through small groups.

His reply reveals much of the practical dilemma facing lead-worshipers who long to pursue big-picture worship. They know God might have a better purpose for worship, but they have to live with realities of small-picture worship.

Perhaps, understandably, this pastor looks elsewhere in ministry and small groups for community building. Yet his statement that "community can't simply be created by worshiping together" challenges a central conviction of big-picture worship: when properly understood and practiced together, worship actually leads people to deeper places of shared values, purpose, and mission. People may thrive separately in their own musical preferences, but doesn't this cause us to lose something vital from God's building his multigenerational, multicultural people together? This argument will rage long and hard with no easy answers. A friend commented, "Something will be sacrificed—either musical preferences or building community. What's really at stake is our values. We may ask why we should sacrifice anything, but the better question is: What must *not* be sacrificed?" Music choices always need to be made in the context of community formation as worshipers develop maturing appreciation of differences while seeking to offer their best together for God's sake.

Application of Questions

Lead-worshipers also need to agree that they will apply the so-called question toolbox. These six questions represent significant aspects of big-picture worship and are relevant to each and every aspect of gathered worship.

Question Toolbox

1. *Gift*: Are we thankfully receiving this gift from the Triune God of grace?
2. *Magnification*: Are we expressing its richness toward God?
3. *Scripture*: Are we allowing Scripture to direct?
4. *Audiences*: Are we addressing two audiences?
5. *Community*: Are we building community by story?
6. *Mission*: Are we enabling community to scatter?

I was amused by Paul Scott Wilson's mnemonic in *Four Pages of a Sermon*. To remember six principles about sermon unity—one text, one theme, one doctrine, one need, one image, and one mission—he suggests *TTDNIM*: This Tiny Dog Now Is Mine.[21] Oddly sticking in the memory, it prodded me to create a mnemonic for my six questions. What about *GMSACM*: God Makes Some Amazingly Connected Misfits? Though less memorable, it does at least capture something of the extraordinary work God has committed to do in worship. As worshipers praise God, he builds his new community by connecting them together as living stones. I know the word *misfit* seems awkward, but it aptly emphasizes that none of us belong naturally within God's new creation. Once we were no people, and now we are his people, owing our togetherness entirely to his amazing grace at work with us.

I remember one Sunday morning at my Cambridge church when three new members joined the community at the Lord's Supper. A university professor with a stellar reputation and his gifted professor wife stood alongside a disheveled man who, as local road sweeper, often cleaned the street outside the church building. Delightfully down-to-earth, normally unshaven, with a grubby yellow fluorescent vest and dust-covered glasses, the road sweeper stood before us full of joy at his new commitment. Reaching across, he greeted the other two while beaming around at the church family he was joining. Afterward the professor said, "That was just amazing, seeing how we all belong in Christ as brothers and sisters. I think we saw something of what the kingdom of God is meant to be like." *God makes some amazingly connected misfits* belong together for his big worship purposes.

Whether the mnemonic helps or not, these six questions should probe every aspect of gathered worship, from the largest elements, such as worship structures, baptism, and the Lord's Supper to smaller choices of music and prayer. They continually remind planners of the major issues such as the role of Scripture and the need for community formation.

Hand Qualifications

After considering heart and head qualities, Malefyt and Vanderwell identify four hand qualifications:

1. willingness to volunteer
2. willingness to schedule the necessary time
3. fulfillment of all assigned tasks
4. practice and growth in God's gifts[22]

Agreement on best practices, with accompanying readiness to serve, adds practical commitment to heart and head qualifications. Some of these practicalities have already been mentioned, such as planning weekly work patterns and timing assigned tasks.

Practice varies dramatically from church to church. Within the boundaries of set liturgy (tennis courts), worship may already have a prescribed flow, making some aspects of planning easier. In less-formal contexts (open fields), preachers and worship planners have more freedom but also more responsibility to think through worship design. Much also depends on personalities, experience, and size of worshiping community. Obviously, the deeper a team's unity, the smoother it will be to work through the practicalities of weekly planning.

I am always intrigued by lead-worshipers' stories. For example, one senior pastor told me he began as director of music within a traditional church with responsibilities for the overall shape and content of the weekly liturgy, which included a choir. Since rehearsal time was limited, he devised a scheme that not only prepared for the upcoming worship service but also anticipated following weeks. But how far could he reasonably look ahead? Gradually he developed a pattern that anticipated six weeks ahead. Choir rehearsal began with a taster of something envisaged for five and six weeks ahead, to be followed by other material relating to weeks two, three, and four. Finally, the choir would concentrate on the upcoming service. As the pattern developed, choir members became used to preparing ahead and bringing their learning into each current worship event. Later, when he became senior pastor of the same church, he discovered that he could apply exactly the same technique to preparing his sermons and worship. Now, working with equally limited time constraints, he and his team look ahead for six services with a rolling pattern. Continually working backward from anticipated future services, they focus on the current one last.

Few are likely to share this particular experience or be so disciplined, but in so many imaginative and creative ways, lead-worshipers can plan out their work. For a number of years I received a copy of a weekly publication from Second Baptist Church, Lubbock, Texas (following my visit to lead a weekend retreat). One page was divided along the middle; in the top half the senior pastor wrote about ministry in the church; in the bottom half the pastor for music and worship, Tommy Shapard, wrote about worship issues.[23] Both wrote extremely well, and I never missed reading what they had to say, especially about music and worship. Immense care was taken each week to explain issues such as moving through seasons of the Christian year. In an article titled "Why Not Sing Christmas Carols in Worship during Advent?" Shapard explained why traditional carols would not be sung until Christmas Eve. Singing them earlier "may seem harmless, but in fact, it is not, for our sensibility to appreciate the *fullness* of the Gospel narrative of Christ's coming into the world is numbed in our stressful scurrying to consume and celebrate. As Christians we are sometimes called to live a bit differently than the world around us."[24]

He carefully introduced new worship happenings such as Tenebrae singing on Good Friday and celebration of U2eucharist (using the music of the rock band U2). At other times he took up big, controversial issues. In a powerful article titled "Worship Authenticity: 'What Does the Lord Require?'" he rejected mistaken criteria for authentic worship, such as "it produces financial and membership growth; it creates more conversions; it is comfortable and therapeutic." Instead, referring to Micah 6, he wrote, "What pleases God is not the kinds of offerings or the manner in which they are presented in worship, but the restoration and inclusion of the poor and needy to the community. . . . I'm still waiting for the publication, *Cutting Edge Worship: How to Attract the Poorest of the Poor to Your Sanctuary*."[25] Taking such trouble to reflect on worship with the whole congregation can only benefit understanding of big-picture worship.

Developing Core Values

Some lead-worshipers take agreement on heart, head, and hand qualifications to a more formal level by developing core values—the values and beliefs that drive vision and action. They have become an important tool for leading transformation because they identify what really matters to an organization and help explain *why* it behaves in the way it does.[26] Aubrey Malphurs describes a Christian organization's core values as "the constant, passionate, biblical core beliefs that drive its ministry."[27] Because core values look to the present and the past, they are very different from discerning vision or mission. Rather, they describe present strengths. "A ministry's key values or beliefs are the shaping force of the entire institution. They beget attitudes that specify behavior. They affect everything about the organization, the decisions made, the goals set, the priorities established, the problems solved, the conflict resolved, and more."[28]

Again, much depends on the church tradition to which the worship planning team belongs. Some open field church leaders have not only worked through their core values but also published them in order to provide a basis for congregational ministry. For example, Faith Baptist Fellowship in Sioux Falls, South Dakota, developed eight core values titled "What Is the Philosophy of Worship That Unites Us?"[29] This is an abbreviated list of their uniting values about worship:

God-focused: Our supreme aim is that of magnifying the worth of God.

Gospel-centered: We join God the Father and God the Holy Spirit in proclaiming, exalting, and cherishing the redemptive work of God the Son.

Expecting the powerful presence of God: We earnestly seek his drawing near to us (James 4:8).

Bible-based and Bible-saturated: The content of God's Word will be woven through all we do in worship.

Head and heart: We seek to worship in a way that aims at stirring up real emotions toward God based on objective truth while at the same time avoiding manipulation. We rejoice with trembling (Ps. 2:11), and the tone we seek is one of joy, wonder, humility, grace, reverence.

Undistracting excellence: We will try to sing, play, pray, and preach in such a way that people's attention will not be diverted from the substance of our worship.

They add three additional principles: gift-based ministry as participants demonstrate giftedness; fruit of the Spirit that recognizes worship ministry is led by the Holy Spirit; and leadership development. The last reads: "We are intentional about team building and identifying those among us whom God is summoning into worship ministry leadership. It is our aim to nurture, develop, and deploy these called and gifted ones into worship leadership roles."

Note how these core values resonate with many issues raised in this book. In their own language, these lead-worshipers have expressed the importance of the role of Scripture and of magnifying God with trinitarian theology. Faith Baptist's stated values introduce a document that then describes how they guide functions and priorities as well as the roles and goals of worship leadership (in nineteen pages). One section details the need "to offer leadership that is prepared spiritually, relationally and musically." Its four subsections are: (1) ultimate priority is spiritual preparation; (2) harmony on and off the field; (3) identify those whom God is summoning into worship leadership—nurture and develop them and deploy them; and (4) find a pace to finish the race.

Time spent sharing and articulating such values not only proves the high seriousness and deep team commitment of those leading worship but also provides a solid foundation for ongoing ministry and even for negotiating through conflict. Divisive issues, such as tension over styles and preferences for music in worship, should be addressed within the context of each congregation's distinctive core values. I suspect that some *worship war* outbursts could be softened by clearly defined core values identified and published for the whole congregation.

Throughout this stage, I hear exasperated lead-worshipers complain, "How can I fit anything else in?" To spend time working through such commitment, seeking to unite hearts, heads, and hands, seems too demanding. But worshiping God together truly is our number one priority. For this reason we are alive. So much busyness fails to be motivated by seeking God's glory. So many routines dull us to God's bigger intentions. God calls us to a fresh reordering of priorities in stage 1 of the worship swim.

12

Being Directed

Worship Swim Stages 2 and 3

> If God were small enough to be understood, he would not be big enough to be worshiped.
>
> from a church sign

Recently, I went to a gym where I have a membership but attend only erratically. I have followed the same ritual over a few years. One routine involves a lateral pull-down of weights that is supposed to strengthen my upper shoulders and back muscles. Sitting on a bench, you reach up for the weights and then pull them down below your chin. As I was pulling down, a trainer came alongside me. "Do you mind if I interrupt?" he said, already interrupting me. "Not at all," I replied. "Well, you are not using the machine properly. Do you mind if I sit down?" Taking my seat, he explained, or rather modeled, how the exercise demands sitting upright with head slightly tilted upward in order to pull the weights down vertically. "You are leaning back pulling outward, and that way the exercise won't help your shoulder or back muscles," he said. "Probably, you need to decrease the weights, sit up, and try again." Self-consciously I reduced the weights, sat upright, and began pulling afresh. Yes, it felt *completely different*. Other muscles between my shoulder blades were complaining. "Now, it's helping you properly," he said.

Without realizing it, I had fallen into sloppy habits that defeated the point of the whole exercise.

Returning from the gym and opening this book manuscript to pick up where I had left off, I realized my gym experience illustrates how preachers, preparing sermons and worship over many years, can develop myopic habits that actually miss out on God's bigger purpose. I also thought of gathered worshipers dutifully repeating exercises week after week yet expending effort ineffectively. Instead of pulling the right ways by God's grace into big-picture worship—developing praise, forgiveness, reconciliation, mission, and service over the long term—some worshipers participate in weekly worship practices that fail to make any difference. Unfortunately, they may even reinforce weaknesses. Where no trinitarian language is used, no celebration around the Lord's Table occurs, and no creeds or great prayers of the church are said, casual spirituality may foster Jesus-only worship, encouraging individuals to do their own thing. Or when people never confess together or pray for others, over the long term this may lead to less honesty together in community and less compassion for the surrounding community. Key Scripture passages about community formation such as Ephesians 4:12 and 1 Peter 2:9 become empty slogans, and the word *maturing* is excluded from the vocabulary.

As we now consider Scripture's role (stage 2) and designing sermons (stage 3), worship planners must keep alert to past bad habits and be willing to work in ways that may feel *completely different*.

Let Scripture Shape the Sermon for Gathered Worship

This second stage opens up the responsibility for listening to Scripture to other worship planners alongside preachers (see fig. 8). Scripture is no longer the sole property of preachers and is set free from being locked up in a *sermon box*. Of course, preachers' own experiences and imagination remain vital as they continue to be accountable for designing sermons (stage 3). But opening up Scripture to all worship planners marks a significant difference (perhaps the biggest difference) from many previous work habits. Scripture becomes the single most important source impacting worship, inviting new ways of working together, and flowing over into worshipers' daily lives, Sundays through Saturdays.

Figure 8. Worship Swim Stage 2

	Preacher	Worship planner(s)
Let Scripture shape the sermon for gathered worship		
Prayerfully read text aloud	X	X
Listen and investigate	X	X

	Preacher	Worship planner(s)
Check out investigations	X	
Interpret for today	X	X
Identify *focus* and *function*	X	X
State *main impact*	X	
Consider worship opportunity	X	X

I hope you sense my enthusiasm for such collaboration. In several contrasting contexts, I have experienced dramatic differences as others have responded to Scripture alongside me. Instead of participating in myopic, isolated preparation fenced into its own small corner, preachers open themselves up to share in vital community learning. They hear what God's Word is saying to *us* and wanting to do with *us*. To reiterate key aspects of stage 2, let me describe two such experiences: blogging at Calvary Memorial Church, Oak Park, and preparing lectionary worship with Karen Roberts.

Glorious Blogging

Preachers and worship planners can collaborate in many ways, but I have found blogging to be especially effective. I remind collaborators of four key responsibilities. First, as partners in preparing gathered worship, they need to pray that its outcome gives God glory. Second, time and space are needed to read prayerfully chosen Scripture texts aloud. Inevitably, those with theological training will likely identify more issues, yet if they approach it seriously, anyone can hear God's Word. Third, they should understand that great care is necessary to consider the original context, investigate the text's meaning, and explore what is said in commentaries. Obviously, this task best suits preachers, yet I have discovered that some of my readers actually did their own exegetical work and consulted commentaries in order to share highlights with me. After asking what the text originally said and did, preachers need to interpret what it says and does today. Each week, as a result of listening to others, I post this outcome of my Scripture work as the *main impact* for the following worship service. Fourth, because worship involves all church life and witness, everyone should be alert to connections with mission issues in wider community life.

I could quote many examples of collaboration during stage 2 and of many surprises along the way. One worship service at Calvary Memorial Church focused on God's promise of peace in Romans 5:1–11 and 12:17–21. I posted four times in preparation for this service and immediately afterward. Perhaps something of the flavor of the process can be seen in the first and last postings on Sunday, January 20, 2008, and the following Sunday, January 27. Early in preparation I learned that some members had attended a conference on Christian peacemaking a few months before, which led to training as conflict coaches to help others in the church and community. Someone suggested that perhaps these coaches might be commissioned in the service. Of course! What a wonderful opportunity for community formation within gathered worship—not just preaching about peace but doing peace.

Blogging God's Promises (7)

Sunday, January 20, 2008

It is eyes down for my next sermon on God's promise of PEACE. It's going to be a little different, because it accompanies the launch of a peacemaking ministry, "Solomon's Way," at Calvary. A number of people have been trained as conflict coaches/mentors by Peacemaker Ministry. I love the idea of "peace activists" at work in the church and community. I also appreciate the ready application this provides the preacher!

After collaboration, I have chosen Romans 5:1–11; 12:17–21 as my text. It makes clear how peace and reconciliation are key words in God's vocabulary. First comes doctrine with the glorious promise that we are at peace with God. You cannot explain his work for us without these words—PEACE, RECONCILIATION. What a promise to seize by faith! Second, the verses in chapter 12 are intensely practical with the challenge to believers to be peacemakers.

You know how I like to summarize the "main impact" of the Scripture passage for the sermon (what the text says and does, the sermon should say and do). For this next sermon my "main impact" is:

> By God's grace what this sermon will *say* is that peace and reconciliation are at the heart of God's work, delivered through Jesus Christ on the cross, so that we are at peace with him and with each other.

> And what the sermon will *do* is challenge us to seize the peace promise and be peace activists in his power and for his sake.

As always, I would value any help you can give me. Any stories where you have been in conflict resolution for the sake of the Prince of Peace? Please keep praying that God will use my preparation.

Lack of space prevents me from including the many lively posts from a wide range of collaborators who interacted with these Scripture verses and shared insights.

Blogging God's Promises (8)

Sunday, January 27, 2008

What a morning at Calvary Memorial, seizing God's promise of peace (Rom. 5:1; 12:18). At one point, I asked the congregation(s) to self-test on two areas of creativity, on a scale of 1 to 10 (1 means no skill; 5 average skill; 10 maximum skill).

The first test relates to "peace-wrecking." Where do we place ourselves on this scale? Here average skill is well-developed since most are naturally gifted, with so many techniques for falling out with people, taking umbrage, misunderstanding, being jealous . . . and otherwise creating bad chemistry. Frankly, we can do it with our eyes shut. We don't even need to say or do anything—just subtle body language can create hostility. So, if you are at a six or seven, you really are proficient! Some people are lethally subversive, adroitly agitating spirit and firing up hostility. At least a nine! A black belt. Mensa class.

The second test concerns "peacemaking." Here skill levels are far less developed. In fact, the average ability is very low. So to be average is really very poor, with low amounts of imagination, creativity, and sheer energy. Of course, the two complement each other. The higher you are on the peace-wrecking scale, inevitably the poorer you are as a peacemaker!

Well, we had some fun. But the implications are devastatingly serious. If we claim Romans 5:1, "Therefore, since we have been justified by faith, we have peace with God through our Lord Jesus Christ," then we, of all people, should know the cost of Jesus's sacrifice to reconcile us to God and heed his command to be peacemakers. If God's people don't cope with conflict with above-average peacemaking skills (by his Spirit), what hope is there? Every little bit of indulgent peace-wrecking sabotages God's peace. And every moment of peacemaking counts. "If it is possible, as far as it depends on you, live at peace with everyone" (Rom. 12:18 NIV). I heard sober stories this morning of people who know that peacemaking is a priority this week. And I want to develop more imagination, creativity, and trust in God's energy for better peacemaking too. What about you?

Six further postings came after this blog and many more verbal comments as worshipers continued responding to God's call to be peacemakers in homes, work life, and the wider community.

Another worship service focused on God's promise relating to prayer.

Blogging God's Promises (11)

Monday, February 4, 2008

What a God-incident! Many weeks ago, as an interim preacher, I planned to preach on God's promises about prayer on February 10. At their recent retreat, the church leaders felt challenged to call the church to forty days of prayer and fasting. And, it just so happens (oh, really!) that one leader contacted me afterward: "We wonder, in your series, if you could introduce the promise of prayer, say on February 10?" "It's

*already planned for that date," I replied, to his great astonishment—
and mine too.*

*Over the last three months I have received more stories about an-
swers to prayer promises than any other kind. One woman told me
how important John 16:23–24 (NIV) has been throughout her life:
"My Father will give you whatever you ask in my name. Until now
you have not asked for anything in my name. Ask and you will receive,
and your joy will be complete." She first memorized these verses when
she was twenty-three years old (during a Navigators Bible study), and
her life ever since, with some dramatic turns (and downturns), has
seen this promise repeatedly delivered. Actually, this promise in its
setting was not well known to me. However, seen in context, as Jesus
leaves grieving disciples, it is very appropriate as we approach Lent
and Easter.*

*So, I am preparing hard on this particular passage. . . . Any insights
you can share will be very welcome.*

Blogging God's Promises (12)

Thursday, February 7, 2008

*Over the last few days I have been immersing myself in John 16:23–
24 (and its context): "My Father will give you whatever you ask in my
name. Until now you have not asked for anything in my name. Ask
and you will receive, and your joy will be complete."*

*In the light of the church challenge about forty days of prayer and
fasting, this promise needs careful preaching. It is no good dashing off
into a prayer program without God refreshing us. And so, I see this
sermon's main impact:*

> By God's grace . . . this sermon will *say*: Effective prayer depends
> on asking the Father in Jesus's name, with joy.

> And this sermon will *do*: Encourage us all to pray in renewed
> ways over forty days.

*I am sure all who will be present at Calvary on Sunday morning
want authentic commitments only. Please pray with me that God
will speak powerfully through this particular promise. Seize the
promise.*

275 Responses

Sunday, February 10, 2008

*At this morning's services I had mixed feelings. 290 packets of
prayer materials sat at the front, waiting for people to sign up for
"forty days of prayer and fasting." Of course for the preacher, it's encouraging to have a practical response built into the service. No one*

*could fail to notice that something specific was supposed to happen
after the sermon! Too many sermons can disappear into thin (hot) air.
. . . At least here tangible action was expected.*

*But as I mentioned at the sermon's beginning, I had mixed feelings
because people might easily see these packets as yet another "church
program"—another good thing the pastors and leaders had planned
for them! How often we are asked to sign up for forty days of this, or
that, or something else! So I pleaded for people to respond in spirit
and truth to the promise in John 16:23–24. To make a commitment
only if they had a measure of: (1) childlike wonder trusting God as
Father; (2) wanting to ask him specifically as Giver; (3) desiring to use
Jesus's powerful name; and (4) anticipating joy.*

*Pastor Howard, who had organized these packets, told me after-
ward that he prayed for 275 people to take them. (I am not quite sure
why 275 exactly—presumably to leave a few spare packets!) Anyway,
at the end, 275 packets had gone with sign-up forms in their places. Of
course this is only the beginning of seizing this prayer promise. Forty
days lie ahead. But praise God for such a beginning! I am humbled as
well as committed.*

Of course, throughout the next forty days, continuing encouragement and
support were necessary as lead-worshipers reiterated their own involvement.

These two examples highlight something of the exhilaration and wonder
of collaboration as others become involved in listening to Scripture. Can you
imagine what a difference it makes to preachers and worship planners who,
through interacting with my blog, saw Scripture's implications not only for
sermons but also for designing the whole act of gathered worship? Chapter 13
will deal with follow-up aspects of stage 4.

Working with the Lectionary

Lectionary readings involve more complicated collaboration because of
the number of texts and greater need to be aware of the Christian year. When
Karen Roberts and I were asked to design a worship service for the 2007 Ancient Evangelical Future Conference held at Northern Seminary, we decided to
record the different steps as class material for students. Since the service was
scheduled for the Saturday immediately prior to the first Sunday in Advent,
we focused on the beginning of the Advent season, using the same Scriptures
that the lectionary chose for the following day (in year A):

Isaiah 2:1–5
Psalm 122
Romans 13:11–14
Matthew 24:36–44

The following comments from Karen (K) and me (M) represent some of our work. Though it looks rather formal and terse when written down, we enjoyed face-to-face meetings with prayer and interaction as well as keeping in touch through emails.

1. Read Scriptures prayerfully out loud.

Immersing ourselves in the Scriptures, we read them out loud, engaging with the content and mood of the various passages. Bearing in mind warnings about how some lectionary texts might skip important verses, we read each in its full biblical context to ensure no verses were omitted and the context was understood. This reading occurred before consulting commentaries or other sermon aids.

> M: These Advent passages have markedly different tones. Isaiah rings with prophetic anticipation and is lively and positive about the glorious future God will work in Jerusalem. Psalm 122 worships with the same spirit as the Isaiah passage. Romans 13:11–14 presents a series of commands with urgency. Matthew 24:36–44 gives Jesus's teaching about the endtimes.

> K: I also read the Scriptures prayerfully aloud. I believe this step can easily be skipped by worship leaders, but I agree with Michael that it is where we should begin. As I read I noted the *tone* of the verses. They were all familiar, yet reading them as lectionary choices, one after the other, connected them in fresh ways for this Advent season.

2. Investigate the texts separately, taking note of their contexts.

This step required the use of commentaries to provide adequate contextual details and explanations.

> M: Isaiah 2:1–5 is uplifting (in contrast with the second part of chap. 2), anticipating people streaming up to the mountain of the Lord in the last days. Here it says that God will teach his ways, judge between nations, and grant universal peace. These are future-tense promises.

> K: This is a visual picture of worship that will take place in the last days. Twice the invitation is given: "Come, let us go up to the mountain of the LORD, to the house of the God of Jacob. . . . Come, let us walk in the light of the LORD!" God is calling his people to the time and place where he will judge and peace will reign.

> M: Psalm 122 expresses worship along similar lines to Isaiah as it talks of rejoicing and praying for peace. This expresses present-tense worship.

> K: The context is worship that involves giving thanks and praying for the peace of others. There is an expression of individual gladness

by David, but there is also a corporate expression in the words, "Let us go to the house of the LORD!" and, "Our feet are standing within our gate, O Jerusalem."

M: Romans 13:11–14 commands an understanding that the endtimes are near. Acts of darkness must be put aside, and instead believers should prepare to live in the light of Jesus Christ's return. This is a strong, ethical call in the light of Christ's return.

K: Christ's return is imminent, and we are to live in light of that promise.

M: In Matthew 24:36–44, Jesus stresses the suddenness of his return and the need to keep watch with spiritual readiness.

K: The context of these verses is Jesus instructing us to be awake, diligent, and ready for his return because no one knows the hour.

3. Consider carefully the opportunities this particular Sunday offers within the Christian year.

We then asked what was significant about the themes and spirituality of that particular Sunday within the Christian year.

M: The first Sunday of Advent particularly anticipates the future coming of the Messiah. It celebrates God's promises and also stresses the need for *preparation* (a meaning of *Advent*). Three readings have this future theme, with the Old Testament texts stressing Jerusalem's role with God's future judgment and realm of peace. The New Testament texts warn of ethical and spiritual responsibilities placed upon believers as they await Christ's return.

K: The Advent season is both a journey backward and a journey forward. During the first two weeks of the season, we look forward to the second coming of Christ. We start with the future and declare that the kingdom and reign of God are coming—prepare. As we wait for his coming, we are to be his people assembled in worship and prayer, living our lives in light of his coming again.

4. In the light of both of their own particularities, the overall theme of the Christian year and the worship context itself, seek to identify for each text the focus and function.

Its *focus*: What does it say? Its *function*: What does it do? This required care. How best can the preacher summarize each Scripture's main impact? With growing experience we have found this exercise becomes easier.

M: Isaiah 2:1–5 *says*: God will reign from his holy mountain, to whom all nations will stream and from which judgment and peace will come. It *does*: anticipate great promise.

Psalm 122 *says*: let's rejoice now, as we go into the temple. It *does*: worship and pray for peace right now.

Romans 13:11–14 *says*: Christ's return is coming soon and we need to make lifestyle changes. It *does*: command us to put on the armor of light and be clothed with Christ.

Matthew 24:36–44 *says*: Christ's return will be very sudden. It *does*: challenge us about spiritual alertness.

K: I agree completely with Michael's summary statements.

This particular worship service took place at the Conference on the Primacy of the Biblical Narrative, Nov. 30–Dec. 1, 2007, at Northern Seminary, Lombard, IL.

5. Ask whether there are common issues through all four texts so that the sermon can be based on all of them. If not, determine which of the passages will provide the main text on which the sermon will be based.

This is a major task for the preacher. No officially prescribed method exists for dealing with these texts. A preacher may be able to combine them all effectively or may use one or more as the main text(s), with or without reference to the others.

M: Though the Old Testament texts have a common theme based on Isaiah's future prophecy, Psalm 122 has little sense of the last days; its prayers for peace are in the present.

On the other hand, both Romans 13 and Matthew 24 connect about Christ's imminent and sudden return, although with a difference of emphasis in the required responses. Because of Advent Sunday's focus on the future and Christ's return, the sermon will be based on the two New Testament passages.

6. Let the main impact of the text(s) influence not only the shape of the sermon but also the shape of gathered worship.

Because the conference to which this sermon was addressed focused on telling and living out God's story in Scripture, it was appropriate to speak of *story* as the controlling metaphor for anticipating Christ's return.

M: The focus of the conference, therefore, influenced my summary for the main impact of the sermon. What this sermon will *say*: anticipating Christ's future return in God's big story clashes with culture's Christmas rush. What it will *do*: challenge hearers to stop running (at least a little) and pray counterculturally this week.

K: As I reflected on how these Scriptures might further influence the worship, I considered their possible use:

    Isaiah 2:1–5 could be incorporated into a call to worship.

    Psalm 122, as with the Isaiah passage, could be used as a call to worship and also be incorporated into the time of prayer, as we pray for peace.

    Romans 13 could be used as a call to worship, calling people to *wake from sleep*, or be used in a prayer of confession as well as in the sermon.

    Matthew 24:36–44 might be used as the basis for the opening prayer as well as be used in the sermon.

Over time such new habits of working together, while perhaps appearing clumsy and time-consuming, can become second nature as worship planners grow in relationship together. Of course, throughout stage 2, both preachers and worship planners are likely to be thinking ahead how Scripture's implications impact sermon and worship design. Already, in her last comment, Karen was anticipating how Scripture might be used in the service. After preachers have benefited from working with others, gaining new insights and fresh perspectives, they move into taking responsibility for the next stage.

Design the Sermon

The third stage of the worship swim reveals more clearly the extent to which preachers have embraced big-picture worship as they now set about designing the sermon. Here their worship *worldview* is laid bare. Just how far have they been able to correct myopia? One of the saddest signs of myopic preaching listed earlier was the last: worshipless sermons. Theologically thin, spiritually disconnected, empty of God, silent about his grace, self-satisfied, and self-oriented, such sermons are devoid of worship. Paradoxically, listeners may rate them highly because they are lively and interesting. Consumers who belittle worship, trapped in practical unitarianism, reckon that when preachers quote Scripture, tell good stories, and make applications, they are doing a good job. "Good job, pastor!" Crowds and applause cap their success. But before the God of glory, whose worthiness requires living sacrifices from preachers and the people, offering their all in his call and in their response of big-picture worship, they are shallow, paltry mouthings.

Designing the sermon in stage 3 obviously follows key tenets of homiletics. Many books describe the necessary steps that preachers should take as they work from exegesis and interpretation to sermon design.[1] But big-picture worship makes extra demands that design is shaped by three key issues: worshipfulness, integration, and outcomes.

Worshipfulness

Worshipfulness speaks of overflowing hearts and attuned minds. Preachers come to the task of sermon design as worshipers first and foremost. All six questions in the toolbox apply to preaching design, but especially questions 1 and 2 concerning thankfulness for the gift of worship and the desire to magnify God. These provide the right motive for preaching. With awe and wonder at their part in God's call and response, preachers thankfully offer themselves and their work to magnify God. Nothing matters more than joining in with fellow worshipers in fellowship with the Triune God, placing their particular call and gifting to preach within the rich call and response dynamics of worship. Worshipful preaching thrills to the pulse of praising God's glory and rests in awe before his holiness.

This worshipfulness should be evident in small and obvious ways. For example, Keith and Krystin Getty comment: "When we visit churches Sunday to Sunday, the churches that sing the best seem to be the ones where the pastor is singing. If he's singing, people sing. For the musician at the front, having the pastor singing with you makes all the difference in the world."[2]

But in hidden ways, worshipfulness should also be present in humble dependence on God at every step of sermon preparation. Worshipful preaching practices "Be still, and know that I am God" (Ps. 46:10); revels in proclaiming Scripture's great worship passages such as Isaiah 6:1–13, John 4:21–24, and Romans 12:1–2; exults in the Psalms, and celebrates in Hebrews. Worshipfulness means unstoppable wonder—each sentence prepared with reverential wonder that dares to speak God's transforming Word.

Integration

Integration recognizes that preaching itself is worship. Preaching belongs within trinitarian worship and is intimately related to singing, praying, hearing Scripture, offering, and sharing the Lord's Supper, all initiated, activated, and motivated by the Triune God. Obviously question 3, "Are we allowing Scripture to direct?" is most clearly answered in preaching, but this belongs with everything else that happens in the worship cycle of call and response (see fig. 3) as God's community journeys inwardly in fellowship and outwardly for mission. Sermons remain the main way by which God discloses Word and will, yet Scripture's main impact is also proclaimed through other worship elements such as singing, praying, giving, baptism, and the Lord's Supper.

Not only are sermons designed with thankfulness in order to magnify God and directed by Scripture as preachers seek to expound God's Word, but they also address the worshiping community with the big purposes of growing in formation for fellowship and mission (questions 4, 5, and 6). Collaborating with other lead-worshipers, preachers should ensure that the preached Word is integrated with every other part of gathered worship and that the structure and content of the whole is directed by Scripture. Such integration enables sermons to worship and worshipers to proclaim, as God's people join in giving glory with all creation (Rev. 4:11; 5:9–13). In far-reaching dimensions way beyond weekly gatherings, God's new creation worships with full-orbed living.

Outcomes

Preaching has a major role in shaping outcomes to God's Word. Sermons are charged to say and do what the Scripture text says and does. But now in big-picture worship, this *doing* (along with the rest of the liturgy) helps shape personal and community formation. Instead of myopic sermons that specialize in isolated swatches of individualistic teaching, preachers use big-picture preaching to proclaim the joined-up, glorious gospel story, inviting worshipers to respond by God's grace to live it out together.

In order that God might build his people in community, many different kinds of preaching are needed (see fig. 5). Initiation requires preaching that is variously evangelistic, doctrinal, and celebrative so that seekers hear and respond to the gospel challenge and learn how they belong in faith to Christ and his community. Preachers should ensure that baptism remains central to initiation, as it opens up new Christian language and new relationships. Integration of new believers highlights the need for liturgical and salvation history preaching that helps them understand how they belong within God's unfolding story, focused on celebrating the Lord's Supper. For character formation and growth in unity, there needs to be pastoral preaching, and helping congregations learn about conflict and reconciliation requires skills of leadership through preaching. For the ultimate outcome of community formation in missional living, both missional and prophetic preaching are necessary to help form new culture in witness to the world.

Making lists of different kinds of preaching is easy, but developing a preaching repertoire for the sake of God's community likely stretches solo preachers almost to the breaking point. Used to working in their own small boxes, they probably see current strengths in only one or two types of preaching. Big-picture worship mightily widens the scope and, by God's grace, gives strength and energy for the task. Always grounded in what Scripture is saying and doing, it calls preachers into lifelong learning about fresh ways of worshipful preaching. When, for example, David Schlafer and Timothy Sedgwick urge preachers to help hearers develop moral discernment in the light of Scripture by centering Christian moral life in key practices, this means new territory for many of us. Similarly, confronted by the need to preach prophetically for a missional church working with a missionary model,[3] many preachers feel inadequate. Yet the wonder of being involved with God's big picture, empowered by triune grace, is that preachers can grow ever more worshipful in their preaching.

In one of my intensive doctoral courses, I ask pastors to bring three of their best sermons that have *built up* their people. Then, using criteria relating to community formation, they analyze these sermons using a questionnaire. Here is a sample of four questions relating to *individualistic language*, *spineless theology*, *generic application*, and *missional defectiveness*.

1. Look at the language. Is *you* always about the personal, individual lives of hearers, and how often are *you* (plural) and *we* related to the community? Does "the kingdom of God" feature in your language? Can a hearer walk away thinking that Christ's challenge is only about *my* life, *my* purpose, *my* future?
2. Underline where there is a theology of Father, Son, and Holy Spirit. Is it explicit or implicit? Where else do you share theological truth to undergird continuing Christian experience?
3. Look at the illustrations and applications. Do they connect specifically with this group of worshipers? In what ways did the personal relationship of preacher with church community and surrounding context make the sermon particular rather than general?
4. In what ways does the sermon challenge the church to live as missional people, expressing Christ's life and love in its witness before the world?

With honest reflection, students are always able to identify some weaknesses because often they have long practiced small-picture worship, preparing stand-alone sermons in solo fashion. It is encouraging to see how, even over the relatively short duration of the teaching course, awareness of big-picture worship makes so much difference to sermon design.

Big-picture worship demands so much more. Preaching can never be only a matter of explaining Scripture well or helping individuals apply its message. Worshipful preachers belong within the great sweep of worship as God calls his people to be a holy nation, a royal priesthood—gathering together in order to be scattered into daily living. Such preachers believe that outcomes of hearing Scripture in worship change people. Rather than individuals walking out as they came in, without any sense of belonging or responsibility to each other and settling for objectives more in taste with contemporary culture than gospel, worshipers encounter the real God in three persons and respond with repentance, faith, and new behavior by walking in the Spirit. They want to offer worship in every part of their lives. They thrill to William Temple's definition:

To worship is to quicken the conscience by the holiness of God,
To feed the mind with the truth of God,
To purge the imagination by the beauty of God,
To open the heart to the love of God,
To devote the will to the purpose of God.[4]

13

Continuing Strong

Worship Swim Stages 4 and 5

I should be sorry if I had only succeeded in entertaining them; I wished to make them better.

Handel, after first London performance of *Messiah*, 1743

A s a teenager I was intrigued by a neighbor who lived down the street. When walking past his house, I sometimes saw him conducting an orchestra in his front room, baton in hand with arms outstretched, beating extravagantly. Strains of recorded orchestral music could be faintly heard, but no musicians were in evidence. I don't know if he was practicing for the real thing, following a score and testing tone and tempo before trying it out on actual musicians, or (much more likely) whether he just enjoyed role-playing, imagining himself effortlessly conducting glorious music, exercising such power.

Of course, genuine conducting is not effortless. Although sometimes composers conduct their own work, most often conductors are working with material composed by someone else. They are responsible for interpreting the composition and then leading others to produce music by combining the musicians' skills. This complicated task requires deep knowledge of the particular piece of music and the many instruments involved combined with skillful leadership that brings out the best in others. And all this is done for the sake of doing justice to the composer's intentions.

Some similarities with leading worship may be obvious. The musical term *transposing*—playing in a different key from the one originally designated—has been applied by writers to the preaching task. For example, Paul Wilson sees the preacher transposing by connecting the original text with contemporary context.[1] Russell Mitman widens this transposing to apply to the whole act of worship "so each prayer, each response, each hymn becomes a transposition of the text in its new context and, if crafted carefully, will retain a recognizable connection with the shapes and contours of the text." From this it is a small step for him to describe worship planners as "orchestrating" gathered worship, though he is anxious to avoid any manipulative or performance overtones. Rather, their "offering in worship is a countercultural endeavor in which leaders give away attention and talents to God in gratitude and obedience."[2] They arrange texts and their transpositions so that the whole community is led to worship. Like conducting, this complicated process requires not only a combination of knowledge and skills but also character (heart and head qualifications) in order that overall content, tone, and tempo do justice to God's intentions.

Russell Mitman develops this idea of orchestrating with language such as "scoring the flow," "scoring the splendor," "finishing the score," and "rehearsing." Throughout, Scripture should shape transpositions whether "verbal or nonverbal, musical or graphic" that belong as "an integrated whole so that there can be a *communal* experience of the Word of God."[3]

Stage 4 moves into this task of helping shape gathered worship. Just as stage 2 opened up Scripture to lead-worshipers, now preachers are invited to join in with other lead-worshipers.

Help Shape Gathered Worship

Figure 9. Worship Swim Stage 4

	Preachers	Worship planner(s)
4. Help shape gathered worship		
Use the question toolbox	X	X
Shape structure and content	X	X
Delegate responsibilities		X
Ensure planning is complete		X

Stage 4 is complicated and calls for sensitive creativity and use of music, liturgical resources, images, and many other imaginative elements with careful selection and arrangement. In the practical business of design, worship planners must never lose sight of God's grace at work throughout the process. Though some aspects are pragmatic, their practicalities must never blind us to the spiritual necessity of depending on God in every part of worship design. Rigorous application of the question toolbox dominates this entire process of selection and arrangement, but it should be viewed as a spiritual tool. Though its six questions are listed in order (God makes some amazingly connected misfits), in practice they rarely work in straightforward, linear fashion. Rather, applied by the Holy Spirit, they all buzz in worship planners' minds simultaneously, probing every aspect of worship design and keeping planners ever alert to God's big purposes in preparation for worship. They become part of the worship planning spiritual mind-set (1 Cor. 2:16). While some questions are necessarily difficult to answer, especially questions 5 and 6, failing to ask them risks slipping back into worship myopia.

Use the Question Toolbox

Question Toolbox

1. *Gift*: Are we thankfully receiving this gift of worship from the Triune God of grace?

2. *Magnification*: Are we expressing its richness toward God?

3. *Scripture*: Are we allowing Scripture to direct?

4. *Audiences*: Are we addressing two audiences?

5. *Community*: Are we building community by story?

6. *Mission*: Are we enabling community to scatter?

Let's be reminded how essential these questions are. Question 1 is foundational, undergirding how worship planners approach their task. Does thankfulness truly motivate attitudes and action? Question 2 values the rich breadth of resources for magnifying God, always setting the bar high for the quality of responses offered to God, looking beyond initial, obvious choices to see deeper and higher possibilities. Question 3 reinforces Scripture's role in directing the whole of gathered worship. Question 4 checks how different parts of gathered worship properly focus on the Triune God—who he is in three persons and what he has done. Yet at the same time, it ensures that worshipers are addressed as God's community. Question 5 asks directly about community formation, probing whether worshipers are being helped to learn new language, relationships, and patterns *within* the story of God's people as they grow and mature in his purposes. Question 6 asks how worshipers will be encouraged to think and act, offering daily lives as a "living sacrifice" (Rom 12:1) when they are sent out from gathered worship to live for God in the world. It considers how well worshipers will continue worshiping through evangelism and social action.

Every part of gathered worship, large or small, comes under scrutiny. How a worship service praises God, for example, needs to be questioned. *Praise* should typically begin worship and be motivated by profound gratitude.

Question 1: "Enter his gates with thanksgiving, and his courts with praise" (Ps. 100:4). Praise extols God's attributes such as holiness, power, wisdom, and love as well as his actions in past, present, and future tenses. Praise magnifies God as richly as humans know how.

Question 2: Scripture should inform the words used in praise, specifically directing God's purpose for each act of worship.

Question 3: Yet even as praise focuses on the Triune God, it involves two audiences.

Question 4: David Edwards comments, "There is a spiritual protocol for every believer who wants to enter into the presence of the King. . . . Praise opens the way for worship to take place. The whole time we are praising, . . . the Holy Spirit is using that praise to whittle away at what's wrong on the inside of us."[4]

Question 5: Although personal praise is essential, worshipers need to learn to praise *together*, ensuring that worship does not merely result in personal feel-good emotion. Rather, it unites people in a corporate praise commitment to participate in God's continuing story.

Question 6: Even as God is being praised, so his people are being formed into a holy nation and a royal priesthood before a watching world.

In subjecting everything about worship design to these questions, nothing should be left out as too small. For example, the *offering* has been downgraded in some churches into almost nonworship, as mere organizational necessity.

Question 1. Giving should not be motivated by duty to meet church budgets but by deep thankfulness for *all* God's gifts to us (2 Cor. 9:15). God loves cheerful givers who do not respond reluctantly or out of compulsion (2 Cor. 9:7) but out of appreciation for God's immense material and spiritual gifts (2 Cor. 8:9).

Question 2: Giving money should always focus on God and include a wider scope of stewardship through gifts of our time, talents, and treasure.

Question 3: Scripture's command about giving what each has "decided in his heart" (2 Cor. 9:7 NIV) needs to be taught clearly, with an emphasis on the important role of money in worship as part of being a living sacrifice.

Questions 4, 5, and 6: Giving to help others, both within the worshiping community as well as beyond, is essential for community formation and missional living (2 Cor. 9:12–13).

Mark Labberton's stark warning that evangelical Christians give away only 2 percent of their income emphasizes how the offering needs to be reevaluated as one of the most practical ways that worship engages with the world.

Missional living also raises profound issues about the stewardship of all God's gifts, including money, as worshipers live for him Mondays through Saturdays.

Over and over again these questions probe every aspect of gathered worship. Too often key aspects such as celebration of the Lord's Supper and baptism have become routine and need careful reexamination, especially in light of community and mission questions. Prayer and music are two elements in gathered worship that particularly require careful questioning.

Prayer

Sadly, prayer is often Cinderella in the basement. Of course, liturgies that contain set prayers ensure some representation. But for preachers in non-liturgical traditions, too often it appears that only 5 percent effort is expended on preparing prayers as compared with 95 percent on preparing sermons. But not only preachers are guilty. I have been in worship services containing very thoughtful, skillful music arrangements only for music leaders to give trite, spur-of-the-moment thoughts instead of leading corporate prayer. R. Kent Hughes quotes Horton Davies: "Free prayers, under the guidance of a devout and beloved minister who knows well both his Bible and his people, have a moving immediacy and relevance that set prayers rarely attain. At the same time, if prayers are not prepared, they can become a stream of clichés and repetitions that numb the mind and ice the heart."[5]

Prayer deserves rigorous attention, especially by those who choose to practice extemporaneous, free prayer. Isaac Watts commended "conceived prayers" that were carefully worked out yet open to the Spirit. To safeguard against free prayer degrading into banality, lead-worshipers must learn the discipline of preparing prayers—both writing their own and drawing from the rich range of prayer resources. "Ordered, carefully worded, historic prayers give objectivity and stability to the service, scriptural soundness, . . . historical awareness, and continuity with the prayers of the church at all times and places."[6] On the other hand, those who always use set prayers need to balance these with carefully prepared prayers that specifically arise out of community life and missional concern. Whatever the worship tradition, the six questions should be applied.

1. Gift: When considering the heart qualifications of lead-worshipers (see chap. 11), we noted the wonder of prayer as trinitarian participation. Prayer joins us with God through Jesus as Mediator and High Priest who ever intercedes for us (Rom. 8:34; Heb. 7:25) and is supported by the Holy Spirit helping us in our weakness (Rom. 8:26). With thankfulness and humility, we join in God's great gift of relationship through prayer.

2. Magnification: Commonly, six types of prayer enrich gathered worship.

Opening/Invocation: In this prayer, worshipers invoke or call upon the Lord, acknowledging that he is the initiator.

Confession: Through confession, worshipers together seek God's forgiveness for sins.

Illumination: Spoken while gathering, before the reading of Scripture or the sermon itself, this explicitly opens up worship to God's Spirit.

Prayers of the people: These include petitions and intercessions for people within the congregation but also for the wider community. It is a key time to express the heart of the people on its mission.

Offering prayers: Such prayers ensure that monetary gifts are part of being living sacrifices as worshipers.

Concluding prayer: Often combined with the benediction, the dismissal is a vital part of the whole.

Earlier we noted that omission of any of these, such as confession and intercession, impoverishes congregational worship. Lead-worshipers need to take seriously these different kinds of prayer and their complementary roles. Those who always pray extemporaneously are in danger of reducing congregational prayer life to predictable words with limited focuses. Magnifying God means taking the trouble to enrich words and participation through conceived prayer and thoughtful use of resources.

3. *Scripture*: The Word of God teaches the importance of prayer, provides models of biblical characters at prayer, and gives practical direction, particularly in Jesus's teaching (Luke 11:1–13). Its text contains explicit prayers—especially some psalms that express not only praise but lament and confession. Scriptural language and content should inform all prayers. Harold Best claims that "the prayers of Scripture should be studied and assimilated as our prayers and we should learn to craft parallel prayers, using these as templates and using our best thought and best language."[7] Because Scripture directs both general patterns of liturgy as well as specific outcomes of particular services, it should have significant influence on all the praying that occurs.

4. *Audiences*: Corporate prayer should always seek to address God in worthy language that enables the whole gathered church to pray. "Prayer is above all about who God is and what he wants. By praying in his name, we pray *for* his sake—not on his behalf, neither to rescue him nor to inform him."[8] Extemporaneous prayer requires careful preparation to ensure its language is worthy of God and can enable others to participate. William Willimon wisely counsels that "public prayer is not private prayer said publicly"[9] but prayer intentionally offered on behalf of the whole people. Instead of expressing personal feelings (with *I* language), so easily captive to individual mood swings and ability, corporate prayer intentionally embraces collective desires and needs. Sensitive language with inclusive and thoughtful content ensures congregations can identify with lead-worshipers' prayers. Again, using prayer resources can enrich ways by which people can make responses together.

5. *Community*: By praying corporately, communities also learn to see God's vision and enter his mission for the world. Prayer that focuses on what God *is doing and will do* lies at the heart of community life. We have noted that the language of togetherness is writ large in the New Testament—*you* plural dominates. Designing prayers with plural language shows sensitivity to others, and as congregations learn to pray *we*, they open up to the Holy Spirit's power to unite (see Eph. 4:3). From opening invocation to sending out, prayers should therefore express the desire and willingness of God's people to live for him. As different voices lead prayer and all voices respond in prayer, gathered worship builds *living stones* together. By the ways that worshipers pray together, they own God's new reality.

6. *Mission*: Such praying together also looks outward to God's mission purposes. Don Saliers claims that the most powerful formative prayers are petition and intercession because they reveal how large a congregation's heart is for mission. He quotes three stanzas of prayer, beginning:

> Remember, Lord, Christians at sea, on the road, abroad, our fathers and brothers (and sisters) in chains and prisons. . . .
> Remember, Lord, those in old age and infirmity, those who are sick, ill, or troubled. . . .
> Remember, Lord, all . . . for good; on all have mercy. Master, reconcile us all, bring peace to the multitudes of your peoples.[10]

This prayer, first spoken around AD 400, repeatedly requests, "Remember, Lord." Bringing such needs of others before God identifies with God's love and care for his world. Saliers bluntly challenges, however, "Our impoverished experience of common prayer for the world is directly traceable to our inability to know and to minister to others in his name."[11] When a community learns to share in prayer for others, it grows in mission awareness for both its inner and outer spiritual journeys.

I have never forgotten participating in intercessory prayers at All Souls Church, Langham Place, London. We were asked to keep our eyes open to focus on pictures shown on a screen while being led in prayer. While concentrating, for example, on a hungry child and mother in desperate poverty, the image was seared into our consciousness. I realized not only how much I should respond but also that I belonged within a community that cared for God's world. Prayer compassion flowed over into practical responses through budget priorities and missionary commitment. When communities pray like this, you know they care in practice.

Further, the final sending-out prayers as communities prepare to scatter as God's missionary people speak volumes about their willingness to live out God's mission in their everyday lives. By the ways that worshipers pray together, they own responsibility in God's mission.

MUSIC

Designing music in worship is much more complicated than preparing prayers. Already we have seen the need for lead-worshipers to think hard about the role of music in their congregations (head qualifications). What a contrast lies between the best experiences of music in worship and the worst!

Early in my interim preaching at Calvary Memorial Church (before I experimented with my blog), I worked face-to-face with a group of musicians. At one Saturday morning meeting, I handed out sheets of paper with details of all six sermons in a new series. Each Scripture text and sermon title was accompanied by a main impact sentence: *By God's grace this sermon will say . . . and will do . . .* I shared how Scripture directs sermon outcomes in a wide variety of ways: it may rebuke, teach ethics, increase praise, drop you to your knees, raise you with wings as eagles, call you to repentance and faith, motivate you to service, or press you into mission.

Then it happened! The music director spoke up excitedly:

> Would you believe it? That's exactly how I believe music in worship works. *Exactly!* It's not just the words of hymns and songs that matter but it's how the music functions and how the congregation will be led. Every time I choose something, I ask what the music is saying and doing and how it helps shape the direction and flow of worship.

I was elated! Nothing unites people more effectively and expresses worship more deeply than words in music, and this lead-worshiper clearly believed his choices should be directed by Scripture. This is music in worship at its best.

In contrast, other experiences may reveal music in worship at its worst. At one large pastors' conference, I mentioned music and was surprised by the anger that spilled out afterward. One preacher said:

> My music pastor went to a worship conference and heard the speaker say, "There is nothing more important than worship. As worship leader, no one has a more important job than you." And my worship leader took that literally and now treats me as though I am irrelevant. Music has become everything—and the people love it! I understand why a pastor friend says that he has to fire his worship leaders every four years because they become so prideful.

Some others, crowding around, bitterly agreed that music had grown too powerful and divided congregations. I guess that at a parallel conference for music pastors (maybe the one just referred to) there might be similar rage at controlling pastors' disregard for their worship role.

Sadly, in too many places churches are in a mess musically. "It's all about God" regresses to "it's all about us." Instead of worshipful communities becoming more Christlike, with members of the body of Christ maturing in obedience under his headship, they snap, snarl, and divide over worship preferences. Because music in worship raises such big issues about community life, its role in formation is strongly emphasized (see fig. 5). Now, aware of the best and the worst, the six questions need to be posed concerning weekly music choices.

1. *Gift*: Let's state the obvious. Music is one of God's greatest gifts to all. "The human voice is the only musical instrument that God has directly created with equal access to music. By doing so he has provided equal access to music and singing for everybody."[12] Scripture is full of music. "The morning stars sang together" to herald creation (Job 38:7); Jubal is "the father of those who play the harp and the flute" (Gen. 4:21 NIV); Moses and Miriam lead singing after escaping Pharaoh's army at the Red Sea (Exod. 15); David's harp refreshes King Saul (1 Sam. 16:23); and King David organizes temple worship (1 Chron. 15:16). Psalms is a hymnbook, packed with lyrics from praise to lament, with choirs and instruments of every kind gloriously joining in (Ps. 150:3–6). Music accompanies Christ's story in Mary's Magnificat (Luke 1:46–55); over the Bethlehem fields (Luke 2:14–15); and at the end of the Last Supper (Matt. 26:30). The early church is exhorted to make melody (Eph. 5:19); Paul and Silas sing in prison (Acts 16:25); and the multitudes fill the heavens with singing (Rev. 4:8–11).

Music inspires, heals, and renews. Popular science suggests that music releases endorphins as pleasurable chemical brain reactions, and few doubt that profound links exist between music and emotions. Indeed, the Institute of Brain and Music Sciences in Massachusetts has found vital correlations between music and positive treatment of neurological conditions. Undeniably, music is an essential part of our lives. Take away music, and life becomes immeasurably poorer.

All of God's gifts can be abused, however, and music is no exception. Musicians may become puffed up with pride in their own gifts and even compete with others. Question 1 brings us back to basics: the only attitude permissible is thanksgiving before God, who gives musical gifts. Accompanying such gratitude, in humility we should seek always to encourage others to share their musical abilities too. Thankfulness and humility show the Holy Spirit's presence among musicians. The command, "Speak to one another with psalms, hymns and spiritual songs. Sing and make music in your heart to the Lord," is prefaced, "Be filled with the Spirit" (Eph. 5:18–19 NIV).

2. *Magnification*: Lead-worshipers must continually ask, "Does this music serve to glorify God by centering upon him?" Unfortunately, words and gestures sometimes express more about the worshipers than the one worshiped. This is wrong! By every appropriate means, God should be exalted. Musical offering is *all* for him.

The string of examples above from Old and New Testaments well illustrates music's rich variety of content, style, and accompaniment. In the early church, diversity is evident: "With gratitude in your hearts sing psalms, hymns, and spiritual songs to God" (Col. 3:16). How different these musical forms were from each other is open to debate.

> No rigid distinctions should be made between "psalms," "hymns," and "spiritual songs." . . . If any differences are made, "psalms" may be taken to refer to the Old Testament psalter, "hymns" and "spiritual songs" to distinctly Christian compositions. The great periods of renewal in Christendom have always been accompanied by outbursts of hymnology.[13]

But importantly, the commentator adds, "Paul is simply emphasizing the rich variety in Christian song." Already this young church reveals different ways of magnifying God. Such variety is God's idea. The fact that God intentionally gives such rich differences enables extraordinary breadth of worship by God's people. No one can decree that there is only *one* way to express congregational praise.

I find Keith Getty's insight provocative:

> Church music fights did not begin twelve months after The Beatles started and the church realized that there was new music. These arguments about what Christians should sing have gone on for all of time, from rival monasteries to rival cathedrals. They're not going to end. And so anybody who prescribes a musical solution is blowing smoke. There's a reason why the Lord made the church a multigenerational, multiclass, multi-ethnic, diverse group of people. I doubt that everybody in Acts had the same musical tastes, if they were Jews and Greeks, and slaves and free.[14]

Certainly lead-worshipers can seek to reduce tension by music choices. For example, one says his policy is "to lead with variety so that there is some familiarity for all but also some unfamiliarity. I am convicted—if I am going to withhold praise because I don't like the style, how far does my love for God go?" Loving God may mean singing other styles and experiencing other kinds of music in gathered worship, but it should always focus on magnifying God. The ultimate solution for resolving tension lies in asking what magnifies God and what best helps God build community that genuinely unites such diverse people (question 5).

In so many ways the question of magnifying God can be obscured. For example, lead-worshipers can magnify music's own power. Contemporary music especially has the ability to build mood. Some music directors outline *progressions* of songs by means of flowcharts, combining tempo, rhythm, key structures, and changes in different forms termed *classic, earthquake,* and *mild.* Moving worshipers to particular outcomes, however, can neglect magnifying God and building his community. Music can become too important. Harold Best warns that faith can be misunderstood as bringing substance *to* music rather than being its own substance (Heb. 11:1). He continues, "I can quite easily forge a connection between the power of music and the nearness of the Lord. Once this happens, I may even slip into the sin of *equating* the power of music and the nearness of the Lord."[15]

3. Scripture: Because Scripture influences worship's overall structure—such as the fourfold gathering, Word, thanksgiving or Lord's Supper, and sending out—music choices need to be appropriate to the rhythm of God's call and response. Clearly, *gathering* requires very different music from *sending out*.

All the collaboration work through stage 2 now bears fruit. Music leaders have benefitted from working with Scripture and can respond with specific music choices for each gathered worship occasion. The music director at the Saturday morning meeting knew instinctively that Scripture influences music choices, not in some vague manner but by directing what words in music would say and do. As with prayer, Scripture also informs the content and language of the words in music; words remain vitally important. "Let the word of Christ dwell in you richly; teach and admonish one another in all wisdom; and with gratitude in your hearts sing psalms, hymns, and spiritual songs to God" (Col. 3:16; see also Eph. 5:19). The Word of Christ, which teaches and admonishes (a task that seems very much like preaching), is intimately connected with the quality of responses in singing.

4. Audiences: Words in music should be directed to God in praise, but they should also allow us to teach and affirm one another—both "gratitude in your hearts to God" (Col. 3:16) and "speak to one another" (Eph. 5:19 NIV). First and foremost, music should *please God*. Psalm 96:1, "Sing to the LORD a new song," commands singing that is directed "to the LORD"—an offering for God's sake. Harold Best notes that while "a new song" speaks of a newness arising out of vital faith, it also suggests that we should sing *newly*. "We can sing a truly new song only once, and thereafter we repeat it, . . . singing a song newly means that we must sing the thousandth repetition *as if for the first time*."[16] Pleasing God is primary; worship celebrates *his* deeds of salvation and *his* ongoing building work. Words addressed to God need to be worthy of God's worthship and are best drawn from Scripture. Marva Dawn asks, "Is the text theologically sound? Is it true to God's nature? . . . Is it a Christian thought? Is it carefully expressed?"[17] Will it confirm the testimony of the preached Word? Special care is needed to ensure trinitarian balance between Father, Son, and Holy Spirit, for hymns and songs can easily neglect the trinitarian perspective. While it may not be possible to give balance to God's three persons in every act of worship, care should be taken to do this over a sequence of worship services.

Second, "speak to one another with psalms, hymns and spiritual songs" (Eph. 5:19 NIV). Worshipers testify to one another in community. Each person, when singing with others, sounds out personal faith in God that contributes toward the group's corporate faith and unity. The Reformers preferred congregational singing in unison, without instruments, so as to emphasize both the human voices and unity of the whole. Words can also express honesty about worshipers themselves. A couple of weeks ago in morning worship, I was introduced to Fred Pratt Green's hymn "When Our Confidence Is Shaken." Earlier in the week I had listened to someone who was wrestling with doubt and complained that there never seems to be room for questions in church. Yet this hymn acutely acknowledges trouble:

> When the spirit in its sickness seeks but cannot find a cure,
> God is active in the tensions of a faith not yet mature.[18]

Of course, words should also teach faith. Contemporary hymn writers Keith and Kristyn Getty write songs with a key principle in mind:

> Songs should teach the faith, telling truths about God and telling God's story.
> . . . Take "In Christ Alone" for instance. A lot of people are moved by the fact that through the verses, Jesus takes on flesh as a helpless babe and ends up on the cross. . . . They've sung through half of Romans by the end of the song, but because you've taken them through a story rather than just giving them didactic truth, it really communicates to them.[19]

It hardly needs to be added, but songs also should be singable. Getty claims,

> Good melody transcends musical style. . . . We often cite "Be Thou My Vision" as an example. The lyrics date to around the sixth century, but it's still being sung. And you've heard it with a big rock band, and you've heard it just voices. That's a great example of how a song continues to be relevant. It's not bound by any generation or style.[20]

Important technical issues are raised here that are far beyond the competence of this author. Planners need to ask, "Does the music style serve the text? Is the melody fine for solo singing but difficult for corporate singing? . . . Does the style disrupt worship in any way? How appropriate is it to the musical ability of the congregation and the music leaders?"[21]

5. *Community*: The controversial issue of music's role in building community has already received attention. At the initiation and integration stages, music helps worshipers learn new Christian language to praise God and express new relationships, patterns, and story. As with prayer, words in music should be plural whenever possible, using *we* often. Marva Dawn asks of the text, "How appropriate is the piece with respect . . . to the diversity of congregation members?"[22]

First, Steve Guthrie comments how music helps *instruct one another* in three ways: by applying the individual texts, by framing the entire service, and by *doing* the Word.[23] Words of an individual text can be *prosody*, with intonation, rhythm, and emphasis conveying emotions by gestures and movement. But when music combines with words, its rhythm, melody, and harmony powerfully reinforce impact. "As we sing Holy, holy, holy we express hushed reverence before God. In the way we marry these words to other sound, we *explain something* about holiness. . . . The music ends up being a kind of exegesis of the text."[24]

Second, "music . . . can provide the interpretive frame for an *entire service*— or an *entire church.* . . . Music can help the congregation make sense of what the minister says. Or more tremblingly—it can make nonsense out of what the minister says—('The pastor said that the church lives and values each of us, but the worship band acted like the rest of us weren't even here')!"[25] Such *felt elements* contribute to an understanding of what is said.

Third, music in congregational hymns and songs offers opportunities not only to hear the Word but also to *do* it. For example, when a congregation sings, "A new command I give you: Love one another" (John 13:34 NIV), "we have the . . . opportunity to *do* this truth—to enact it. As we sing, we don't just imagine one church composed of many individuals; we actually hear the many voices of the body of Christ, joined into one voice."[26]

This *doing truth* is critical for resolving the tension about contrasting music preferences. Loving one another in spirit and in truth requires maturing sensitivity as worshipers ask themselves, "In love for God and for other brothers and sisters, how far will we go in foregoing personal preferences for the sake of others?" We have noted that conflicting music preferences seriously damage community at the higher levels of personal and community formation (see fig. 5). Dawn therefore poses another test: "Is it true to God's nature, conducive to the formation of character, inclusive for the whole community?"[27] Inclusivity should always be part of lead-worshipers' ongoing concern in order for music to play a positive role in community formation.

6. *Mission*: Words in music should also embrace the wider calling of God's mission before the watching world. Before describing music, Ephesians 5:15–16 (NIV) challenges: "Be very careful, then, how you live—not as unwise but as wise, making the most of every opportunity, because the days are evil." Commitment to wise living in service and witness to the world should be made through words in music. As the community seeks to journey outwardly in God's mission, music choices should reinforce responses to God's Word and accompany the sending out of God's people to live as missionaries.

So much more could be written about music in worship, but even this brief survey may dismay preachers by its range of responsibilities. Yet music is too significant an issue to be left to others. Preachers cannot opt out of responsibility for understanding, interpreting, and helping develop music within big-picture worship.

Shape Structure and Content

By asking the six toolbox questions, always seeking the Holy Spirit's help, worship planners help shape the structure and content of gathered worship.

Just as orchestral conductors prepare hard before leading complex orchestration, attending to details as well as overall shape, so worship planners prepare *the trees* and *the forest*.

In common with many worship planners, I possess several bulging files containing countless details of worship services, designed over four decades of ministry. Each worship service has unique features, testifying to hours of collaboration over choices and creativity. It is fascinating to pull out old worship bulletins and be reminded of the individuals who took part, drama that was written, artwork celebrated, songs composed, and testimonies given, always seeking to respond to God's Word and will through Scripture. Reasons for many of the choices are still in my memory bank. At some point I will need to dispose of all this paperwork so my children are not left with mountains of old files. But at present I am loathe to throw away a single one because each one speaks of hours of loving care about worship. How easy it would be to fill several more chapters with examples drawn from these files.

Sometimes planning is straightforward. For example, in designing the Advent service with lectionary readings (described in chap. 12), I used the fourfold pattern: gathering, Word, thanksgiving, and sending out. In collaboration, Karen added many suggestions. Romans 13:11–12 (slightly amended) was chosen as the call to worship. From resource books she found a powerful prayer of confession with an assurance of pardon especially written for the first Sunday in Advent. Of the many possible traditional hymns, "O Come, O Come, Emmanuel" was chosen for the gathering.

My sermon developed the theme that anticipating Christ's future return as the concluding act in God's big story confronts and subverts our Christmas priorities. I challenged worshipers to stop running (at least a little) and invited them to pray counterculturally every day through Advent, using an Advent prayer that was shown on the screen.

> Lord Jesus Christ, as I await your coming
> Show me your ways,
> Teach me your paths.
> For you are the God of my salvation,
> On you I wait all the day.
>
> adapted from Psalm 25:4–5

Appropriately, this prayer came from *The Book of Daily Prayer* by Robert Webber,[28] who was the conference founder but was unable to be present because of his final illness.

For the response to God's Word in thanksgiving, Karen wrote a pastoral prayer that included elements from Psalm 122 and was put on the screen to be prayed by the whole congregation. "Love Divine, All Loves Excelling," by Charles Wesley, was the hymn of response, chosen because of the eschatological expectation in its final two verses. The sending out involved the congregation repeating in unison the Advent prayer above immediately prior to the benediction. Various lectionary readings enabled rich biblical language and thought to flow through the whole act of worship. Yet the specific invitation to pray the Advent prayer encouraged ongoing commitment through the rest of Advent.

As with all worship planning, practical details included preparing words of hymns and prayers for projection onto a screen, especially the Advent prayer, to focus attention both during the sermon and then at the conclusion. Organizing other visuals—electronic images, banners, and candles—was necessary, particularly preparing the Advent candle not only to make explicit connection with the Advent theme of light coming into the world but also to mark the beginning of the longer Advent process. As it was lit, the congregation responded, "We light this candle as a sign of the coming light of Christ."

Other services are much more complex, particularly when they need to integrate larger new elements into their structure. For example, the service on *peace* (also mentioned in chap. 12) required thoughtful placement of the commissioning of conflict coaches within the pattern of singing, praying, and preaching. How could this practical commitment, setting apart some peacemakers, best relate to the challenge of God's Word in worship? Elements such as drama, video, and other visual helps obviously needed to be strategically placed within the rhythm of God's call and response.

On every occasion, music choices remain critically important. Sometimes even finding music relating to particular Scriptures is difficult. When planning another service in the God's promises series on the topic of resisting temptation (1 Cor. 10:13), we couldn't find an appropriate response song to be used in contemporary worship. I asked for help.

Temptation—Out of Fashion?

Wednesday, February 13, 2008

I asked one of next Sunday's music leaders whether the theme of "facing temptation" emerges much in contemporary songwriting. I mentioned that when I was young there were some old-fashioned hymns like: "Yield not to temptation, for yielding is sin." I questioned: "Do you think this theme is out of fashion?"

He bounced back: "I can't think of any worship songs in my library that address temptation as explicitly as this hymn. That said, modern worship tunes are less verbose and don't develop themes as comprehensively as hymns. In any case, I'm happy to hear that you are addressing temptation. While the topic may be out of fashion in today's music, it is as relevant as ever in our oversexed, materialistic, instant gratification culture."

Anybody out there aware of appropriate contemporary worship material for 1 Corinthians 10:13?

To my surprise, many replied. I blogged later:

Worship Collaboration

Tuesday, February 19, 2008

One great joy in last week's blogging was the buzz that followed my query about appropriate music for dealing with temptation. Several people replied. And, as a result, the worship leader was able to use some new music he had never heard before. So many worship tributaries flow in from every side. Nobody can keep in touch with them all, . . . but how wonderful to receive others' suggestions and act on them. Worship was enriched. . . .

How rarely do preachers and worship leaders collaborate over preparing public worship. They seem to work in separate boxes—preachers choosing texts and themes while worship leaders choose music. Their choices are then fed into the worship order that has become routine for their particular local church—from set liturgy to informal (though often ordered) worship.

What a difference it makes when they BOTH take greater responsibility for the whole, when the preacher cares about the shape of the worship service and the content of its different elements, and when the worship leader bothers about engaging with the Scripture to be preached and asks what impact this might have upon worship.

This posting brings us back full circle to the importance of collaboration. The last steps in stage 4 involve delegating responsibilities and ensuring that planning is complete. Preparing music, liturgy, and images takes time and energy. Many churches benefit from volunteers who help prepare PowerPoint, print service bulletins, and organize visual materials. Obviously, with greater creativity the more people need to be involved and the more complex organizing worship becomes. At this point of the worship swim, lead-worshipers other than the preacher necessarily take most responsibility for overseeing preparations. After all, the preacher still has the sermon to prepare. Such oversight should never cut corners or take chances; it should support others in fulfilling their responsibilities to ensure the outcome. Indeed, some lead-worshipers rehearse the whole sequence of activities to ensure optimum worship preparation.

I recently participated in a Good Friday service called "The Way of the Cross." The congregation was divided into four sections (each comprising fifty people or so), and then each group moved through a progression of stages in different parts of the building. Over twenty of us were involved in leadership. Two members had painted pictures of journeying with Christ and others helped display them. Each different worship space in the building was prepared in contrasting ways using visuals, lighting, music, and practical activities to encourage participation. Responsibility for preparing each of these spaces was delegated to individuals who drafted others (musicians, readers, artists) to provide support. Having worked on details for several weeks beforehand, we all met together the night before and spent two hours running through the practical issues as well as practicing a joint Scripture presentation that preceded dividing up the congregation. On Good Friday we met again, an hour before the service, to pray together and ensure final preparations were completed. After a time of extended prayer, the music pastor whispered to me, "Just look at all these different people united in bringing worship together. This is the wonder of church family." Yes! Afterward, several friends testified how this experience of worship helped them journey with Christ to his cross in significant ways.

Deliver the Sermon and Lead Worship

Stage 5 marks the outcome of all this work of preparation. Every part of the preparation process belongs within the Trinity's empowering grace, and now the Holy Spirit brings the work to fruition. Lead-worshipers give their best preparation for God's use knowing he can bless it in surprising ways. One such leader described his experience:

> There have been occasions when I prepared my transitions so exactly that I felt too rehearsed. It came off as something that was supposed to have meaning but never really *hit*. The times when I have not prepared at all, well, sometimes that worked and sometimes it didn't. But the times when I prepared and went with whatever happened at the moment, those are the times that I felt like I was really leading in the Spirit. As long as the leader has been in prayer and preparation, there's a good chance that *whatever* does come out will be a result of that prayer and preparation.

The Holy Spirit never despises hard work when it is offered to him thankfully and humbly.

Of course, key practical issues matter too, especially lead-worshipers' voice and body language. I was intrigued to read an Internet discussion on "10 Tips for Worship Leaders: How to Enhance On-Stage Presence."[29] The title immediately troubled me with its overtones of performance, but I was encouraged to read on and find a plea for lead worshipers to show servant leadership that always *facilitates* corporate worship. The ten tips are:

1. Watch what you do (be aware of body language and gestures).
2. Keep your eyes open (interact with the congregation).
3. Sing it like you mean it.
4. Cut down on "downtime."
5. Use readings and transitions wisely.

6. Show and tell (connect with scriptural truth).
7. Get engaged (make sure the focus is not on yourself).
8. Listen to your mom (practice, practice, practice).
9. Embrace imperfection (the unexpected happens, but it is not a performance to entertain but family at worship).
10. Pray.

These ten points led to considerable positive online feedback as other lead-worshipers interacted. The list, however, did not emphasize use of the voice. Matters such as breathing and diction also need close attention. Sadly, nothing wrecks good content more than mumbled or confused delivery. When I teach preachers, I encourage them to work on improving their voices as well as their body language.[30] As G. Robert Jacks says, "God loves us enough to accept us as we are. But he loves us too much to leave us that way."[31] Occasionally I have encountered lead-worshipers who seem to presume that because they have a microphone they have no need to modulate their voices. They express no variety in rate, volume, stress, and inflection and have a total absence of intentional pauses. By deadpan, flat delivery they dull the wonder of worship. Refusing to work on delivery can sabotage the best efforts of preparation.

This chapter began by noting similarities between orchestral conductors and lead-worshipers. I was intrigued to read a rave review of a recent visit by English conductor Mark Elder to conduct English orchestral music with the Chicago Symphony Orchestra. The headline read: "Mark Elder Inspires CSO." Reviewing his conducting, the critic wrote, "His energy was always flexible, mindful of the long view as well as of telling instrumental detail. You really have to have this music in your blood to be able to infuse it with such warm glory and deeply elegiac feeling. The playing Elder drew from the orchestra was robust, lucid, alive, full of character."[32]

Lead-worshipers really need such love for God that worship is in their blood. Reveling in their relationship with God and longing for others to join in so that God can work his purpose through all his people, they help infuse every part for God's glory. And yes, they need to draw out the best from everyone taking part—robust, lucid, alive, and full of character. Our Triune God inspires worship, but he needs men and women willing to be inspired to give their best in worship leading.

14

Evaluating and Building Forward

Worship Swim Stage 6

The true test of worship is whether it does produce such a high tide in the hearts of the Christian community as overflows with cleansing and fruitfulness into homes, fields, schools, business houses and into the many channels of national and international life.

E. C. Rust[1]

On July 30, 1988, in the Americas Shopping Center, Lisbon, Portugal, Antonio Gomes dos Santos stood motionless for fifteen hours, two minutes, and fifty-five seconds to establish the latest world record for standing still. What lengths people will go to attain a world record! Physical motionlessness, however, is much easier to gauge than spiritual motionlessness. In gathered worship, much can appear to be happening with impressively buzzing activity as worship services are well planned, lively, and popularly received. Yet in terms of any genuine growth of God's people maturing together, there may actually be precious little movement. Worship marks time on the spot. Myopic preaching reigns, and nothing much happens week after week.

But when worship opens up to God-centered, God-empowered, all-inclusive, continuous living for God's glory, it has no limits. It claims every waking minute and every ounce of energy, every private moment and every relationship. It throws worshipers down in adoration, throws worshipers out in loving God and loving neighbor, and throws worshipers together living in love and unity. Nothing lies beyond its scope. It is transformational, over time making deeper, more Christlike people who belong in maturing communities. It unites people in spirit and in truth (John 4:24). It propels worshipers into presenting their bodies as a spiritual sacrifice, no longer conformed to this world but transformed by the renewing of their minds (Rom. 12:1–2). It binds living stones together that they might be a spiritual house, a royal priesthood, and a holy nation "proclaiming the mighty acts of him who called you out of darkness into his marvelous light" (1 Pet. 2:9; see vv. 1–9). The language of worship reaches out for huge realities—spirit, truth, transformation, proclamation. God in his big-picture purposes enables believers to put away childish things (1 Cor. 13:11) so that growing in the unity of faith and the knowledge of the Son of God, they come to maturity (Eph. 4:13). Big-picture worship makes Christian adults who are marked by personal and community maturity, thinking and living differently. "Once you were not a people, but now you are God's people" (1 Pet. 2:10).

But for many, such talk and this chapter's opening quotation seem far out of reach. Some will smile at its idealism, and others may go on the defensive: "Have you any idea what my church is like, full of problems and tension— many actually caused by worship services?" After sketching out some of the possibilities of big-picture worship, we can easily settle back with less than God's best. As when I believed the postcard picture of the Swiss mountain range was not real (see chap. 1), we can assume that no breathtaking possibilities actually lie beyond the familiar and humdrum. Great worship claims can flounder, and pulse-raising Scripture worship claims can sound unrealistic, sabotaged by cold realities. Pilgrims' progress turns into pilgrims' regress. Worship outcomes are lost in low expectations.

But if we have high expectations, because as lead-worshipers we are committed to big-picture worship, then we should expect great things to happen. After all, worship outcomes depend on the Triune God of grace, whose extraordinary interaction with us makes 360-degree worship possible. Because of our God, we *can* dare to grasp how worship throws open expansive possibilities that are far bigger than any of us can even imagine. Let's stop thinking that worship is something for which we are solely responsible. Too often we have allowed human limitations and current problems to blind us to God's mercy and power. Worship challenges the direction of everything we are living for and throws wide open before us the reality of living in God's new creation in Christ. The only faithful way to respond is to declare:

Now to him who by the power at work within us is able to accomplish abundantly far more than all we can ask or imagine, to him be glory in the church and in Christ Jesus to all generations, for ever and ever. Amen.

Ephesians 3:20–21

Worship means going to deeper places together. And God in three persons makes it possible.

At a recent church meeting in Oak Lawn, Illinois, that was part of a project on worship renewal, I was asked to describe some markers for personal and community transformation. The organizers posed the question, "How do we know we are growing personally and communally?" What an important question! As the worship swim progresses, we need honest evaluation in order to continue building forward as God's community. Indeed, stage 6 is called "evaluate the outcomes." The question forced me to think afresh how to address the complicated issue of assessing worship outcomes.

Frankly, the whole idea of evaluating Christian worship seems fraught with difficulty because it assumes we can assess spirituality. For some, that very idea is almost blasphemous. How can we talk about quantifying a spirit and truth event designed for God's glory? Surely only God can say whether worship is valuable, because the human perspective is notoriously suspect. God continually warns about hypocrisy and the importance of heart attitudes that only he sees (1 Sam. 16:7; Amos 5:21–24; Matt. 5). So spiritual reality does seem, by definition, inexpressible. Those metaphors I used in this book about seeing a magnificent mountain range hidden from view or stepping out of a preaching *dome* into a new reality speak of tingling senses and fresh actions alive to extraordinary new possibilities—more mystery, wonder, and danger pointing beyond to things unseen (2 Cor. 4:18). But how can we be sure that God is truly at work? C. S. Lewis warns that beauty should not be mistaken for things we think beautiful: "For they are not the thing itself; they are only the scent of a flower we have not found, the echo of a tune we have not heard, news from a country we have never yet visited."[2]

Keeping this warning in mind, I suggest that some evaluation is possible at two levels. Level 1 is not as difficult because it reviews the practical details of gathered worship. This primarily concerns lead-worshipers reviewing their preparation and outcomes. Level 2, however, goes much more profoundly into assessing responses to big-picture worship. In spite of the inherent limitation that only God knows the depth of spiritual response, it asks what we see happening as week after week we gather for worship and then scatter for worship.

Level 1: Evaluating Practical Details of Gathered Worship

At this basic level, the worship planning team needs to evaluate its work. Musician Keith Getty says:

> The effective pastor-and-worship leader teams we've seen are totally geared to serving their congregations every week. They continually ask, "What really worked here and what didn't?" It's so easy to make the unimportant things the

important things. So the music in itself or the sermon or the production values become the thing.[3]

Of course, every aspect of worship planning, including the music, should be assessed. Most teams need to work strenuously to develop necessary disciplines of time, energy, and accountability. But after having spent hours in preparation and delivery, even devoting a few minutes to review the past can seem a luxury in the face of urgent demands to prepare the next worship service. Also, tiredness so often hits, anticlimactically sapping energy levels. Further, evaluation makes heavy psychological demands. Few of us enjoy honest examination, especially when the subject is so large and accessible to others' opinions as gathered worship. Since so many are able to offer opinions (out of different motives), sifting out constructive criticism from destructive requires maturity from leaders. Yet only through such feedback can leadership develop.

Norma Malefyt and Howard Vanderwell list several benefits of worship evaluation, including its ability to encourage, balance out negative criticism, fuel and stir creativity and motivation, provide a healthy corrective, and provide a safeguard against hyperevaluation.[4] Looking back on my ministry, I recognize that I have benefited far more from constructive criticism than from praise. Indeed, my journey from myopia traced in this book owes much to listening to others' (sometimes hard-hitting) critiques. Making time for serious evaluation, with willingness to learn from feedback, must occur.

Elsewhere, I urge preachers to evaluate their own preaching by using four *R*s: reflect, review, record, receive.[5] *Reflect* is about asking what difference the sermon's main impact should make on the preacher's own life. Having preached a sermon to challenge others does not excuse preachers from making a personal response too. Indeed, because preachers have dwelt longer in God's Word and wrestled with its contemporary implications, they should be more likely than others to perceive and respond to its message. A preacher said to me recently, "I find preparing sermons spices up my spiritual life. It keeps me on the edge." But even more importantly, living out the message of those same sermons is vital for the integrity of long-term spiritual life. Preachers who remain unaffected by their own messages are unlikely to be effective, period. *Review* involves asking about the sermon's structure and content—did its various parts work together? Were any parts too long, complex, or rushed? Experienced preachers are often very aware of weaknesses and strengths even while preaching. Listeners look puzzled at one point, become restless at another, or visibly light up. *Record* concerns organizing material for future use. And then back to *receive*, which emphasizes the importance of being open to others' responses. Did comments afterward reveal strengths and weaknesses? The one golden rule of preaching is that God's preachers never cease needing to improve.

Just as preachers should reflect, review, record, and receive feedback, so too members of the worship planning team should scrutinize their work. Of these four aspects, *reflect* makes the most spiritual demands and consequently is often the least practiced. It is much easier to review how well different parts of the service worked together and what visible participation occurred. Did elements keep within time limits and were transitions smooth? Were music choices helpful? Getty comments on the way he evaluates music:

> The ministers have two goals, to teach the faith and to support the congregation. On Monday morning the pastor and music minister need to get together and ask: "How well did we achieve these goals?" They need to look at the words they put in the congregation's mouths and minds. So we need to print out all the words from Sunday and ask, "Are these true words? Are these words giving people a bigger vision of God?" Next you have to ask, "Did the congregation sing?" If the congregation can't sing, then it doesn't matter how good it is for the worship band or the lead singer.[6]

Much more could be said about the wide range of practical issues that need to be reviewed, and good resources are available, such as Malefyt and Vanderwell's provision of several sample worship evaluation sheets with helpful practical advice.[7] Evaluation, however, involves much more than assessing how well sermons and services seemed to work out. The step of *reflect* should take us to deeper levels. It is possible for worship planners to be self-congratulatory about how their planning worked out when bathed in immediate, positive feedback. But what happened to them as worshipers? For the worship swim is never just about the mechanics of how well we gathered; it is also about whether in praising and responding to God the worshipers were moved closer in his community for missional living. Worship outcomes over the long term are far-reaching in their transformation. That's why evaluation should always go on to this second level.

Level 2: Evaluating Big-Picture Worship Responses

Beyond the practical responsibility of lead-worshipers to evaluate their own part in designing gathered worship, it is much more important to look for evidence of growth in worshipers themselves. Back to that question from the church meeting organizers: "How do we know we are growing personally and communally?" Do we see any signs of growth and change? Where is God's action evident? Gathered worshipers can only give back their best in word and action because of God's initiating work in their lives. Participating in fellowship with God—Father, Son, and Holy Spirit—enables worshipers to magnify God and grow together in Christ for his mission. Sharing by the grace of the Triune God in community and mission is the heart of true worship.

As Thomas Long writes, "Worship is best measured not by how popular, inspirational, beautiful, educational, musically rich, poetic, or exciting it is. . . . In essence worship is what happens when people become aware that they are in the presence of the living God."[8]

Worship's purposes are the grandest ever offered to humankind through Jesus Christ. "When we leave the worship service has our character been nurtured by visions of God's reign so that we will be agents of Triune righteousness and faithfulness in the world—God's purposes to feed the hungry, combat oppression, expose the lies, live the truth?"[9]

It is these grand purposes that need our attention. Everything within the worship swim offered in gathered worship should have wider repercussions—building a community of maturing persons to be a missionary people every day of the week. Jesus said that "by their fruits you will know them" (Matt. 7:20), both warning of bad fruit as well as encouraging good. The apostle Paul challenged that our building with gold, silver, costly stones, wood, hay, or straw will be revealed on the judgment day by fire (1 Cor. 3:12–13). But in the meantime, how can we recognize good fruit or gold? How can we know that people are aware they are in the presence of God? What evidence should we look for in assessing whether a high tide in the hearts of the Christian community is impacting the world with cleansing and fruitfulness?

Such evidence should be signs of God at work in the lives of his people. Many church actions and commitments can be sustained by human energy only. It's an old (sad) joke that 90 percent of church activity could continue if it was proved conclusively that Jesus Christ was not raised from the dead and there is no Holy Spirit. Practical unitarians can ensure that worship services run smoothly and church organizations prosper, but just where do we see Father, Son, and Holy Spirit sustaining fruit as worshipers build with gold and silver? Big-picture worship should show evidence of actions and commitments that can be sustained *only* by the grace of God working in people's lives and the community. Where are worshipers living beyond themselves, showing signs of God's love and power in their lives? To quote Henry Moore again (see chap. 1), where are people evidently devoting their entire lives to "something they cannot possibly do"?

This deeper level of probing should begin with the lead-worshipers themselves. If all their planning resulted in well-constructed, Scripture-directed gathered worship, there is a positive review of their efforts and skills (with ever-lurking pride). Now they must ask questions about their own growth as worshipers. Alongside the easier task of evaluating what happened in gathered worship, they must evaluate what happened in their own lives because they worshiped God.

Lead-worshipers need to ask about *their own responses to God.* All kinds of questions can be raised, such as:

- Are we transparently thankful and filled with reverential wonder and awe that make us give the very best of ourselves in worship?
- Do we listen prayerfully together to God's Word in Scripture and seek to direct everything in obedience?
- Are we preachers preaching sermons that enlarge wonder before God, thrilling imaginations about who he is and what he is doing now, moving worshipers to action?
- Are we really lead-worshipers—first responders to each new worship challenge?

Closely connected with their worship response to God, they need to ask questions about *their relationships with each other*:

- Does every member of the worship planning team love each other, exhibiting willingness to share heart, head, and hand qualifications, surrendering personal ambitions to the highest purpose of loving God?
- Do we share largeness of spirit with generosity in all our preparation work together?

Lead-worshipers should model wonder at God's awesome power, gratitude for his forgiving love, and commitment to peacemaking and reconciliation. Together they seek to lead the community into greater maturity for God's mission even as they are growing by his grace into greater maturity themselves.

But we must also ask about the wider congregation of worshipers. Are there ways in which the whole community reveals signs of what God is doing in their lives both personally and in community? Are there characteristics that show good fruit or building with gold, silver, and precious stones?

Several authors have studied church congregational life in order to identify positive characteristics of spiritual life. For example, Thomas Long discerns nine signs of churches that are building vital and faithful worship:

1. They make room somewhere in worship for the experience of mystery.
2. They make planned and concerted efforts to show hospitality to strangers.
3. They have recovered and made visible the sense of drama in Christian worship.
4. They emphasize congregational music that is both excellent and eclectic in style and genre.
5. They creatively adapt the space and environment of worship.
6. They have a strong connection between worship and local mission, and this connection is expressed in every aspect of the worship service.

7. They have a relatively stable order of service and a significant repertoire of worship elements and response that the congregation knows by heart.
8. They move to a joyous festival experience toward the end of their worship service.
9. They have a strong, charismatic pastor as worship leader.[10]

Is it possible to focus some of these signs into even more specific characteristics? Recently, a church leader said to me, "I always think that the number of people remaining in the church building after a service is one of the best signs of worship. A few years ago nobody stayed—within two or three minutes the place was empty. People couldn't wait to get home. Now the whole place buzzes up to half an hour and beyond. That's got to be a very good sign." Listening, I wondered if such a specific sign has value. *Do* numbers of people remaining in church buildings after services signify something important?

I guess much depends on whether practical unitarians can organize the same outcome without depending on God's grace. If people remain in church because of normal social behavior as friends meeting together, then there is little chance it is a sign of God's empowering and community formation. But if people remain because God makes some amazingly connected misfits into his community where depths of love and unity demonstrate something beyond normal social behavior, then yes, this shows God's grace at work. Practical unitarians cannot manufacture love and unity like that which binds dissimilar people together, moving hearts and minds to adore and serve and transforming them into community with love for others. Here all the talk about participating within the life of the Trinity because of the relationships, movement, and power of God in three persons should show.

Are there other signs? As I offer some suggestions, I invite you to be creative about what signs you might look for in your own worshiping congregation. The following four signs relate to the stages of community foundation and contain starter questions to stimulate your own thinking.

Transformed by the Renewing of Minds (Rom. 12:2)

Obviously, how worshipers actually think and talk about worship reveals how big their picture is and how much God is working in their lives. Are worshipers able to say the following?

We understand that worship is *not* just:

- going to church on Sundays
- singing our favorite songs and hymns
- following through the liturgy
- listening to sermons

We understand that worship *is* about:

- who God is and what he has done and is doing
- everything we do and every day we live in response to him
- offering our lives as living sacrifices (Rom. 12:1–2)
- belonging with brothers and sisters in Christian family
- being changed to be more like Christ together
- living as Christian missionaries among our neighbors

We believe that:

> we gather because God loves us and longs for fellowship with us, and so we bring the best of our praise, love, commitment, money, and time to share together; we prepare to be sent out to take the best of our praise, love, commitment, money, and time to share it in the world.

When worshipers think of worship like this, then we know that God is truly at work.

Presenting Sacrifice in Worship (Rom. 12:1)

Offering sacrifice, holy and acceptable to God, lies at the heart of gathered worship and everyday living for Christian believers. Signs of such sacrifice can be grouped under three headings: awe, Scripture, and participation.

Awe. Encountering God in his holiness is vital for authentic worship. What questions help us recognize awe in worship?

- Did our praise focus on God, using worthy language grounded in trinitarian theology so that it expressed awe and adoration not only in gathered worship but also during the week in private praise?
- How much quietness invited stillness and knowing that he is God (Ps. 46:6)?
- How honest were we before God, making confession that shows we *really* see ourselves before our holy God?
- How did we encourage preachers to preach deeper sermons?
- Did we see an awakened sense of dependence—not *doing our own thing* but desiring to depend on God's grace at work? Was there wariness about knee-jerk activism?
- Was there longing for more space and time to take part in the Lord's Supper as we expect spiritual encounter?
- Do we drop on our knees every day before God, who grants life and grace afresh?

Scripture. In big-picture worship, Scripture directs the whole of gathered worship. The Bible is uncaged. Positive signs relate to these questions:

- Did we pray for the preacher and share in any preparation before hearing the preached Word?
- How seriously did we attend to Scripture within worship, actively listening for God's Word?
- Did we bring our own Scriptures to gathered worship and then open them up again (preferably with others) to reflect on the same text in our own homes later the following week?
- How sensitive and obedient are we to what God says and wants to do through his Word?

Participation. One music leader commented, "It's not just the volume of singing that goes up when people get involved but the whole congregation's body language expresses conviction. You can *see* their engagement. But at other times there's just no connection at all."

- How much did we share in collaborating with the worship planners and wider congregation beforehand and afterward?
- What visible signs of engagement did we and the congregation show with elements of worship and the flow of the worship service?
- How many different voices took part, and how many different gifts were used within gathered worship?
- How much does our worship continue in homes and neighborhoods?
- How generous is our financial giving?

Growing Maturity in Character (Eph. 4:13)

Gathered worship seeks to form individuals into community by growing them together inwardly. Those who hunger for God seek spiritual authenticity, and those who hunger for community long for genuine relationships with others. Without losing awe before God's holiness, worshipers also seek mutual acceptance within his loving community.

- How genuine was the welcome we gave others as we worshiped? Some traditions are more reserved than others, but no stranger should feel unwelcome. Sensitive ushering is necessary.
- How inclusive were the music choices? Did they allow all members of the community to participate?
- What level of *we*-ness was expressed by the language in music and preaching that encouraged us to own togetherness?

- Was there an authentic exchange of greeting or peace within worship that was expressed by continued sharing at the conclusion of gathered worship?
- How many people continued in fellowship within the church buildings?
- What proportion of volunteers gladly support the life of the fellowship?
- What proportion of the congregation is committed to meet in small groups during the week?
- How willing are worshipers to speak the truth in love and develop maturity of relationships?
- What amount of hospitality is given by members to each other in an average week?

Worshiping in the World (1 Pet. 2:12)

One of Long's signs of a vital and faithful congregation concerns the strong connection between worship and local mission, with this connection expressed in every aspect of the worship service. Awareness of the wider community and world should be stamped into prayers, sermon, and offering. Connections between Sunday and Monday should be evident throughout, and at worship's conclusion the responses should include commitment to God's mission.

- Did the list of matters that the church prays about week by week include concerns for the community and world?
- What specific responses of service and action occurred as the congregation was sent out?
- Did moral discernment connect Scripture with life in the world, demonstrating distinctive Christian values especially in households as communities of faith?
- What percentage of the church budget is given away to others in need?
- How many secular community organizations are members involved with, especially community care agencies?
- Is there a high level of awareness of such community work within the fellowship?
- How much hospitality is given to unchurched friends?

What a Challenge!

How markedly different all these signs of effective worship are compared to where we began with myopic preaching. Remember those ten characteristics? How cripplingly limited they now seem as preachers settled for small-picture worship—mere organized events bounded by music or liturgy or Sundays only.

Putting the most emphasis on what *we* must do to make worship effective rather than thrilling to the full (and demanding) theology of trinitarian grace as God—Father, Son, and Holy Spirit—invites us to join in, empowering our responses. Too often Scripture has been caged as a resource book to provide sermons that educate (and possibly inspire) listeners rather than liberated as God's two-edged sword moving and directing everything that is important about being alive. And the whole experience of rich liturgy, with God-ordained elements like the Lord's Supper and baptism, has been treated as less-than-vital encounters with the Lord who commanded them.

Tragically, myopic preaching has allowed individuals to walk away from gathered worship with no more sense of belonging to others than shopping in the same mall. Community life has been woefully neglected as personal choice and preferences reign supreme. Church resembles its surrounding culture, living the same way and organizing its success-oriented goals on business principles. Music has often been allowed to become *the* determining factor that gives life and purpose to services that lumber from one separate event to another with no sense of progressing through God's bigger story.

You can see how dramatically my earlier myopic preaching has been deconstructed. This book has charted my journey to a new worship worldview. Earlier I expressed the ambitious hope that I might open preachers' eyes with wonder and excitement to big-picture worship, that they might recognize how everything important in their lives and ministry is called *worship*. Worship is the integrator that holds all of life together in God's biggest purpose. Before all else, preachers are worshipers and their preaching is worship. And responding in worship is all by grace, as we are caught up in participating with our Triune God, reveling in his relationships, movement, and power that enable us to live together for him.

Several times in this book I have resorted to recounting various experiences to express the wonder of big-picture worship—like seeing mountains and climbing a tower. Perhaps my most intense experience occurred on my first visit to the John Hancock Tower in downtown Chicago on a snowy winter day. This striking building soars from street level up to 1,127 feet. Visiting its top-floor viewing lounge is a tourist's must-do. On that day, however, there were few others. My family and I were alone as the elevator propelled us up ninety-five floors, and we found ourselves wandering in comfort around the spacious viewing area, gaping at the city and lakeside far below. Unhurriedly, we studied information posted about famous buildings and landmarks.

Then we noticed the revolving door leading to an outside deck. No warning was given about what lay on the other side. Passing through, suddenly, invigoratingly, we were exposed to an unforgettable raw, noisy, whole-body experience. Wind whipped our clothes and bitter cold pinched our cheeks. Perched high, we were now *in* the city. Sights and sounds hit us from below, ricocheting off buildings. Lights sparkled on the horizon. Instead of viewing scenery behind safe insulation, we had *entered* the scenery. A high wind chill made this even more dramatic. One minute we were protected inside with cerebral calm; the next we were exposed outside with all our senses in overdrive. Out of warm, protected space, we were unexpectedly thrust into an extraordinary experience. Our response was sheer exhilaration. Actually, the word *exhilaration* stems from the Latin *hilarare*—to make cheerful—and *exhilarate* is defined: "to cause to feel happily refreshed and energetic; to invigorate, stimulate."[11] Yes, that's what happened!

This provides a vivid analogy for my worship journey. Formerly I looked at worship from behind glass as something other than preaching to be kept at a distance. Now I have entered its full-on impact. Instead of feeling comfortable detachment, I have awakened to the reality of preaching as worship within God's big picture. Instead of seeing worship as a dimension to be added to the preaching task, I have discovered that worship is the best way to describe preaching. Convicted that worship had become shrunken in scale, captured by lesser motives, I knew I had to attempt to redefine worship in bigger ways to restore its scale of living every day for eternity. I saw that worship leading—lead-worshiping—was my responsibility as preacher too. And in order to experience big-picture worship, I had to step out and join in with the gathered community of saints, both militant and triumphant, entering into the whole-body, raw experience of living in the tumultuous call and response of God's grace.

This wonderful discovery about worship meant I had to reinterpret some of the events in my ministry. In particular, my ministry experience in Cambridge, a church come alive to God in its life and mission (told at the end of chap. 2), needed to be understood within the perspective of big-picture worship. Stepping out from the safe and known, that whole community experienced worship that led outward to daring and exhilarating mission. Worshipers tasted heaven on earth, living more largely and breathing more deeply. God makes some amazingly connected misfits.

I now know that churches that see afresh the possibilities of being built as God's worshiping communities sound and look different. Instead of individuals judging worship by whether it helped them or not, leaving church with little sense of belonging to the people of God or sharing his mission for the world, they are enlarged in spirit and in truth and dare to act as chosen people and holy nation. Rather than participating in services of worship that are personally oriented, plagued by worship wars as music preferences battle for supremacy, they grow in spiritual formation to include others in the royal priesthood. Instead of being criticized by culture as un-Christian, they live such good lives that others see their "good deeds and glorify God" (1 Pet. 2:12 NIV). Rather than giving out invitations that say, "You must come to our church—you'll love the music," "I really want you to hear our pastor," or "We've got a great program for youth," now they say, "Come and meet

God with my Christian family," "Come, you'll want to belong in our mission together," "Come, let's worship together."

I end this book knowing that I am only at the beginning of working through the implications of big-picture worship. I dream that one day my preaching class will combine with those on worship and spirituality so that future pastors can learn together about Scripture directing worship, not just sermons, and about worship holding together everything that is important in their future ministries. I dream that preachers reading this will want to commit themselves unreservedly to this adventure of big-picture worship and take risks for God's sake. I dream they will step out boldly from myopic preaching and be willing to allow God to reconstruct all their work within his dynamic gift of worship. Then they can pray:

> O gracious God, Father, Son, and Holy Spirit,
> Help me to worship you with everything I am—
> Heart, soul, mind, and strength.
> Awaken me to worship you with brothers and sisters,
> Loved by Christ, who unites us more deeply than we presently know
> In Word and Table,
> In God's ongoing story,
> In gathered worship and scattered worship.
> Challenge my little ways and prejudices that presume to know best,
> My solo preparation,
> My preferences that shut others out,
> My laziness too easily satisfied.
> Help me say "we" and "love" more with other lead-worshipers,
> Not just to those who gather in community but to those who live
>   around.
> And put my sermons in perspective that, with the whole of gathered
>   worship, they will give glory to you
> And do immeasurably more than I can ask or imagine.
> In Jesus's name. Amen.

Appendix

Some Definitions of Worship

1. Authentic worship is a continuous outpouring of all that we are and can ever hope to become in the light of the saving work of Christ. It reaches into every quarter of our living, informing all of our actions and safeguarding them within the arena of Spirit, truth, and sacrificial living. Harold Best in *Unceasing Worship*, 2003, 111.
2. Worship is a display, a performance commanded by God so that all of creation may see the life-transforming glory of God. Tod Bolsinger in *It Takes a Church to Raise a Christian*, 2004, 86.
3. Worship is a gift between lovers who keep on giving to each other. C. Welton Gaddy in *The Gift of Worship*, 1992, xi.
4. Worship is God's conversation with the people of God and the community's communication with the divine Communicator. F. Russell Mitman in *Worship in the Shape of Scripture*, 2001, 40.
5. Christian worship is nothing more nor less than the Spirit enabling us to join in with Christ's worship of the Father. Robin Parry in *Worshiping Trinity*, 2005.
6. Here is the essence of Christian worship. As members of a people whose storyline includes creation, sin, and grace, we commune with our Creator and Savior—with God, through Christ, in the power of the Holy Spirit. Worship is narrative engagement with the Triune God. Cornelius Plantinga and Sue Rozeboom in *Discerning the Spirits*, 2003, 126.
7. At its best, Christian worship presents a vision of life created, sustained, redeemed, and held in the mystery of God. What we do together in acknowledging God *schools* us in ways of seeing the world and of being in it. Don Saliers in *Worship and Spirituality*, 1996, 2.

8. True worship is Spirit touching spirit. Worship happens when the presence of God is bridged with people's felt needs in their life context. Michael Slaughter in *Out on the Edge*, 1998, 73.

9. Worship [is] the acknowledging of the holiness of God and the passionate love borne to all creatures by a God of justice. Until preachers get that straight we will not be at ease in our office. Gerard S. Sloyan in *Worshipful Preaching*, 1984, 11.

10. Christian worship is . . . our participation through the Spirit in the Son's communion with the Father, in his vicarious life of worship and intercession. It is our response to our Father for all that he has done for us in Christ. James B. Torrance in *Worship, Community, and the Triune God of Grace*, 1996, 15.

11. Worship names what matters most: the way human beings are created to reflect God's glory by embodying God's character in lives that seek righteousness and do justice. Mark Labberton in *The Dangerous Act of Worship*, 2007, 13.

12. Worship is all of us for all of God. Thomas Troeger in *Preaching and Worship*, 2003.

13. The reason we gather for worship is: to celebrate and honor God, to engage and build up the congregation to live out Christian discipleship; to provide hospitable communication that welcomes others into a fresh experience of and relationship with the living God. Ron Weber in *Reconnecting Worship*.[1]

Notes

Chapter 1 An Ocean and a Bucket

1. Dan Kimball, *The Emerging Church* (Grand Rapids: Zondervan, 2003), 15.

2. Lytton Strachey, quoted in Joseph J. Ellis, *Founding Brothers* (New York: Vintage House, 2001), ix.

3. Susan J. White, *Foundations of Christian Worship* (Louisville: Westminster John Knox, 2006), 13.

4. Robert Webber, *Worship Is a Verb: Celebrating God's Mighty Deeds of Salvation* (Peabody, MA: Hendrickson, 2004), vi.

5. Ibid., 1–6.

6. Ibid., 34.

7. Robert Webber, "The Call to an Ancient Evangelical Future," May 12, 2006, www.aef-center.org/read.html.

8. Robert Webber, *Signs of Wonder: The Phenomenon of Convergence in Modern Liturgical and Charismatic Churches* (Nashville: Abbott Martyn, 1992), 25.

9. See Harold M. Best, *Unceasing Worship: Biblical Perspectives on Worship and the Arts* (Downers Grove, IL: InterVarsity, 2003); Mark Labberton, *The Dangerous Act of Worship: Living God's Call to Justice* (Downers Grove, IL: InterVarsity, 2007); F. Russell Mitman, *Worship in the Shape of Scripture* (Cleveland: Pilgrim Press, 2001); James B. Torrance, *Worship, Community, and the Triune God of Grace* (Downers Grove, IL: InterVarsity, 1996); Marva Dawn, *Reaching Out without Dumbing Down* (Grand Rapids: Eerdmans, 1995); Kimball, *The Emerging Church*; Don E. Saliers, *Worship and Spirituality* (Akron, OH: OSL Publications, 1996); Tod E. Bolsinger, *It Takes a Church to Raise a Christian: How the Community of God Transforms Lives* (Grand Rapids: Brazos, 2004); Cornelius Plantinga and Sue A. Rozeboom, *Discerning the Spirits: A Guide to Thinking about Christian Worship Today* (Grand Rapids: Eerdmans, 2003); D. A. Carson, ed., *Worship by the Book* (Grand Rapids: Zondervan, 2002); and Norma deWaal Maleyft and Howard Vanderwell, *Designing Worship Together: Models and Strategies for Worship Planning* (Herndon, VA: Alban Institute, 2005).

10. William Hendricks, *Exit Interviews* (Chicago: Moody, 1993), 250.

11. Dawn, *Reaching Out*, 281.

12. Sally Morgenthaler, *Worship Evangelism* (Grand Rapids: Zondervan, 1995), 24.

13. David E. Fitch, *The Great Giveaway: Reclaiming the Mission of the Church from Big Business, Parachurch Organizations, Psychotherapy, Consumer Capitalism, and Other Modern Maladies* (Grand Rapids: Baker, 2005), 100.

14. Ibid., 103.

15. Tex Sample, *The Spectacle of Worship in a Wired World* (Nashville: Abingdon, 1998), 63, 69.

16. Ibid., 3.

17. Warren W. Wiersbe, *Real Worship: Playground, Battleground or Holy Ground?* (Grand Rapids: Baker, 2000).

18. William H. Willimon, *Preaching and Leading Worship* (Philadelphia: Westminster, 1984), 16–25.

19. Brainyquote.com/quotes/authors/h/henry_moore.html.

Chapter 2 Preaching and Worship: Is There a Problem?

1. Charles Rice, quoted in Mitman, *Worship in the Shape of Scripture* (Cleveland: Pilgrim Press), 14.

2. John Killinger, *The Centrality of Preaching* (Waco: Word, 1969), 51.

3. Mitman, *Worship in the Shape of Scripture*, 28.

4. Kevin Navarro, *The Complete Worship Service: Creating a Taste of Heaven on Earth* (Grand Rapids: Baker, 2005), 37.

5. Sam Hamstra Jr., *Principled Worship* (Eugene, OR: Wipf & Stock, 2006), 49.

6. Thomas Troeger, *Preaching and Worship* (St. Louis: Chalice Press, 2003).

7. William H. Willimon, *Preaching and Leading Worship* (Philadelphia: Westminster Press, 1984).

8. Barbara Brown Taylor, *The Preaching Life* (Cambridge: Cowley, 1993), 70.

9. Michael J. Knowles, *We Preach Not Ourselves: Paul on Proclamation* (Grand Rapids: Brazos, 2008), 13–14.

10. In no way do I want to downplay the significance of preaching for proclaiming the gospel, and I stand by my past writing that trumpeted its key role. In *360-Degree Preaching* (2003) and *360-Degree Leadership* (2006), however, I wrote enthusiastically about the role of preaching with minimal reference to worship.

11. Timothy L. Carson, *Transforming Worship* (St. Louis: Chalice Press, 2003), 14.

12. Mitman, *Worship in the Shape of Scripture*, 20.

13. Thomas Long, personal conversation during the E. Y. Mullins Lectures, Southern Baptist Theological Seminary, Louisville, KY, 1993.

14. J. G. Davies, *Worship and Mission* (London: SCM Press, 1966), 21.

Chapter 3 Beware Myopic Preaching

1. *American Heritage College Dictionary*, 3rd ed. (Boston: Houghton Mifflin, 1993), 902.

2. Gary Parrett, *9.5 Theses*, PulpitTalk CD, *Worship and Preaching*, vol. 2 (South Hamilton, MA: Center for Preaching, Gordon-Conwell Theological Seminary, summer 2004), 4.

3. Paul Beasley-Murray, *Faith and Festivity: Guide for Today's Worship Leaders* (Eastbourne, East Sussex, UK: Marc, 1991), 10.

4. Willimon, *Preaching and Leading Worship*, 39.

5. Ibid., 27.

6. A. E. Garvie, *The Christian Preacher* (Edinburg, UK: T & T Clark, 1920), 5.

7. Mitman, *Worship in the Shape of Scripture*, 27.

8. R. Kent Hughes, "Free Church Worship: The Challenge of Freedom," in *Worship by the Book*, ed. D. A. Carson (Grand Rapids: Zondervan, 2002), 140.

9. Robin Parry, *Worshiping Trinity* (Carlisle, UK: Paternoster, 2005), 144.

10. Michael Pasquarello III, *Christian Preaching: A Trinitarian Theology of Proclamation* (Grand Rapids: Baker, 2006), 39.

11. Ibid., 42.

12. Gardner Taylor, quoted in "Is Our Preaching Christian?", April 29, 2009, www.theafrican americanpulpit.com/post/Is-Our-Preaching-Christian.aspx.

13. Torrance, *Worship, Community, and the Triune God of Grace*, 20.

14. Karl Rahner, *The Trinity* (London: Burrs and Oates, 1970); and Thomas A. Smail, *The Forgotten Father* (Grand Rapids: Eerdmans, 1980).

15. Torrance, *Worship, Community, and the Triune God of Grace*, 27.

16. Ibid., 29.

17. Ibid., 20.

18. Navarro, *Complete Worship Service*, 144.

19. See Thomas G. Long, *The Witness of Preaching* (Louisville: Westminster John Knox, 1989), 86.

20. Mike Graves, *The Sermon as Symphony* (Valley Forge, PA: Judson, 1997).

21. Jeffrey D. Arthurs, *Preaching with Variety* (Grand Rapids: Kregel, 2007).

22. J. Kent Edwards, *Effective First-Person Biblical Preaching* (Grand Rapids: Zondervan, 2005), 18–19.

23. Morgenthaler, *Worship Evangelism*, 51.

24. Mitman, *Worship in the Shape of Scripture*.

25. Timothy Carson, *Transforming Worship*, 13.

26. Ibid., 18.

27. Robert Webber, *Ancient-Future Worship: Proclaiming and Enacting God's Narrative* (Grand Rapids: Baker, 2008), 148.

28. Willimon, *Preaching and Leading Worship*, 17.

29. Craig van Gelder, "From Corporate Church to Missional Church: The Challenge Facing Congregations Today," *RevExp* 101 (2004): 425–50.

30. Ibid.

31. Ibid.

32. Dallas Willard, quoted in Bolsinger, *It Takes a Church*, 111.

33. Bolsinger, *It Takes a Church*, 57.

34. Saliers, *Worship and Spirituality*, 2.

35. Fitch, *Great Giveaway*, 111.

36. Dawn, *Reaching Out*, 105–6.

37. Fitch, *Great Giveaway*, 111.

38. Plantinga and Rozeboom, *Discerning the Spirits*, 57–74.

39. David Wells, quoted in Dawn, *Reaching Out*, 9.

40. Dawn, *Reaching Out*, 8.

41. Ibid., 55.

42. Kimball, *Emerging Church*, 59–61.

43. Fitch, *Great Giveaway*, 96.

44. Ibid., 97.

45. Ibid., 103.

46. Ibid., 151.

47. See Sample, *Spectacle of Worship*.

48. *A Call to an Ancient Evangelical Future: On the Primacy of the Biblical Narrative*, conference at Northern Seminary, Lombard, IL, November 30–December 1, 2007.

49. Webber, *Ancient-Future Worship*, 174–75.

50. Plantinga and Rozeboom, *Discerning the Spirits*, 163.

51. Thomas E. Boomershine, *Story Journey: An Invitation to the Gospel as Storytelling* (Nashville: Abingdon, 1998), 16.

52. H. Benton Lutz, quoted in Dawn, *Reaching Out*, 207.

53. William Temple, *Readings in St. John's Gospel* (London: Macmillan, 1950).

Chapter 4 A Fuller Definition and Deeper Theology

1. Best, *Unceasing Worship*, last chapter.

2. Webber, *Worship Is a Verb*, 3.

3. Donald Coggan, *A New Day for Preaching* (London: SPCK, 1997), 17.

4. Mitman, *Worship in the Shape of Scripture*, 22.

5. Ibid., 21–22.

6. P. T. Forsyth, quoted in Richard Lischer, *The Company of Preachers* (Grand Rapids: Eerdmans, 2002), 412.

7. See David Norrington, *To Preach or Not to Preach?* (Carlisle, UK: Paternoster, 1996).

8. "Liturgical Committee Report," Acts of Synod of the Christian Reformed Church (Grand Rapids: Christian Reformed Church, 1968), 135–36, quoted in Hamstra, *Principled Worship*, xvii.

9. Morgenthaler, *Worship Evangelism*, 39.

10. Note the title of Kevin Navarro's book: *The Complete Worship Service: Creating a Taste of Heaven on Earth*.

11. Marva Dawn, *A Royal "Waste" of Time: The Splendor of Worshiping God and Being Church for the World* (Grand Rapids: Zondervan, 1999), 59.

12. Morgenthaler, *Worship Evangelism*, 9.

13. Hughes, "Free Church Worship," 140.

14. Best, *Unceasing Worship*.

15. Mitman, *Worship in the Shape of Scripture*, 35.

16. G. Robert Jacks, *Getting the Word Across: Speech Communication for Pastors and Lay Leaders* (Grand Rapids: Eerdmans, 1995), 25.

17. Best, *Unceasing Worship*, 17–18.

18. Ibid., 10.

19. Ibid., 19.

20. Stephen F. Winward, quoted in Ronald C. D. Jasper, ed., *The Daily Office* (London: SPCK, 1968), 23.

21. Ibid., 20.

22. Rick Warren, *The Purpose Driven Life* (Grand Rapids: Zondervan, 2002), 63–64.

23. Evelyn Underwood, *Worship* (London: Collins, 1962), 13.

24. D. A. Carson, *Worship by the Book*, 26.

25. Troeger, *Preaching and Worship*, 21.

26. Labberton, *Dangerous Act of Worship*, 13.

27. Theological giants like Karl Barth, Karl Rahner, Wolfhart Pannenberg, and Jurgen Moltmann set about reinvigorating the classic doctrine, with a ferment of writing that continues until the present with Leonardo Boff, Catherine Mowry LaCugna, and John Zizioulas.

28. See authors such as Harold Best, Tod E. Bolsinger, Marva Dawn, James B. Torrance, Kevin Navarro, Robin Parry, and Jonathan R. Wilson, whose works are referenced elsewhere in the endnotes.

29. Parry, *Worshiping Trinity*, 5.

30. Bruce A. Ware, *Father, Son and Holy Spirit: Relationships, Roles and Relevance* (Wheaton: Crossway, 2005), 15.

31. Parry, *Worshiping Trinity*, 6–8.

32. The creed's language has remained seminal for all subsequent reflection. It formulated that God is one in his essential being (*ousia*), but he subsists eternally in three persons (*hypostases*)—Father, Son, and Spirit. Two prime models emerged: (1) The "Immanent Trinity" (sometimes called the "ontological," "psychological," or "individual" model) describes who God is in his oneness, as triune being. Focusing on the Godhead's essential nature, his inner dynamics shared

by three persons apart from creation underscore God's freedom and graciousness of salvation. This model stresses the *transcendent* nature of God, who is independent of humankind yet created humankind in his "own image." (2) On the other hand, a model of the "Economic Trinity" expresses how God in three persons has revealed himself in the story of creation—in the act of creation itself and through the events of incarnation, crucifixion, resurrection, and Pentecost.

33. Jonathan Wilson, *Why Church Matters: Worship, Ministry, and Mission in Practice* (Grand Rapids: Brazos, 2006), 55.

34. Christopher Cocksworth, quoted in Parry, *Worshiping Trinity*, 95.

35. Parry, *Worshiping Trinity*, 31.

36. Ibid., 32.

37. Ibid..

38. For a fuller treatment, see three consecutive articles on "Trinitarian Preaching," *Preaching* 13, nos. 3, 4, and 5 (2008).

39. John D. Witvliet, quoted in Leanne Van Dyke, ed., *A More Profound Alleluia* (Grand Rapids: Eerdmans, 2005), 15–25.

40. Personal communication.

Chapter 5 Preaching in 360-Degree Worship

1. Martin Luther, quoted in Christoph Schwobel, "The Preacher's Art: Preaching Theologically," in *Theology through Preaching*, ed. Colin Gunton (Edinburgh, UK: T & T Clark, 2001), 2.

2. Arthur F. Holmes, *Contours of a World View* (Grand Rapids: Eerdmans, 1983), 4.

3. Michael J. Quicke, *360-Degree Preaching* (Grand Rapids: Baker, 2006), 52.

4. Ibid., 49.

5. I gave less than five pages to *worship* in the book.

6. E. C. Rust, *The Word and Words: Towards a Theology of Preaching* (Macon, GA: Mercer University Press, 1982), 107.

7. Best, *Unceasing Worship*, 33.

8. C. Welton Gaddy, *The Gift of Worship* (Nashville: Broadman, 1992), xi.

9. Dawn, *Reaching Out*, 82.

10. Coggan, *A New Day*, 20–21.

11. Bolsinger, *It Takes a Church*, 100.

12. Pasquarello, *Christian Preaching*, 10.

13. Troeger, *Preaching and Worship*, 20–22.

14. Torrance, *Worship, Community, and the Triune God of Grace*, 20.

15. Richard Foster, *Celebration of Discipline* (London: Hodder & Stoughton, 1980), 147.

16. Michael Green and R. Paul Stevens, *New Testament Spirituality* (Guildford, UK: Eagle, 1994), 7.

17. James B. Torrance, quoted in Bolsinger, *It Takes a Church*, 100.

18. Labberton, *Dangerous Act of Worship*, 13.

19. Ibid., 8.

20. Ibid., 33.

21. Ibid.

22. See, for example, Stanley Hauerwas and Charles Pinches, *Christians among the Virtues* (Notre Dame, IN: University of Notre Dame Press, 1997).

23. Fitch, *Great Giveaway*, 104.

24. Wilson, *Why Church Matters*, 14.

25. Ibid., 13.

26. Ibid., 11.

27. David J. Schlafer and Timothy F. Sedgwick, *Preaching What We Practice: Proclamation and Moral Discernment* (Harrisburg, PA: Morehouse, 2007), 149.

28. Dawn, *Reaching Out*, 8.

29. Saliers, *Worship and Spirituality*, 2.

30. From the Westminster Shorter Catechism.

31. Schlafer and Sedgwick, *Preaching What We Practice*, 27.

32. "10 Tips for Worship Leaders: How to Enhance On-Stage Presence, the Worship Community," July 24, 2008, www.theworshipcommunity.com.

Chapter 6 Directive Scripture with Thoughtful Liturgy: Part 1

1. Michael J. Quicke, "Issues of Integrity Facing Proclaimers of the Gospel," Christian Ethics Commission, Baptist World Alliance Meeting, Prague, Czech Republic, July 2009.

2. Kenton C. Anderson, "Squeaky Clean," in *The Art and Craft of Biblical Preaching*, ed. Haddon Robinson and Craig Brian Larson (Grand Rapids: Zondervan, 2005), 85–88.

3. John Huxtable, *The Preacher's Integrity* (London: Epworth, 1966), 17–19.

4. Hamstra, *Principled Worship*, x.

5. Mitman, *Worship in the Shape of Scripture*, 33.

6. Gerald L. Borchert, "Responding to the Mystery," paper presented at BICTE, International Baptist Theological Seminary, Prague, Czech Republic, July 2008, 3.

7. R. T. Beckwith and Martin J. Selman, eds., *Sacrifice in the Bible* (Carlisle, UK: Paternoster, 1995).

8. Temple, *Readings in St. John's Gospel*, 68.

9. John P. Burgess, quoted in Mitman, *Worship in the Shape of Scripture*, 10.

10. Mitman, *Worship in the Shape of Scripture*, 150–51.

11. Morgenthaler, *Worship Evangelism*, 50–51.

12. Gordon Lathrop, quoted in Mitman, *Worship in the Shape of Scripture*, 39.

13. Mitman, *Worship in the Shape of Scripture*, 46.

14. Ibid., 50–51.

15. For example, Webber, *Worship Is a Verb*, 45.

16. Michael Horton, *A Better Way: Rediscovering the Drama of Christ-Centered Worship* (Grand Rapids: Baker, 2002), 147–60.

17. William Willimon, *Pastor: The Theology and Practice of Ordained Ministry* (Nashville: Abingdon, 2002), 77–79.

18. Mark Ashton, "Following in Cranmer's Footsteps," in *Worship by the Book*, ed. D. A. Carson, 80, 89.

19. Hughes, "Free Church Worship," 147–48.

20. Timothy J. Keller, "Reformed Worship in the Global City," in *Worship by the Book*, ed. D. A. Carson, 217.

21. Ibid., 233.

22. Mitman, *Worship in the Shape of Scripture*, 33 (italics his).

23. David Peacock, "Preparing for Sunday Worship," *Ministry Today* 4 (June 1995): 27.

24. Long, *Witness of Preaching*, 70.

25. Mitman, *Worship in the Shape of Scripture*, ix.

26. Elizabeth Achtemeier, *Preaching from the Old Testament* (Louisville: Westminster John Knox, 1989), 37.

27. Ibid., 32.

28. Mitman, *Worship in the Shape of Scripture*, 60.

29. Ibid., 96.

30. Morgenthaler, *Worship Evangelism*, 51.

Chapter 7 Directive Scripture with Thoughtful Liturgy: Part 2

1. Laurence Hull Stookey, *Calendar: Christ's Time for the Church* (Nashville: Abingdon, 1996), 127–28.

2. Robert Webber, *The Younger Evangelicals* (Grand Rapids: Baker, 2004), 182–86.

3. Maleyft and Vanderwell, *Designing Worship Together*, 106.

4. *Liturgical Year: The Worship of God*, Presbyterian Church U.S.A., 19.

5. Vicki Black, *Welcome to the Church Year: An Introduction to the Seasons of the Episcopal Church* (New York: Moorehouse, 2004), 1–2.

6. Anscar J. Chupungeo, *Handbook for Liturgical Studies*, vol. 5, *Liturgical Time and Space* (Collegeville, MN: Liturgical Press, 2000), 322.

7. Robert Webber, *Ancient-Future Time* (Grand Rapids: Baker, 2004), 11.

8. Malefyt and Vanderwell, *Designing Worship Together*, 99–103.

9. Best, *Unceasing Worship*, 73–74.

10. Eugene L. Lowry, *Living with the Lectionary* (Nashville: Abingdon, 1992), 35.

11. Mitman, *Worship in the Shape of Scripture*, 11.

12. Barbara Day Miller, *The New Pastor's Guide to Leading Worship* (Nashville: Abingdon, 2006), 58.

13. Thomas G. Bandy, *Introducing the Uncommon Lectionary* (Nashville: Abingdon, 2006), 32–33.

14. Lowry, *Living with the Lectionary*, 15.

15. Ibid.

16. Ibid., 17.

17. Ibid., 19.

18. Jim Herrington, Mike Bonem, and James H. Furr, *Leading Congregational Change: A Practical Guide for the Transformational Journey* (San Francisco: Jossey-Bass, 2000), 17.

19. See Hoyt Hickman, Don E. Saliers, Laurence Hull Stookey, and James E. White, *The New Handbook of the Christian Year* (Nashville: Abingdon, 1992); and Kenneth Lawrence, ed., *Imaging the Word: An Art and Lectionary Resource* (Cleveland: United Church Press, 1994).

20. Malefyt and Vanderwell, *Designing Worship Together*; Tim Wright and Jan Wright, eds., *Contemporary Worship: A Sourcebook for Spirited, Traditional, Praise, and Seeker Services* (Nashville: Abingdon, 1997).

21. Troeger, *Preaching and Worship*, 25.

22. Best, *Unceasing Worship*, 180–85.

23. John D. Witvliet, quoted in Van Dyke, ed., *More Profound Alleluia*, 10–11.

24. Karmen Krahn and Leslie James, *Proclamation by Design: The Visual Arts in Worship* (Scottdale, PA: Faith and Life Resources, 2008), 5–9.

Chapter 8 Toward Community Formation

1. A. Skevington Wood, quoted in Frank E. Gaebelein, ed., *The Expositor's Bible Commentary*, vol. 11 (London: Pickering and Inglis, 1978), 42.

2. Quicke, *360-Degree Leadership*.

3. The Gospel and Our Culture Network emerged out of Lesslie Newbigin's call for "the missionary encounter of the gospel with our Western culture." See G. R. Hunsberger and Craig van Gelder, eds., *Church between Gospel and Culture* (Grand Rapids: Eerdmans, 1996), xiii–xix.

4. Kimball, *Emerging Church*, 59–61.

5. Van Gelder, "From Corporate Church to Missional Church," 425–49.

6. Ibid., 426 (italics his).

7. Ibid.

8. Alan J. Roxburgh and Fred Romanuk, *The Missional Leader: Equipping Your Church to Reach a Changing World* (San Francisco: Jossey-Bass, 2006), xv.

9. G. R. Hunsberger, "The Newbigin Gauntlet: Developing a Domestic Missiology for North America," in *Church between Gospel and Culture*, 3–25.

10. George Barna, quoted in Morgenthaler, *Worship Evangelism*, 18.

11. Dawn, *Reaching Out*, 57.

12. Ibid., 69.

13. Anthony B. Robinson, quoted in Van Dyke, ed., *More Profound Alleluia*, 137.

14. William H. Willimon, *The Intrusive Word: Preaching to the Unbaptized* (Grand Rapids: Eerdmans, 1994), 39.

15. Wilson, *Why Church Matters*, 63.

16. Dawn, *Reaching Out*, 105.

17. Bolsinger, *It Takes a Church*, 57.

18. Saliers, *Worship and Spirituality*, 2.

19. Wilson, *Why Church Matters*, 71.

20. Bernd Wannenwetsch, *Political Worship: Ethics for Christian Citizens* (Oxford: Oxford University Press), 7.

21. Ibid., 3.

22. Ibid., 6.

23. Ibid., 14.

24. David Stubbs, quoted in Van Dyke, *More Profound Alleluia*, 140–43.

25. George Barna, *A Fish Out of Water* (Nashville: Integrity, 2002), xxv.

26. Mark Driscoll, *Confessions of a Reformission Rev.: Hard Lessons from an Emerging Missional Church* (Grand Rapids: Zondervan, 2006), 32.

27. Labberton, *Dangerous Act of Worship*, 13.

28. See Jonathan Wilson-Hartgrove, *New Monasticism: What It Has to Say to Today's Church* (Grand Rapids: Brazos, 2008).

29. Fitch, *Great Giveaway*, 111.

30. Saliers, *Worship and Spirituality*, 5–6.

31. Robert Webber, *Ancient-Future Evangelism: Making Your Church a Faith-Forming Community* (Grand Rapids: Baker, 2003), 24.

32. Leslie D. Weatherhead, *Key Next Door* (London: Hodder & Stoughton, 1968), 39.

33. Wilson, *Why Church Matters*, 85.

34. Dawn, *Royal "Waste" of Time*, 184.

35. Ibid., 185.

36. Saliers, *Worship and Spirituality*, 30.

37. Ibid., 38.

38. Ibid., 1–2.

39. Wilson, *Why Church Matters*, 112–15.

40. Hamstra, *Principled Worship*.

41. Saliers, *Worship and Spirituality*, 24–26.

Chapter 9 Integrating Elements of Community Formation

1. Torrance, *Worship, Community, and the Triune God of Grace*, 9.

2. Ibid., 77.

3. Ibid., 78–79.

4. See James W. Thompson, *Preaching Like Paul: Homiletical Wisdom for Today* (Louisville: Westminster John Knox, 2001), 39.

5. Dawn, *Reaching Out*, 238.

6. See Frank A. Thomas, *They Like to Never Quit Praisin' God* (Cleveland: United Church Press, 1997).

7. Webber, *Worship Is a Verb*, 22–38.

8. Ibid., 30.

9. Saliers, *Worship and Spirituality*, 73.

10. David C. Buttrick, "A Sketchbook: Preaching and Worship," a paper presented at the meeting of the Academy of Homiletics, Princeton Theological School, 1980, 10.

11. Bolsinger, *It Takes a Church*.

12. Torrance, *Worship, Community, and the Triune God of Grace*, 39.

13. Mitman, *Worship in the Shape of Scripture*, 83.

14. Plantinga and Rozeboom, *Discerning the Spirits*, 126.

15. Karl Barth, *Church Dogmatics: The Doctrine of Reconciliation*, IV.3.2, trans. G. W. Bromiley (London: T & T Clark, 1961), 866–67.

16. Dawn, *Reaching Out*, 175.

17. Plantinga and Rozeboom, *Discerning the Spirits*, 106–7.

18. Leadership interview with Keith and Kristyn Getty, "With One Voice," January 30, 2009, www.christianitytoday.com.

19. H. E. Fosdick, quoted in John Killinger, *The Centrality of Preaching in the Total Task of Ministry* (Waco: Word, 1969), 54.

20. See James W. Thompson, *Preaching Like Paul*, 106, see also 85–106.

21. Quicke, *360-Degree Leadership*.

22. David Kinnaman, *UnChristian: What a New Generation Really Thinks about Christianity . . . and Why It Matters* (Grand Rapids: Baker, 2007), 15, 41–90.

23. Fitch, *The Great Giveaway*.

24. Wilson, *Why Church Matters*, 11.

25. Milfred Minatrea, *Shaped by God's Heart: The Passion and Practices of Missional Churches* (San Francisco: Jossey-Bass, 2004).

26. Schlafer and Sedgwick, *Preaching What We Practice*, 149.

27. Ibid., 48–49.

28. Ibid., 48.

29. Ibid., 49.

30. See Michael J. Quicke, "Prophetic Preaching for a Missional Church," in *Text and Task: Scripture and Mission*, ed. Michael Parsons (Carlisle, UK: Paternoster, 2005), 218–33.

31. D. S. Long, "Prophetic Preaching," in *Concise Encyclopedia of Preaching*, ed. William Willimon and Richard Lischer (Louisville: Westminster John Knox, 1995), 386.

32. W. Brueggemann, *The Prophetic Imagination* (Philadelphia: Fortress, 1978), 111.

Chapter 10 Toward a New Pattern for Big-Picture Preaching

1. Matt Redman, "Who's Really the Worship Leader?" March 3, 2002, www.worshiptogether.com/resources/article.

2. This pattern forms the basis for sermon preparation in Quicke, *360-Degree Preaching*.

3. See, for example, Donald Coggan, *The Sacrament of the Word* (London: Fount, 1987); John McClure, *The Round Table Pulpit* (Nashville: Abingdon, 1995); and Doug Pagitt, *Preaching Reimagined* (Grand Rapids: Zondervan, 2001).

4. Mitman, *Worship in the Shape of Scripture*, 26.

5. Bolsinger, *It Takes a Church*, 98–100.

6. See Quicke, *360-Degree Preaching*, 188–93.

7. Quicke, *360-Degree Leadership*, 117–21.

8. Maleyft and Vanderwell, *Designing Worship Together*, 4.

9. Ibid., 8–15.

10. Ken Gosnall, "Preaching and Blogging," *Preaching* 22, no. 2 (September/October 2006): 6–9.

Chapter 11 Beginning Well: Worship Swim Stage 1

1. Hughes Oliphant Old, quoted in Hamstra, *Principled Worship*, 7.

2. Maleyft and Vanderwell, *Designing Worship Together*, 15–23.

3. Ibid., 17.

4. Eugene Lowry, "Listening to the Dark," E. Y. Mullins Lectures, Southern Baptist Theological Seminary, Louisville, KY, March 3, 1992.

5. Dawn, *Reaching Out*, 78.

6. J. S. Whale, *Christian Doctrine* (Cambridge: Cambridge University Press, 1941), 152.

7. Gerard S. Sloyan, *Worshipful Preaching* (Philadelphia: Fortress, 1984), 13.

8. Ibid., 20, 22.

9. Ibid., 12.

10. Hamstra, *Principled Worship*, 14.

11. Malefyt and Vanderwell, *Designing Worship Together*, 17.

12. Thomas G. Long, *Beyond Worship Wars: Building Vital and Faithful Worship* (Herndon, VA: Alban Institute, 2003), 22.

13. Willimon, *Pastor*, 58.

14. Dietrich Bonhoeffer, *Life Together* (London: SCM Press, 1954), 16.

15. Malefyt and Vanderwell, *Designing Worship Together*, 18–21.

16. Ibid., 18.

17. Hamstra, *Principled Worship*, 4.

18. Malefyt and Vanderwell, *Designing Worship Together*, 4.

19. Troeger, *Preaching and Worship*, 59.

20. Ibid.

21. Paul Scott Wilson, *Four Pages of the Sermon* (Nashville: Abingdon, 1999), 36.

22. Malefyt and Vanderwell, *Designing Worship Together*, 21–22.

23. First Baptist Church, Lubbock, TX, senior pastor Philip Wise and pastor of music and worship Tommy Shapard.

24. *The Second Page* 46, no. 50 (December 13, 2005): 2.

25. Ibid., 46, no. 36 (September 6, 2005): 2.

26. For fuller treatment of implementing core values, see Quicke, *360-Degree Leadership*, 141–45.

27. Aubrey Malphurs, *Values-Driven Leadership* (Grand Rapids: Baker, 1996), 34.

28. Ibid., 141.

29. "What Is the Philosophy of Worship That Unites Us?" Faith Baptist Fellowship, Sioux Falls, SD.

Chapter 12 Being Directed: Worship Swim Stages 2 and 3

1. See survey of the most influential preaching books of the past twenty-five years in *Preaching* 25, no. 25 (March/April 2010): 18–19.

2. Getty, "With One Voice."

3. Quicke, "Prophetic Preaching," in *Text and Task*, ed. Michael Parsons, 218–33.

4. Temple, *Readings in John's Gospel*.

Chapter 13 Continuing Strong: Worship Swim Stages 4 and 5

1. Paul Scott Wilson, *Imagination of the Heart* (Nashville: Abingdon, 1988).

2. Mitman, *Worship in the Shape of Scripture*, 59, 98.

3. Ibid., 99.

4. David Edwards, *Worshipthreesixtyfive* (Nashville: Broadman & Holman, 2006), 99.

5. Hughes, "Free Church Worship," 175.

6. Willimon, *Preaching and Leading Worship*, 43.

7. Best, *Unceasing Worship*, 102.

8. Ibid., 99.

9. Willimon, *Preaching and Leading Worship*, 41.

10. Saliers, *Worship and Spirituality*, 69.

11. Ibid., 73.

12. Best, *Unceasing Worship*, 143.

13. Curtis Vaughan, "Colossians," in *The Expositor's Bible Commentary*, vol. 11, ed. Frank E. Gaebelein, 216.

14. Getty, "With One Voice."

15. Best, *Unceasing Worship*, 30.

16. Ibid., 146.

17. Dawn, *Reaching Out*, 202.

18. Fred Pratt Green (1903–2000), "When Our Confidence Is Shaken" (Carol Stream, IL: Hope Publishing, 1971).

19. Getty, "With One Voice."

20. Ibid.

21. Dawn, *Reaching Out*, 202.

22. Ibid.

23. Steve Guthrie, "Music and Lyrics," *Worship Leader* 18, no. 1 (January/February 2009): 24–30.

24. Ibid., 28.

25. Ibid., 29.

26. Ibid., 30.

27. Dawn, *Reaching Out*, 202.

28. Robert Webber, *The Book of Daily Prayer* (Grand Rapids: Eerdmans, 1993), 11.

29. "10 Tips for Worship Leaders," www.theworshipcommunity.com.

30. See Quicke, *360-Degree Preaching*, 188–93.

31. Jacks, *Getting the Word Across*, 191.

32. John von Rhein, "Mark Elder Inspires CSO," Classical Review, *Chicago Tribune*, April 3, 2010, 15.

Chapter 14 Evaluating and Building Forward: Worship Swim Stage 6

1. Rust, *The Word and Words*, 126–27.

2. C. S. Lewis, *Weight of Glory* (New York: HarperCollins, 2001), 31.

3. Getty, "With One Voice."

4. Malefyt and Vanderwell, *Designing Worship Together*, 157–60.

5. Quick, *360-Degree Preaching*.

6. Getty, "With One Voice."

7. Malefyt and Vanderwell, *Designing Worship Together*, 173–75.

8. Long, *Beyond Worship Wars*, 18.

9. Marva Dawn, quoted in Malefyt and Vanderwell, *Designing Worship Together*, 162.

10. Long, *Beyond Worship Wars*.

11. The American Heritage College Dictionary, third ed., s.v. "exhilaration."

Appendix

1. Ron Weber, *Reconnecting Worship: Where Tradition and Innovations Converge* (Nashville: Abingdon, 2004).

Index

Michael J. Quicke is Charles W. Koller Professor of Preaching and Communication at Northern Seminary in Lombard, Illinois. He previously served as principal of Spurgeon's College in London.

from the author of **360-Degree Preaching**

michael j. quicke

> **preaching** to transform congregations

360-degree
leadership

foreword by Mike Bonem, Jim Herrington,
and James H. Furr

"The book is thick with practical insights drawn from the best leadership teaching of recent years, flavored by an author who 'walked the walk' as a pastor of two local churches, and who has spent his most recent years training a new generation of preachers. . . . As an experienced pastor as well as a talented teacher and writer, Michael Quicke understands leadership well and helps us understand it better. This is an excellent and helpful book that deserves a place on any pastor's bookshelf."

—**Michael Duduit**, *Preaching* Magazine

A *Preaching* Magazine Book of the Year*

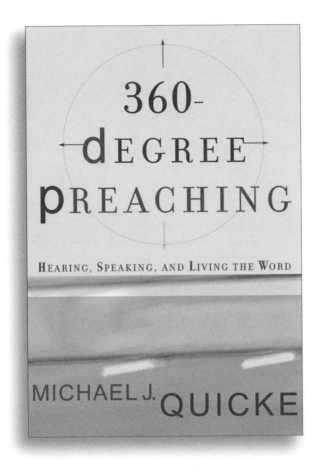

"[Quicke] challenges a popular metaphor for preaching, suggests a better alternative, and encourages preachers. The result is a book that takes seriously the challenges of preaching in the 21st century but faces them with a hopefulness rooted in God's character and activity."—**Evangelical Homiletics Society**

With *360-Degree Preaching*, veteran preacher Michael Quicke brings expository preaching to a postmodern world. As someone who preaches every Sunday, he has witnessed the transforming power of preaching firsthand for over thirty years. As he teaches students and pastors the art of preaching, his goal is to encourage preachers and those who train to be preachers.

*2003